HOSTAGES
OF EACH
OTHER

HOSTAGES OF EACH OTHER

The Transformation
of Nuclear Safety since
Three Mile Island

JOSEPH V. REES

The University of Chicago Press
Chicago and London

The University of Chicago Press, Chicago 60637
The University of Chicago Press, Ltd., London
© 1994 by The University of Chicago
All rights reserved. Published 1994
Printed in the United States of America

03 02 01 00 99 98 97 96 95   3 4 5

ISBN: 0-226-70687-7 (cloth)

Library of Congress Cataloging-in-Publication Data

Rees, Joseph V.
    Hostages of each other : the transformation of nuclear
safety since Three Mile Island / Joseph V. Rees.
        p.   cm.
    Includes bibliographical references and index.
    1. Nuclear power plants—United States—Safety measures.
    2. Nuclear industry—Safety regulations—United States.
    3. Institute of Nuclear Power Operations (U.S.)—Rules and
practice.
    I. Title.
    TK9152.R427   1994
    363.17'99—dc20   93-35819
                                                      CIP

♾ The paper used in this publication meets the minimum
requirements of the American National Standard for
Information Sciences—Permanence of Paper for Printed
Library Materials, ANSI Z39.48–1984.

For Nancy, Goosey, Nessa, and JoJo

Contents

PREFACE

How has nuclear safety regulation changed since the 1979 Three Mile Island accident? That is this book's main question, and it was prompted by a mixture of personal concern and intellectual interest. Before moving to North Carolina, my family and I had never lived near a nuclear plant. Now we do, a fact I am reminded of each year when my children bring home from school, as required by the Nuclear Regulatory Commission, an evacuation plan in case of a nuclear accident. The first time I studied it was the first time I stopped to seriously consider: "How dangerous is nuclear power?" It was also about this time that the tenth anniversary of the Three Mile Island accident was in the news, and as I read accounts recalling this country's worst nuclear plant accident, I wondered about its aftermath, how nuclear safety regulation had changed over the past ten years. Given all the controversy that has surrounded nuclear power, I assumed there was a great deal written on the matter. Not so; I went to the library in search of an answer and came up empty-handed.

With no published studies addressing the question, I went to the Nuclear Regulatory Commission's Washington, D.C., headquarters, where, in talking with NRC officials, I began to learn how the regulatory system had changed. And, what's more, I discovered that one of the most significant changes involved an organization I was not even aware of—the Institute of Nuclear Power Operations (INPO). From what they told me about this private regulatory bureaucracy created by the nuclear industry itself, I wanted to learn more about INPO, as I have long thought the whole subject of industry self-regulation an important yet neglected area of research on regulation. Scholarly neglect is not something that seems to trouble INPO officials, however, as they refused to answer most of my questions or cooperate with my inquiry when I first tried to learn a bit more about their organization.

Stonewalled, I made contact with leading organizations on either side of the nuclear power debate. Nuclear power proponents, such as NUMARC (Nuclear Management and Resources Council), the industry's key lobbyist in Washington, D.C., spoke glowingly of INPO's role in promoting nuclear safety since the TMI accident. There was nothing surprising in this. The surprise came when I got in touch with groups well known for their opposition to the nuclear industry, such as the Union of Concerned Scientists and Ralph Nader's Critical Mass Energy Project, and they did not dismiss INPO's regulatory role as mere industry window-dressing. Far from it; indeed, one of the most knowledgeable (and frequently quoted) critics of this country's nuclear regulatory system, Robert Pollard, a former NRC inspector now with the Union of Concerned Scientists, thought highly enough of INPO to suggest (only half-jokingly) that the federal government should nationalize INPO and disband the NRC. "INPO is doing the job that the NRC inspectors ought to be doing," as he put it. "And if NRC inspections were even half as good as INPO's, we would not have the types of problems we have today." This was astonishing to hear, not only because it came from a leading industry critic, but because it stands in stark contrast to the prevailing social science view, which has it that industry organizations like INPO are typically weak and ineffective regulators. Could it be that INPO represents a rare regulatory species, I wondered, an industrial association that is an effective regulator?

Searching for an answer has been no easy task. Almost all INPO documents are concealed from the public, and INPO denied me access. Indeed, throughout the course of doing research for this study most INPO officials refused to cooperate in my efforts. As some INPO officials tried to explain it, their relationship with the nuclear plants is a special one, like that of a doctor dealing with her patient, and thus requires strict confidentiality for INPO to carry out its essential tasks. Perhaps. But I would also note that INPO (like many organizations in the nuclear industry) shows signs of a bunker mentality—guarded, suspicious of outside observers. Which is hardly surprising, of course, given that INPO works in such a highly charged political and legal environment, one that has been anything but friendly to nuclear power. However that may be, one thing is certain: INPO is a secretive regulatory bureaucracy.

Fortunately, there are ways to study an organization that hides its activities from public scrutiny. First of all, INPO must deal with other organizations, public and private, and sometimes provide them with information as well. In the case of Congress, for example, INPO officials have testified before its committees on several occasions over the years. And in dealing with the NRC, INPO officials have briefed government regulators numerous times about various INPO programs. I have gathered and read all those hearings and briefings, and thanks to some judicial proceedings, I have also collected some sensitive INPO documents forced into the public domain, such as INPO nuclear plant inspection reports.

But that is not all. INPO must also send a large assortment of written materials to the organizations it regulates, the nuclear utilities, and I have obtained many of those documents through various channels. This includes Freedom of Information Act (FOIA) requests to the Tennessee Valley Authority, the only nuclear plant operator that is also a federal agency subject to FOIA requirements. It includes visits to nine nuclear utility libraries where I located various INPO documents. And, most important, it includes contacts I cultivated among nuclear industry officials willing to assist me in my efforts.

Two further sources of written information should be mentioned. One is the nuclear industry trade press, which I continuously surveyed for any items concerning INPO. The other is the NRC's public document room in Washington, D.C., where I reviewed all NRC reports concerning INPO, as well as the extensive record of correspondence between a wide array of INPO and NRC officials.

All in all, then, I have examined hundreds of relevant documents despite INPO's tight-lipped ways. Yet if written records represent one of the best sources of data on INPO, one must always keep in mind their limitations, especially in the case of many INPO documents, where the "official" perspective often tends to place INPO's activities in the most favorable light. So whenever possible I have sought to double-check and expand upon the written record, particularly through interviews with informants who have (or had) access to privileged information concerning INPO. I thus interviewed 126 individuals (84 in person and 42 by telephone) in a wide variety of positions throughout the industry. They include NRC officials (commissioners, administrators, and inspectors, among others), nuclear utility executives (CEOs, presidents, and vice presidents for nuclear power, among others), nuclear plant employees (managers, supervisors, control room operators, operating experience review personnel, and quality assurance inspectors, among others), nuclear industry consultants, and trade association officials. Along the way, moreover, I systematically searched out INPO's strongest critics, found six at various Washington-based public interest groups—Critical Mass, the Natural

Resources Defense Council, the Nuclear Information and Resource Service, and the Union of Concerned Scientists—and interviewed them. And, despite INPO's general unwillingness to cooperate, I also managed to interview nineteen past and present INPO officials.

As with all interview data, the conscientious researcher, alert to sources of bias and distortion, must not take the respondent's words at face value. I have therefore done my best to maintain a critical eye and to be hard-nosed about the validity of important pieces of information gathered in these open-ended interviews. Is the story plausible? Is it consistent? How confident is the respondent in his account of what happened? Is the respondent's story based on direct experience or secondhand accounts? And most important, can it be corroborated (or disconfirmed) by independent sources, such as the written record, or by asking different people the same in-depth question?

All very well and good, I hear you say, but what does all this evidence show us? Put most simply, it reveals that a remarkable regulatory transformation has been taking place in the nuclear industry, one that began with the TMI accident and continues to this day, and at the vanguard of it all is a little-known organization called INPO. What follows will seek to explain how and why.

For their helpful comments, I wish to thank John Braithwaite, Jonathan Hartlyn, Todd LaPorte, Michael Lienesch, Gordon Whitaker, and Aaron Wildavsky. For his useful advice and encouragement, I also owe a note of appreciation to John Tryneski of the University of Chicago Press. Thanks to Ed Nicolas for his outstanding research assistance. Finally, I owe special thanks to Philip Selznick. By sharing and discussing various chapters of his (now published) *The Moral Commonwealth: Social Theory and the Promise of Community*, he has influenced this book in many important ways.

1
Introduction

It was early in the morning, March 28, 1979, when several water pumps stopped working at Unit 2 of General Public Utilities nuclear plant on Three Mile Island near Harrisburg, Pennsylvania. So began the chain of events that led to America's worst nuclear power accident. More than the breakdown of a nuclear reactor, the accident became a symbol—"TMI"—indelibly etched on the public mind.[1] For all institutions involved in nuclear power the accident was a traumatic shock. Like a revolution, it divided nuclear power history into two parts— before and after TMI—as it utterly transformed all levels of the nation's nuclear regulatory system. The nature of that regulatory transformation is the central focus of this study.

Less than two weeks after the accident, a committee of nuclear utility chief executive officers was formed to coordinate the industry's response to the accident, and their efforts resulted in perhaps the single most important change that has taken place in the post-TMI nuclear regulatory system.[2] On December 3, 1979, a short nine months after the accident, an organization called INPO (Institute of Nuclear Power Operations) began operation in Atlanta, Georgia.

INPO is a regulatory bureaucracy. As in many well-known regulatory agencies operated by the federal government, INPO's approximately four hundred employees develop standards, conduct inspections, and investigate accidents. With an annual budget of nearly $54 million, moreover, if INPO were a federal regulatory agency, it would rank in the top twenty (about equal to the budget of the U.S. Federal Trade Commission). Yet INPO also differs from these governmental regulatory agencies in a fundamental way; it was created not by Congress, but by the nuclear power industry, and its activities are funded not by tax dollars, but by the large industrial institutions that own and operate all the nuclear power plants in the United States. In short, INPO is a *private* regulatory bureaucracy.

Why did the nuclear power industry create INPO in the first place? And why single out INPO's role in a study of nuclear industry regulation? Let's consider how the chairman of INPO's board of directors, Detroit Edison CEO Walter J. McCarthy, Jr., described the circumstances surrounding INPO's creation in a speech to his fellow nuclear utility CEOs:

> It took the shock of a world-focusing event such as TMI to make us realize major changes must be made—in operations, in information exchange, in training, in management, in attitude, in culture overall. For the first time, I believe it hit us that an event at a nuclear plant anywhere in our country . . . could and would affect each nuclear plant.

He then went on to quote a phrase that his audience had heard time and again since the TMI accident, as it had become a root metaphor in the nuclear power industry's basic cultural orientation: "Each licensee is a hostage of every other licensee." Why? Because a single catastrophic accident (think of Chernobyl) at any one U.S. nuclear plant would have ruinous consequences for the entire industry. It was the realization "that we truly were all in this together," McCarthy adds, that led to INPO's creation.[3]

As these remarks suggest (and as we shall see throughout this study), the notion that each nuclear utility is a hostage of every other utility exerted and continues to exert a powerful influence on the nuclear power industry. Acting upon this assumption, the industry created INPO; and by capitalizing on this assumption for more than a decade now, INPO has led the way in transforming the nuclear power industry in fundamental respects. In short, one cannot understand the nuclear industry's post-TMI transformation unless one understands INPO's crucial role in these developments.

INPO's role has also been controversial. A case in point: "We are concerned that the NRC's relationship with INPO may be compromising, rather than enhancing, public health and safety," two congressional overseers of nuclear industry regulation recently wrote. "We are concerned that the NRC may rely too heavily on INPO by delegating its statutory responsibility to this industry-sponsored organization while not maintaining an effective system of reviewing INPO's findings."[4] The NRC, as we shall see, has in fact delegated major regulatory tasks to INPO. (See chapter 4.) Is this appropriate? Is the NRC abdicating its regulatory responsibilities and relying too heavily on INPO? And is this relationship compromising public health and safety?

Compounding these concerns is the fact that INPO is a very secretive regulatory bureaucracy. INPO exercises "quasi-governmental functions," as Ralph Nader and his associate testified before Congress, yet it "functions in complete secrecy."[5] Indeed, INPO goes to great lengths to conceal its activities from public view. Like a black hole in the regulatory universe, INPO appears to exert an intense gravitational influence on the nuclear industry's regulatory system, governmental as well as nongovernmental, yet it remains hidden from public view. Small wonder then that so little is known about this publicity-shy organization.

So we see that there are strong policy reasons for examining INPO's role in U.S. nuclear industry regulation. Also note that INPO's significance is not limited to domestic nuclear regulatory policy, for it now appears to be extending far beyond our borders as part of a larger trend toward the internationalization of nuclear power regulation. A small but revealing example is a U.S. Department of Energy joint nuclear safety initiative with the Soviet Union. "We plan to rely extensively on . . . INPO for assistance in this initiative," said Secretary of Energy James Watkins.[6] Another, more important, example of INPO's growing international significance involves the World Association of Nuclear Operators (WANO), a multinational organization created in 1989 in response to the Soviet Union's Chernobyl nuclear reactor accident. WANO's 139 member organizations operate more than four hundred nuclear power plants worldwide, and WANO's chairman, Lord Marshall of Goring, described WANO's "ambition" thus: "We can see that INPO has produced an enormous increase in the safety of nuclear power plant operations in the United States. Our ambition is to do a similar task for the world as a whole."[7] It remains to be seen, of course, whether WANO will in fact assume an important worldwide regulatory role; but if it does, this examination of INPO can also be viewed as a preview of an incipient worldwide nuclear regulatory system.

Further evidence of INPO's expanding influence can also be found in this country's system for regulating nuclear weapons plants. In the past few years the Department of Energy (DOE) has acknowledged grave safety and pollution problems at active and inactive nuclear plants in more than thirty states. The resulting cleanup effort could cost $200 billion or more over the next thirty years and is destined to become one of the country's largest public works projects.[8] It is now

evident that these widely publicized problems are leading to fundamental reforms in the DOE's regulatory strategies for dealing with
these facilities. Less apparent is INPO's role in all this. There is a
"heavy INPO influence," says a nuclear engineer who has worked at
both the Savannah River and Rocky Flats nuclear weapons facilities.
"The Department of Energy is implementing the INPO standards just
about verbatim." What that heavy influence represents, in the words
of an INPO spokesperson, is a kind of "technology transfer," a movement of regulatory techniques from a private regulatory bureaucracy
to a public one.[9]

Besides such considerations, it is also important that we notice
INPO's significance from an altogether different angle. Adopting the
perspective of the social science literature on regulation and its prevailing view as to the efficacy of self-regulation through industrial associations, there is good reason to think that INPO is a peculiar anom-
aly. As Braithwaite and Fisse write: "Skepticism has often been voiced
about the efficacy of self-regulation through trade associations. . . .
They are commonly uneasy alliances of companies that are trying to
do each other in. It would be expecting a lot of informal social control
to work in such a setting." Self-regulation by industry associations seldom amounts to more than "faint symbolic activity," according to this
line of reasoning, and is therefore generally "devoid of any solid foundation for either informal or formal social control."[10] The conventional view, in short, is that industry associations are weak and ineffective regulators.

Now consider the nuclear industry's safety record since INPO's creation. Today, fifty-four nuclear utilities operate 110 nuclear power reactors located at seventy-four sites throughout the nation, and, by all
accounts, the safety of those plants has increased significantly since
the TMI accident. The nuclear power industry's "average performance
is significantly higher," Secretary of Energy James Watkins (a nuclear
power advocate) told a congressional committee. Before TMI the industry "was probably close to a C-minus, and I think they are now
getting a B-plus."[11] Even critics of nuclear power acknowledge improvement. "It's beyond dispute that the plants are safer," said Robert
Pollard, the nuclear industry critic with the Union of Concerned Scientists.[12]

What is more, the data on safety-related performance indicators appear to support these judgments, as they all show clear signs of improvement over the past ten years. (See Appendix.)

If the nation's nuclear plants have in fact become safer since the

TMI accident, the question is why. No doubt the reasons are complex, but three factors stand out. One involves changes in the governmental sphere, particularly the Nuclear Regulatory Commission's post-TMI regulatory strategies; another involves changes in the corporate sphere, especially the in-house regulatory systems located in the fifty-four nuclear utilities. We shall have more to say about these developments later in this study. But what about nuclear power's industrial association? How has INPO contributed to these improvements in safety?

From what has just been said about self-regulation through industry associations, the answer may seem plain enough: INPO was created by the industry; it is funded by the industry; INPO, in short, is an *industry* organization, with all that that implies about undue industry influence. Given these basic facts, one would thus expect that industry self-regulation through INPO is nothing more than faint symbolic activity. Is it?

Now it is very difficult (perhaps impossible) to measure precisely how much of the nuclear industry's improved safety performance can in fact be attributed to INPO's regulatory efforts, as nuclear plants operate in an extremely complex regulatory environment. California's Diablo Canyon, for instance, is regulated in one way and another by the Federal Emergency Management Administration (FEMA), the Environmental Protection Agency (EPA), the California Public Utility Commission (CPUC), the state Office of Emergency Services (OES), the California Occupational Safety and Health Administration (CAL/ OSHA), the state Nuclear Safety Review Group (NSRG), and various insurance companies, as well as the NRC and INPO.[13] Nevertheless, as we shall later see, and as attested by INPO's growing influence—on the Soviet nuclear program, on federal nuclear weapons facilities, and on the newly formed World Association of Nuclear Operators—there is wide agreement among knowledgeable observers (among proponents of nuclear power as well as every critic I interviewed) that INPO's contribution has in fact been highly significant.[14]

Is this perception justified? The basic answer is yes. Our task, then, is to explain how and why.

I would like to remark briefly on a larger aspiration of this inquiry. If this work has a distinct contribution to make, apart from exploring the post-TMI nuclear regulatory system, it lies in the attempt to understand the regulatory worth of community in a complex technological society.

The question "What is INPO?" can be addressed in many ways. Yet most significant for our purposes is its status as a form of regulatory ordering. What is distinctive about INPO in this regard? What combination of qualities or features distinguishes this regulatory regime from others? At one level, the answer is relatively straightforward: INPO is an industry association that performs a variety of familiar regulatory tasks—developing standards, conducting inspections, and so forth.

But at a deeper level, what truly distinguishes INPO from many other forms of regulatory ordering (including, most notably, the NRC's regulatory regime) is INPO's role in promoting the development of a distinctive kind of community in the nuclear power industry. This movement toward community, I also found, has led to the emergence of a new responsibility-centered industrial culture, a distinctive set of unifying principles and practices that spells out what conduct is virtuous (professional versus unprofessional, for instance) and what goals are legitimate and desirable. I call this form of regulatory ordering "communitarian regulation." To generalize, a well-developed system of communitarian regulation has a well-defined *industrial morality* that is backed by enough *communal pressure* to *institutionalize responsibility* among its members. This is the key to understanding INPO's distinctive regulatory role in the nuclear power industry, for reasons that I hope will become clear as we proceed. So let us adopt this bare-bones formulation as our starting point, and use the rest of the book to add the flesh and blood of real-life illustrations. Our goal? To learn how a little-known organization (INPO) has used a remarkable regulatory strategy (communitarian regulation) to fundamentally change this country's nuclear power industry.

It could be argued that nuclear power in this country is a dying industry, for the simple fact is that not a single reactor has been ordered since the TMI accident. This does not mean that nuclear regulatory policy is a dying issue, however. Today, 110 commercial nuclear power reactors (constituting the largest nuclear power program in the world) are producing about 20 percent of the nation's electricity, up from about 11 percent in 1979. Given the problems associated with readily available alternative energy sources (coal and the greenhouse effect, oil and Middle East politics) it seems likely that most of these plants will continue to operate well into the twenty-first century.[15] In fact, it now appears that the operating life of many of these reactors will be extended well beyond their original forty-year licenses,[16] and that a new generation of nuclear reactors may soon be developed.[17]

So whether we are for or against nuclear power, difficult issues of regulatory policy must be addressed if we are to minimize the risks of a catastrophic nuclear accident. And few issues are of greater importance to that policy debate than the role of industry self-regulation in nuclear power's future.

OVERVIEW OF THE BOOK

The rest of this book is divided into three major parts.

Part 1, "Discovering Institutions," examines how the NRC and the nuclear industry responded to the Three Mile Island accident. Chapter 2 looks into the TMI accident, paying special attention to one of its most important lessons, that nuclear power's institutional arrangements were poorly suited to meeting the special demands of nuclear technology. Chapter 3 then casts a glance at the NRC's response to that lesson, for only against this backdrop can we fully appreciate the emergence and development of nuclear industry self-regulation. Chapter 4 then turns to the nuclear industry's response, to see why it created INPO, and also to see what formative factors have most influenced INPO's subsequent administrative development.

Part 2, "Communitarian Regulation," investigates the twin pillars of INPO's regulatory regime, an industrial morality backed by communal pressure. In discussing the new industrial morality INPO has created, chapter 5 clarifies how INPO spells out for the entire industry what conduct is esteemed and what goals are legitimate and desirable. Chapter 6, in turn, by inquiring into how INPO uses communal pressure as a regulatory enforcement tool, aims to understand what motivates nuclear utilities to take these industrial principles and practices seriously.

Part 3, "Institutionalizing Responsibility," explores communitarian regulation's overall aim in the context of two major INPO programs. Chapter 7 details INPO's efforts to improve the nuclear utilities' ability to learn from industry experience. And chapter 8 analyzes INPO's program to enhance the professionalism of nuclear industry employees.

In conclusion, chapter 9 shifts the discussion from the particular to the general, in order to reflect on the distinctive kind of community produced by the nuclear industry's regulatory transformation, and also to consider what broader lessons this case study may hold.

Part One

Discovering Institutions

2
Lessons of Three Mile Island

The TMI accident began with a simple mechanical failure that immediately shut down the reactor. This triggered water pumps to cool the system and opened a pressure relief valve to let water and steam escape into the reactor's containment vessel. These events were supposed to happen. But the relief valve remained open for two hours, unnoticed by workers. That was not supposed to happen. The reactor began to overheat as a million gallons of cooling water escaped through the malfunctioning relief valve—leaving the top half of the hundred-ton uranium fuel core with no water to cool it. Operators failed to understand what was happening, failed to close the valve, and mistakenly shut off an emergency cooling system that otherwise would have flushed the core and ended the accident immediately. Instead, temperatures in the core shot up to 5,000 degrees, and the top half melted in the volcanic heat. Finally, almost two hours into the accident, reactor operators released a torrent of cooling water into the reactor, shattering the remainder of the core. In industry parlance, the TMI reactor had suffered a "LOCA"—a loss-of-cooling accident.

Nearby schools were closed, residents were urged to stay indoors, and farmers were being warned to keep their animals under cover and on stored feed. The governor ordered the evacuation of children and pregnant women. Frightened by reports of uncontrolled radiation releases and a potentially explosive hydrogen bubble in the damaged reactor, as many as 200,000 people living within fifty miles of the plant fled the region. More than four hundred reporters from around the world were assigned to cover the event, and millions of television viewers watched the chillingly technical description of what they feared would be a meltdown—the "China Syndrome" they had seen at the movies. The reactor was crippled beyond repair; cleanup lasted more than a decade and cost about $1 billion.

In marking the accident's tenth anniversary, the vice president for nuclear power of TMI's parent company was asked to reflect on its most important lessons. "The lessons learned at TMI-2 went well beyond the technical ones. In retrospect, it seems we had in the United States *about as poor an institutional arrangement for the introduction of this demanding new technology as one could devise.*"[1] In singling out nuclear power's poor institutional arrangements, he could have spoken for all the leading TMI accident studies, for they had reached much the same conclusion a decade earlier.[2] More particularly, the collective portrait that emerges from those investigations draws a vital distinction between two types of issues—those that concern the *technological hardware* used in commercial nuclear power generation, and those that involve the *institutional arrangements* for using that technology. And if one all-important lesson attaches to the TMI accident, the accident examinations tell us, it mainly concerns the latter issue—nuclear power's institutional arrangements. In this chapter we seek an understanding of what those institutional arrangements were and why they were so poorly suited to meet the demands of nuclear power.

Why concern ourselves with the lessons of an accident now well over a decade old? The official inquiries into the TMI accident made a real difference, contrary to the oft-remarked futility of most blue-ribbon commissions. Indeed, far from being forgotten by industry and government officials, the lessons of TMI have influenced—and continue to influence—the industry's agenda for regulatory reform in fundamental ways, including almost all of the major developments examined in this book.

Look back with me, then, on those lessons so that we can investigate nuclear power's institutional problems more closely. My crucial point: many of the institutional problems uncovered by the postaccident examinations are best understood in terms of *a fundamental tension between the nuclear utilities' fixed organizational character and their changing technological environment.* In plain language, the nuclear industry suffered from a severe case of institutional lag.[3] Only against this institutional background, observed TMI's vice president for nuclear operations, can we fully appreciate the TMI accident's larger significance for the nuclear industry's historical development.

> TMI . . . provided a traumatic shock to all institutions involved in nuclear energy applications—a shock badly needed to

make those institutions aware of additional requirements for the safe use of this enormous new source of energy.

Such a shock was needed because of the hubris with which we all picked up the momentum of the nuclear age. . . . Unlike the decades which had been available to those applying the new technologies of steam engines or aviation, nuclear power moved from the first submarine experience, to commercial application, to large-scale use in thousand megawatt plants in such a short time that there was little potential for adequate feedback of experience into the overconfident but naive organizations who . . . operated the new plants.[4]

The rest of the chapter falls into two major parts. First we trace the nuclear industry's historical development to shed some light on the emergence of its institutional lag problem. Then, with that as backdrop, we shall discuss four major institutional problems highlighted by the TMI accident.

HISTORICAL DEVELOPMENT

The origins of the nuclear power industry date back to the early 1950s, when a heated debate took place over the future course of nuclear power. The central question—who should own and operate nuclear power plants, the federal government or electric power companies?— was settled by 1956, with the advocates of private nuclear power victorious.[5] Nuclear plants should be owned, managed, and operated by electric power companies. That was the public policymakers' view, although the utilities themselves hardly rushed in to take advantage of this newly created opportunity.[6] In fact only six commercial nuclear power plants began operation during this period, 1956 to 1962, largely because utility executives, traditionally an ultraconservative group, were uncertain about nuclear power as an economical alternative to traditional coal and oil-fired power plants.

The commercialization of nuclear power began as a slow crawl, but starting in 1963 it soon became an all-out sprint as electric utilities rushed to acquire nuclear plants—ordering two reactors in 1963, seven in 1965, twenty-one in 1966, and twenty-seven in 1967. By 1974 utilities had placed more than a hundred orders for nuclear power plants; in fact, almost all the commercial nuclear power plants in operation today were ordered during this period.[7] And as the orders for nuclear reactors rose, so did their size. For example, six of the twenty-one orders placed in 1966 were for units larger than 1,000 megawatts; yet it was not until 1969, a full three years later, that a nuclear plant half that size (500 megawatts) actually went into operation. In any case, by 1974 the great buying spree was over, and now the utilities confronted a new task—learning to operate the many new plants coming on line. Or, to put it another way, the five years preceding the TMI accident, 1974 to 1979, marked the first time that a large number of commercial reactors were in operation and that a large number of inexperienced utilities first tried their skills at managing and operating nuclear plants.

I am oversimplifying a very complicated history, of course, yet it serves well enough to underscore a crucial fact we need to appreciate about the nuclear industry's historical development. However one looks at it, a remarkably rapid change had taken place in the electric utilities task environment. In little more than ten short years an immature small-scale technology, largely developed and operated by a select group of scientists and engineers, was transformed into a large new industry managed and operated by electric power companies. Which leads to the next basic question: how well did the nuclear utilities adapt to these momentous changes?

Boston Edison's experience with its first nuclear plant, Pilgrim, here described by the company's CEO, is a revealing place to begin.

> Our major management shortcoming then [from 1972 to 1979] was the failure to recognize fully that the operational and managerial demands placed on a nuclear power plant are very different from those of a conventional fossil-fired power plant. Boston Edison structured its nuclear organization as part of a traditional operating arm.

With the benefit of hindsight, he went on, it was now very clear why Pilgrim had been beset by so many problems:

> The early management problems can be attributed to Boston Edison's attempt to manage Pilgrim Station *using essentially the same practices as had been established for our fossil units* without an adequate transition and adjustment for differences between the two technologies.[8]

Difficult as it may be to imagine now, most utility executives, like Boston Edison's, saw little practical difference between power plants fired by nuclear fission and conventional fossil fuel–based technologies. "Most utility executives viewed their nuclear plants just like they were another fire box—just another way to generate steam," a longtime nuclear industry official observes.[9] So it is no wonder that they responded to their new task environment in tradition-bound terms and that hardly any notice was taken of nuclear technology's unique demands. If nuclear power was just another way to boil water and make steam, according to this logic, long-established organizational practices for operating fossil fuel plants should be well suited to nuclear plants as well. Or so it seemed until the TMI accident, when those traditional habits of thought—the "fossil fuel mentality," in industry parlance—were seriously challenged by the postaccident examinations.

One moral we may draw from Boston Edison's experience, and others like it, is that electric power companies had a certain way of seeing and responding to the world about them—a fossil fuel mentality—when they first managed and operated nuclear plants. But what exactly is this fossil fuel mentality? We can best begin with Philip Selznick's concept of organizational character.

> Culture is the symbolic expression of shared perception, valuation, and belief. Therefore the idea of "organizational culture" properly emphasizes the creation of common understandings regarding purpose and policy. The character of an organization includes its culture, but something more as well. A pattern of dependency—for example, on a specific labor force, a market, or particular suppliers—may have little to do with symbolism or belief. The character of a company or trade union owes much to the structure of the industry, the skills of employees or members, the alliances that can be fashioned, and many other practical limits and opportunities. Attitudes and beliefs account for only part of an organization's distinctive character.[10]

In much the same vein, the pre-TMI nuclear utilities also possessed a distinctive culture and character, one that evolved over time as they adapted themselves to their internal and external social environment; and in this process of character formation, the utilities developed an attachment to a distinctive way of doing things, a fossil fuel mentality, that colored many aspects of their organizational life, and that provided a basis (explicitly or implicitly) on which personnel were selected, trained, rewarded, and managed, as well as the way tasks got defined. All this needs examples to make it clear, and several follow. However, one further conceptual point is crucial for our discussion—the idea of "distinctive competence." Think here of the way some business firms are good at marketing but less successful in research and development, and, conversely, how other firms are good at research and development but less successful in marketing. The important point here, as Selznick makes us aware, is to see how each firm has acquired a distinctive character that decisively affects its ability (or inability) to carry out a particular activity.

> The hallmarks of character are special competence and disability. "Character" refers to the commitments that help to determine the kinds of tasks an organization takes on. . . . We cannot presume every organization has a definite character. When one does, however, we can usually identify premises that fix, for substantial periods, the association's operative goals and characteristic methods.[11]

With these ideas in mind, let us explore the nuclear utilities' distinctive character before TMI. What were their operative goals and characteristic methods? Their special competencies and disabilities? And most important, how did all this affect their ability to manage and operate nuclear reactors? But first a caveat: it is always tempting to exaggerate a tendency, and it would certainly be going too far to say that all of nuclear power's institutional problems were somehow caused by a fossil fuel mentality. My present point is only that this cultural orientation, as a defining feature of the nuclear utilities' organizational character, conditioned their response to nuclear power— how it should be managed and operated—in some noteworthy ways. In particular, it helps illuminate some of the major institutional problems uncovered by the TMI accident studies, including the problem of management involvement, the problem of regulatory norms, the problem of learning from experience, and the professionalism problem. Each will be discussed in turn.

MANAGEMENT INVOLVEMENT

> When the decision was made to make nuclear power available for the commercial nuclear generation of energy, it was placed into the hands of the existing electric utilities. Nuclear power requires management qualifications and attitudes of a very special character. . . . However, the analysis of this particular accident raises the serious question of whether all electric utilities automatically have the necessary technical expertise and mana-

gerial capabilities for administering such a dangerous high-technology plant.[12]

So said the Kemeny Commission, the presidential board of inquiry that minutely scrutinized the TMI accident. And as these comments imply, there were strong reasons to doubt that existing electric utilities had the "very special character" required to manage a "dangerous high-technology plant." Here we take a closer look at one of these organizational weaknesses—the role of management involvement.

"After TMI," noted INPO's first president, "one thrust of the Kemeny Commission and industry's soul searching was that there needed to be more management involvement."[13] In fact, after conducting two rounds of inspections of all U.S. nuclear power plants, INPO concluded that a lack of management involvement was one of the industry's "foremost safety and reliability issues": "Managers and supervisors at all levels need to be more involved in the details of station operations."[14] This included top-level utility executives. Indeed, it was particularly true for the industry's leadership given INPO's "pervasive finding" that nuclear plant problems "were not known by top management."[15]

Why did they single out the need for more management involvement? In large part this was a tribute to a "deceptively simple" yet "fundamental" lesson of the TMI accident, in the words of TMI's CEO: "Commercial nuclear power is a uniquely demanding energy source and requires extraordinary care and attention."[16] That is so, not just because of the obvious risks inherent in its use, but also because the complexity of nuclear power technology far exceeds that of the other common methods of generating electricity—coal, oil, and water. A good benchmark for power plant complexity is the number of valves it has; a typical nuclear reactor has 40,000—ten times the number in a coal-fired plant. What's more, one cubic foot within a reactor core generates as much power as one thousand cubic feet of raging flame in a coal-fired boiler. So things can happen very rapidly when certain malfunctions occur (remember TMI's stuck valve), thus leaving plant operators but minutes to figure out what went wrong and correct it. Also, a nuclear reactor is very demanding in routine operation. The chemistry of the water flowing through the reactor must be kept within strict tolerances, for instance; if it is not, the plant's piping is subject to severe corrosion and damage. In these and countless other ways, nuclear power technology thus requires extraordinary care and attention. Or, to cite Carl Walske, president of the Atomic Industrial

Forum, "A nuclear reactor requires 10 times the management inten-
sity as a comparable coal-fired power plant."[17] In the words of one TMI
study: "It is extremely important that senior management become
technically informed and be personally familiar with conditions at the
operating plant. . . . *In this way, the pressure will be to maintain the
plant in excellent condition at all times.*"[18]

And there's the rub. "Before March 1979, little management support or attention was given to our nuclear plants." Why? "We had operated fossil plants for many years with little interaction between top
management and the plants," and nuclear plants "were looked on as
just another part of our electrical production group."[19] Comments like
this one, made by a nuclear utility CEO to an audience of fellow
CEOs, could be heard in a number of interviews. As another industry
official recalls: "Utility executives didn't dirty their hands a great deal
at the plant. They had plant managers, and they pretty much left it to
the plant manager to run everything. That's how they used to run fossil plants. So that's how they ran nuclear plants."

One final question. If hands-off management was the prevailing industry practice before TMI, what accounts for this managerial pattern
in the first place? Let me suggest two related reasons.

One was a bottom-line emphasis on *production.* Historically, writes
Cordell Reed, Commonwealth Edison's (Illinois) senior vice president
in charge of nuclear operations, "equivalent availability has been
preached in the industry as *the* parameter of good operations." Transla-
tion: "good" nuclear plant operations means pushing the machinery
to its limits in order to maximize the output of electricity. As another
longtime nuclear industry official tried to explain it:

> In the fossil fuel business the general philosophy is run it till it
> breaks. Then you shut it down, fix it, and run it again. You see,
> the capital investment is enormous. Every minute you don't use
> that capital for production purposes you are running costs, be-
> cause the capital runs continuous costs, but you're not getting
> any return. It's a return on capital problem, and every utility ex-
> ecutive wants a maximum return on capital. So the people that
> run the big utilities, mostly lawyers and financial people, have
> looked upon the power plants and their operation as just a cash
> cow that runs and turns out kilowatt hours. *They weren't really
> interested in how the plant runs, so long as it produced.* "Let's
> run the plant every minute we can and we'll fix it when it
> breaks." That was their basic attitude. [Emphasis supplied.][20]

Leaving the dirty business of actually running the plant to others, utility officials focused on output; how much plant operators produced was far more important than how they went about producing it. Add to this the many millions of dollars at stake in those outputs, plus the fact that those outputs are far easier to observe and measure than the quality of the production process itself, including its safety, and management's production orientation thus becomes quite understandable.

It becomes all the more understandable, finally, when we consider the fact that the *means* for producing those outputs had been relatively unproblematic, at least in the case of hydro and fossil fuel–based power plants. As a mature, undemanding, and trouble-free technology, say industry officials, fossil fuel plants did not place many demands on the attention of utility executives. As one utility executive explains:

> Historically, the utility has been involved in producing electricity by oil, coal, and water. Those operations required very little management attention, mainly because they were relatively simple, relatively trouble-free. In the case of a water-powered system, for example, it'll run and run and run with no failures and no problems. You put a little oil on the bearings once in a while and it keeps on going. So there's nothing to challenge top management at all because everything just runs fine. *That mentality of how you operate a power plant carried over from the fossil fuel systems to the nuclear systems.*

Utility officials, he adds, "just didn't realize that this was a new animal that they were dealing with."

What about the role of management involvement today? How has it changed, if at all, as a result of the post-TMI regulatory transformation? Much more on this later.

NORMATIVE SYSTEM

When the Kemeny Commission explored nuclear power's normative landscape—the totality of rules, principles, and other norms (both governmental and nongovernmental) for governing nuclear plant design, construction, and operation—they found NRC regulations dominating the scene. Probing further, they also discovered that nuclear utility officials were so consumed by the enormous task of complying with a "voluminous and complex" maze of NRC rules that satisfying regulatory requirements—going by the book—was equated with safety.[21] As Thomas Pigford, a member of the Kemeny Commission and a professor of nuclear engineering, tried to explain it: "The massive effort required to comply with the vast body of [NRC] requirements and to demonstrate compliance therewith . . . foster[ed] . . . [the] complacent feeling that all of that work in meeting regulations must somehow insure safety."[22]

If a pervasive formalism bred complacency, it also meant a general industry mind-set of doing no more than what the NRC regulations require. As another TMI study observed:

> We found evidence from our interviews that the prevailing attitude and policies at the time of the accident can be best described as "Operate in accordance with the conditions of the license and applicable regulations." *We found no evidence that . . . regulatory requirements were considered to be goals to be exceeded, or that management had a policy which deliberately encouraged the use of standards exceeding those mandated by regulation.*[23]

In a very concrete way, then, the upper limits of safety that nuclear plant officials aspired to were held down by lowest-limit NRC standards.

But that was not all. Notice further how the above quotation distinguishes between two types of norms—bare NRC requirements, and standards exceeding those mandated by regulations—and put yourself in the shoes of a conscientious nuclear plant manager who vigorously complies with NRC regulations. Because you are a *conscientious* manager, however, meeting minimum requirements is not good enough; you want your plant to rank among the industry's best in all respects, including safety. So where do you turn for guidance? What principles or standards must you honor in your quest for excellence? The fact of the matter is that, in the pre-TMI nuclear industry, you had nowhere to turn. "You didn't have definitive standards you were striving to attain," an industry official explains. "You had minimum NRC regulations that you could aspire to, which was just meeting the minimum regulatory needs. But standards of excellence were not available." In other words, and more generally, nuclear power's normative system did not embody any vision of the best, of the perfected, that provided conscientious nuclear plant managers with criteria for what is worth striving for. The normative landscape, thoroughly dominated by NRC regulations, was curiously silent on such matters.

I say *curiously* because, although one might expect minimum standards from the NRC, one might also expect the nuclear industry itself to develop more demanding norms for conscientious plant managers striving to excel within the industry. Yet the industry did not do so. Why?

Part of the explanation certainly involves the industry's fixation on NRC regulations. (After all, why develop additional standards when existing regulations were considered more than adequate for ensuring nuclear safety?) Part of the answer has to do with the normative system's hardware-centered approach to nuclear safety. (More about this shortly.) But the root explanation, I suspect, has to do with the industry's fossil fuel cultural orientation and its strong tendency to corral industry aspirations within the confines of minimum NRC standards. As one example of what I mean by this, consider the following excerpt from a 1987 NRC inspection report on Commonwealth Edison's Dresden nuclear plant. According to NRC inspectors Dresden was a problem plant whose history of poor performance reflected a distinctive organizational culture. In the NRC's words, Dresden's "attitude and approach . . . had not been directed at achieving or maintaining a high standard of safety performance. Such a level of performance was not demanded, not funded, and not established as a way of life. Instead *an old 'fossil plant' climate flourished where the minimum was good enough; if it is not required, don't do it; and fix it only when it's broken.*" [24] By reason of institutional lag, Dresden was a throwback to the pre-TMI nuclear industry when the fossil plant climate flourished throughout the industry. Like Dresden, the pre-TMI industry did not demand, fund, or establish high standards of safety performance; as in Dresden's case, developing such norms would have been wholly out of character for an industry mind-set steeped in the notion that doing the minimum was good enough.

Finally, one last point must be made: the pre-TMI normative system did not take institutions seriously. Which is to say, the vast majority of standards (governmental and nongovernmental) concentrated on hardware-related issues—how nuclear plants should be designed and constructed—while hardly any notice was taken of the institutional arrangements and processes required to manage, operate, and maintain those plants. Why?

Ideas and historical circumstances both figure in the explanation. Note, first, that the Kemeny Commission explained this one-sided emphasis on hardware standards in terms of the industry's distinctive mind-set—its "preoccupation with the safety of equipment" and its failure to recognize that "human beings who manage and operate the plants constitute an important safety system."[25] (More on this in chapter 3.) Note, second, that most of the NRC's regulatory activities can be divided into two phases: the licensing phase (in which the NRC reviews and analyzes the design of reactors prior to certifying them as fit for operation) and the postlicensing phase (in which the NRC monitors operating plants). Given that division of regulatory tasks, plus nuclear power's rapid commercialization from 1964 to 1975, when most nuclear plants were ordered, it is scarcely surprising to learn that the NRC's licensing process was inundated by the rush to nuclear power. Result: "a regulatory system consisting primarily of an elaborate apparatus for reviewing the safety of nuclear reactor designs."[26] As for the institutional arrangements for managing, operating, and maintaining those reactors—in effect all those matters were largely ignored by a regulatory system consumed by the enormous task of developing hardware standards in response to nuclear power's great construction boom.

Given all this—the fixation on NRC regulations, the absence of high standards of safety performance (doing the minimum is good enough), and the one-sided emphasis on hardware standards that overlooked the all-important institutional side of nuclear safety—it is easy to see why the Kemeny Commission concluded that "the nuclear industry must dramatically change its attitudes toward safety and regulations."[27] Has it dramatically changed? I shall take up this question in chapter 5.

LEARNING FROM EXPERIENCE

Soon after the TMI accident it was discovered that very similar accidents had almost occurred twice before, in 1974 at a Westinghouse reactor in Switzerland and in 1977 at Toledo Edison's Davis Besse plant in Ohio. Yet there were no meltdowns. In a matter of minutes operators at both plants had successfully diagnosed and solved the problem, thus avoiding serious damage. The TMI investigations also uncovered another telling fact. The power-operated relief valves that failed to close on the TMI reactor, the major culprit in the accident, had failed before—nine times—in reactors of similar design. Indeed, the sequence of events that ultimately occurred at TMI, and its possible consequences, had been postulated and analyzed by researchers at the Tennessee Valley Authority and the NRC. Had the TMI operators known about these prior events and analyses, in all likelihood a simple breakdown would not have escalated into a disastrous meltdown. Yet TMI's operators had no information whatsoever about all this.

Here we arrive at a third major lesson of the TMI accident: nuclear power's institutional arrangements for learning from industry experience were seriously flawed.[28] For example, although the NRC required the nuclear utilities to report all abnormal events, there was no system for distributing these reports to other utilities, no system for evaluating their safety significance, and no system for analyzing their applicability to other nuclear plants.

What is more interesting, however, is the fact that no such system existed within the industry itself. And at least part of the reason why can be found in another defining feature of nuclear power's fossil fuel mentality. It was *insular.*[29] In the words of one nuclear utility CEO, here speaking to an audience of fellow utility CEOs:

> As all of us know, the nuclear industry is unique. For years, each of us decided on his own marketing strategy, financing program, labor contracts, and power sales contracts. Although we tried to beat each other on the bottom line, *we ran our business independently, free to give little regard to what our sister utilities did.*[30]

All the nuclear utilities thus behaved as if each were an island unto itself, and did so, I suspect, in large part because they were monopolies insulated from the competitive pressures of the marketplace. Whatever the cause, we can safely say that the nuclear utilities led an isolated existence in many significant respects, and that one noteworthy consequence of their isolationism was that hardly any serious attention was given to the operating experience (including accidents) of other nuclear plants.

Now look at the industry's learning disability from a slightly different perspective. We have already noticed the utilities' tendency to equate good power plant performance (both fossil fuel and nuclear) with output—maximizing the production of electricity. If this meant running the machinery until it broke, it also led utility officials to conclude that "repair and maintenance wasn't a high priority," in the words of one industry official. "What was important was continuous operation, and repair and maintenance means being shut down." Not only that, it was extremely difficult to measure with any precision the direct benefits of repair and maintenance. Did this particular maintenance procedure actually prevent a breakdown? No one really knew. What they did know is that the maintenance procedure required the unit to be shut down, thus reducing output. The *costs* of repair and maintenance were obvious, in the eyes of industry officials, while the *benefits* were vague and uncertain. Hence these were low priorities. It was the same for learning from industry experience as well—even more so, because the practical benefits were even more uncertain and difficult to ascertain, especially when calculated in terms of the nuclear utilities' *real business*—producing electricity.

So learning from industry experience, far from being regarded as a core (production-enhancing) task, was judged to be a peripheral if not wholly expendable undertaking. And so, with only a slight degree of caricature, one might say that the pre-TMI nuclear industry was composed of inward-looking and production-oriented utilities that saw little if any value in joining together to develop an industry-wide institutional mechanism for the collection, analysis, and dissemination of safety-related operational experience. How has all this changed with the post-TMI regulatory transformation? We shall return to this question in chapter 7.

PROFESSIONALISM

The role of a nuclear plant control room operator has frequently been compared to that of a commercial airline pilot. Both jobs deal with extremely complicated machines; both are mundane much of the time, even boring, because the equipment is highly automated; and, most critically, both have the potential for producing disastrous results if the operator or pilot does not react quickly and intelligently when a problem arises. But soon after the TMI accident, industry observers also noted a big difference: commercial airline pilots are very carefully selected and rigorously trained; nuclear plant operators aren't. That, distilled to its essence, was the heart of nuclear power's professionalism problem according to the TMI accident investigations. "The TMI operators were not properly trained," said nuclear engineering professor Thomas Pigford, a member of the president's commission on TMI. "There must be far better education, training, and understanding, and there must be more careful selection of qualified people. . . . A new approach towards training and qualification of all people in the management of safety is required. . . . This is the most important lesson to be learned from the TMI accident."[31]

It was a most important lesson indeed, and still is, as evidenced by the elaborate industry-wide training system the utilities now have in place to address the training-related problems uncovered by the TMI accident studies.[32] By the mid-1980s, however, it became increasingly apparent that this was only part of the industry's professionalism problem. "We are now seeing troublesome events that cannot be traced to inadequate training," said INPO's president. "Instead, our conclusion is that the principal root cause is a shortfall in professionalism."[33]

An extreme but revealing example: in 1987 it was discovered that night-shift operators, while working in the control room of Philadelphia Electric Company's Peach Bottom nuclear plant, frequently broke into rubber-band and paper-ball fights, distracted themselves with video games, and, most alarming, fell asleep (sometimes *all* of them) on several occasions, thus leaving the fully operating reactor unattended. In a nuclear plant this is no trifling matter. Add to this a multiplicity of less flagrant cases INPO has uncovered at other plants—trainees starting a reactor without proper supervision, operators destroying important plant records, "nonconservative" decisionmaking—and you have a pattern of occurrences united by one very troubling common thread. As INPO sees it, they are all symptomatic of *a lack of sufficient professional respect and sense of responsibility for nuclear technology,* otherwise known as a lack of "professional attitude."[34] They are also symptomatic of the industry's institutional lag problem, I might add; for when we investigate these attitudes more closely, we will discover that, here as elsewhere, at least part of the reason for the professionalism problem can be traced to the industry's fossil fuel cultural orientation.

And so it is that nuclear power's current professionalism problem mainly has to do, not with inadequate technical training, but with more subtle and elusive aspects of institutional life—the constellation of values, purposes, and sensibilities informing the conduct of nuclear plant personnel; in short, their "professional attitude." On this deeper level lies the phenomenon with which we will be concerned, for it invites us to consider what has now become one of INPO's most significant, ambitious, and challenging tasks for the 1990s. I will call it INPO's professionalism project, and I will explore its origins, methods, and aims in chapter 8.

Inadequate management involvement, an impoverished normative system, an inability to learn from industry experience, a lack of professionalism—I have only remarked here upon some of the most obvious lessons of the TMI accident. Nevertheless, I hope these examples provide, in a more general way, some sense of why it is necessary to distinguish between nuclear power's technological hardware and institutional arrangements, and why, to once again cite TMI's vice president, "we had in the United States about as poor an institutional arrange-ment for the introduction of this demanding new technology as one could devise." Our task now is to explore the regulatory system's re-sponse to this most fundamental lesson of TMI, first the NRC's and then the industry's.

3

Nuclear Regulatory Commission

"The TMI accident scared the hell out of us," recalls a top-level NRC official. "The possibility of a serious accident ceased to be a theoretical possibility, a highly unlikely event, and from that point on we began thinking much more seriously that accidents can really happen." And from that point on, he adds, the NRC began taking institutions—"the management systems and people that actually run the machines"—much more seriously:

> We gradually began to realize that these were mainly management problems that led to poor operations. It wasn't the design of the plant in most cases that was the real problem. A really good careful driver can probably drive a poorly designed car with no bumpers, but a poor driver can easily wreck a well-designed car.

In this chapter we cast a glance at how the NRC has responded to the lessons of TMI, particularly those concerning nuclear power's institutional arrangements, for only against this background can we fully appreciate the emergence and development of nuclear industry self-regulation. And to find the beginnings of an answer, we must go back to the origins of nuclear power regulation.

HISTORY AND ORGANIZATIONAL CULTURE

Although the NRC was not created until 1975, the origins of its basic regulatory approach can be traced to the end of World War II, soon after the development of the first atomic bomb, when Congress passed the Atomic Energy Act of 1946. In establishing a five-member Atomic Energy Commission (AEC), the statute defined the AEC's principal functions in military terms: to develop and manufacture nuclear weapons. That lasted until 1954, when Congress revised the law and, by allowing nuclear technology to enter the mainstream of American industrial life, broadened the AEC's mandate. Congress declared that the widespread use of nuclear energy was a national goal and that it was the AEC's task to promote that growth.

But the AEC was created with a dual mission. Congress directed the AEC not only to promote nuclear power's peaceful uses, but also "to protect the health and safety of the public." This raised an obvious problem; instructing an agency to both promote *and* regulate an industry was like instructing a driver to step on accelerator and brakes simultaneously. And so, almost from the start, critics expressed serious misgivings over these regulatory arrangements.

To further collapse a very complicated history, years of criticism finally culminated in the Energy Reorganization Act of 1974. Its basic purpose, here described by Senator Abraham Ribicoff, the act's principal author, was straightforward:

> The development of the nuclear power industry has been managed by the same agency responsible for regulating it. While this arrangement may have been necessary in the infancy of the atomic era after World War II, it is clearly not in the public interest to continue this special relationship now that industry is well on its way to becoming among the largest and most hazardous in the Nation. In fact, it is difficult now to determine . . . where the Commission ends and the industry begins. The result has been growing criticism of the safety of nuclear power reactors.[1]

In consequence of the bill's passage, the AEC was split on January 1, 1975. The NRC was given the AEC's regulatory responsibilities, while the Energy Research and Development Administration (now part of the Department of Energy) was given the AEC's promotional responsibilities.[2] But we are getting ahead of our story. To see how the NRC defined its regulatory task, we must first consider how the AEC defined its regulatory role, as the NRC was "mostly staffed by those who staffed the AEC during its last years."[3] Or, to put it another way, the NRC inherited the AEC's "regulatory tradition."[4] So we must ask what that tradition was and how it influenced the AEC/NRC's core regulatory task.

DEFINING REGULATORY TASKS

Students of public administration tell us that there are great differences in how the tasks of government agencies get defined. In some cases, for example, the organization's stated goals may be important. How well could AEC officials infer what they were supposed to do in light of the AEC's stated goals? You are an AEC official, and seeking guidance as to your safety-related responsibilities; you read the agency's authorizing legislation, which tells you this: "Protect the health and safety of the public." Reading further, you find this goal cited frequently throughout the act, but you also find that the act itself, as well as its legislative history, is silent on specifics. So what are your duties? What specific functions are you to perform? Judging by the language of the act, the answer was anything but clear.

If the AEC's stated goals were of little help, perhaps a closer look at the nature of the technology itself, nuclear power, can shed some light on how AEC officials defined their regulatory task. Here is how Edward Teller, a leading figure during the formative years of nuclear power regulation, described the technology's unique demands from a regulatory standpoint:

> We could not follow the usual method of trial and error. This method was an integral part of American industrial progress before the nuclear age, but in the nuclear age it presented intolerable risks. An error in the manufacture of an automobile, for instance, might kill one to ten people. An error in planning safety devices for an airplane might cost the lives of 150 people. But an error allowing the release of a reactor's load of radioactive particles in a strategic location could endanger the population of an entire city.[5]

Nuclear power's special risks thus led regulators to establish what Teller called a "simple procedure." For each reactor, designers were to "imagine the worst possible accident and to design safety apparatus guaranteeing that it could not happen."[6] In Teller's words:

> The committee [the AEC's Reactor Safeguards Committee] reviewed each reactor plan, trying to imagine an accident even worse than that conceived by the planner. If we could think of a plausible mishap worse than any discussed by the planner, his analysis of the potential dangers was considered inadequate. In

most cases, the required discussion created a reasonable spirit of caution, and we could advise the Atomic Energy Commission that the reactor would be sufficiently safe.[7]

Without going into the complex details of how this "simple procedure" developed over time, suffice it to say that it became the foundation of the AEC's licensing review process—the AEC's principal regulatory tool for protecting the public's health and safety.[8] And the first thing to be said about this whole process is that it stressed one principle above all—*engineering safety.* For the AEC and the NRC, nuclear plant hardware was the key to preventing accidents. And from the mid-1950s until the TMI accident, the entire regulatory framework displayed a strong engineering bias.[9] Nuclear plants should be designed *conservatively.* That was the keynote, and a list of design principles of this kind included *wide margins for error* (for instance, the number of control rods used to regulate the nuclear reaction in the reactor core had to be substantially greater than the number actually needed to shut down the reactor); *redundant systems* so that if any safety-related piece of hardware failed there would be a backup to perform that function (for instance, each plant was required to have multiple and independent sources of electrical power, each capable of providing all the power required to run the plant); and *emergency safety systems* (such as emergency high-pressure water cooling pumps) because it was assumed that, despite conservative designs, some components and systems would still fail. In these and numerous other cautious ways, nuclear plant hardware was the regulators' foremost defense against nuclear accidents.

DEFINING REGULATORY TASKS: THE ROAD NOT TAKEN

All of this raises an interesting question. Nuclear power's development in the United States proceeded along two closely related yet distinct paths: the civilian side, led by the AEC/NRC and the nuclear utilities (among others), and the military side, led by the navy's nuclear submarine program, including, most notably, Admiral Hyman Rickover.[10] I say "closely related" because the naval program influenced the civilian side in many important ways. The design of the Three Mile Island reactor, for example, was a descendant of a pressurized water reactor developed in the late 1940s and early 1950s to power a submarine.[11] And many of the land-based reactor program's conservative design principles (wide margins for error and redundant systems, for instance) were modeled after the navy's sea-based reactors.[12] Yet it was a process of selective incorporation, for the AEC stopped short of following the nuclear navy's lead in one particularly noteworthy respect. The naval program, in addition to engineering safety, also pursued a strategy of institutionalizing safety by governing the management and operation of nuclear reactors in light of a complex set of demanding institutional principles. (See chapter 5 for a detailed discussion of these principles.) Engineering safety *and* institutionalized safety were the twin hallmarks of the naval program's safety strategy. Thus, if we take a comparative view of the matter, it is possible to see that the AEC's one-sided preoccupation with nuclear hardware, and corresponding neglect of nuclear power's institutional arrangements, was by no means a foregone conclusion. Why this pattern of selective attention? Why didn't the AEC pursue a strategy of institutionalized safety as well as engineering safety?

Though the answer is far from clear, let me suggest how political considerations might have figured in the explanation. Put most simply, the AEC was responding to the wishes of its key political overseers—the president and Congress—and their desire to rapidly develop atomic energy for civilian purposes. If you were an AEC official, historians tell us, the clear message you received from the president was a goal of minimum regulation: "President Eisenhower had explicitly stated a goal of minimum regulation for the new atomic-energy industry, and his philosophy had been incorporated in the 1954 Atomic Energy Act."[13]

The AEC heard a similar message, prodevelopment and antiregulation, from Congress, particularly the Joint Committee on Atomic Energy, by far the AEC's most important congressional overseer. After meeting with the Joint Committee, for example, the AEC's general manager left the room thoroughly convinced that the majority of its members wanted the fledgling regulatory program "to get into the licensee's business as little as possible."[14] Or, to cite the AEC's chairman, the commission "should not impose unnecessary limitations or restrictions upon private participation in the development of the atom's uses." Most important, he added, the AEC "should not interfere with management practices."[15]

Not interfering with management practices—that was an essential part of the AEC's marching orders during its formative years, and signs

abound that it had a deep-seated and lasting impact on the AEC/
NRC's subsequent development. In stark contrast to the navy's approach to nuclear safety, the AEC/NRC almost completely ignored the
industry's institutional arrangements for managing and operating nuclear plants—that is, until TMI.

DISCOVERING INSTITUTIONS

The TMI investigation revealed overreliance by the regulatory
agency [NRC] on an excessive number of detailed written regulations that seem to specify how a reactor should be designed
and operated for safety. Writing these regulations and evaluating nuclear plants against these regulations has been the preoccupation of the regulatory agency. . . . It is understandable that
the NRC staff may be reluctant to undertake a new approach
that can undermine its extensive investment in regulation by
detailed documentation.[16]

So said a Kemeny Commission member two years after the accident, and in his observation lies an important moral. To this day the
NRC remains a very "rule-ish" regulatory bureaucracy in significant
respects, highly prescriptive and compliance-oriented in most of its
methods, and still very much committed to engineering safety.[17] The
simplest way of showing that is to look at figure 3.1 and note the pro-
liferation of regulatory requirements since the TMI accident. And yet,
despite the continuity in regulatory orientation, it is also central to
recognize how the TMI accident changed the NRC's regulatory posture in some very significant ways.

Most important, the TMI accident led many observers and participants, including the highly influential Kemeny Commission, to reject
a fundamental premise of the AEC/NRC's pre-TMI regulatory regime—not interfering with management practices:

Responsibility and accountability for safe power plant operations, including the management of a plant during an accident,
should be placed on the licensee in all circumstances. It is
therefore necessary to assure that licensees are competent to
discharge this responsibility. *To assure this competency . . . we*

recommend that the agency [NRC] establish and enforce higher organizational and management standards for licensees. Particular attention should be given to such matters as the following: integration of decision-making in any organization licensed to construct or operate a plant; kinds of expertise that must be within the organization; financial capability; quality assurance programs; operator and supervisor practices and their periodic reevaluation; plant surveillance and maintenance practices; and requirements for the analysis and reporting of unusual events.[18]

The "NRC fully agreed with this recommendation."[19] And over the years agency officials have developed a variety of regulatory tools that, in one way and another, focus on the nuclear utilities' management practices. Chief among these are the Systematic Assessment of Licensee Performance program, the Diagnostic Evaluation program, and the Resident Inspector program.

Take resident inspectors first. Frequently described as the NRC's "eyes and ears" in the nuclear plant, the resident inspector program, established throughout the industry shortly after the TMI accident, has NRC inspectors (usually two or three) working full-time in each nuclear plant. "Having resident inspectors there really helps us better

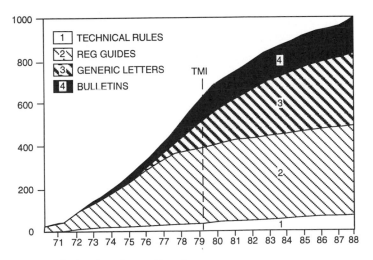

Fig. 3.1 Cumulative Regulatory Requirements

understand what's going on in the plant from a management stand-point," explains an NRC official:

Before TMI, we'd only send in inspectors periodically, and they could only go in and look at records and logs and didn't get the flavor of the day-to-day management of the plant. Our resident inspectors are there full-time, and they form opinions about the adequacy of everybody in the plant by interacting with them. So we get a lot of feedback through them about how well the organization functions.

If the Resident Inspector program is the NRC's eyes and ears, the Diagnostic Evaluation Program (DEP) is the agency's in-house psychoanalyst. Established in 1987, the DEP has as its main goal "to determine the root causes of a nuclear plant's safety problems by strongly focusing on the utility's management and organizational practices," explains an NRC official close to the program. To this end, a twenty-person NRC inspection team spends six to eight weeks (including two weeks at the plant, where they interview more than a hundred persons across the organization) diagnosing the organization's "leadership and management practices" and probing its "organizational environment/operator culture" to determine how all that affects plant performance. "While leadership and management practices deal with effective management principles and skills," according to the NRC, "organizational environment/operator culture focuses on attitudes, norms, practices, and history, and their role in creating an atmosphere that affects nuclear operational performance." [20]

Our final example, the Systematic Assessment of Licensee Performance (SALP) program, is the single most important manifestation of the NRC's post-TMI management-oriented regulatory strategy. Created in 1980, the SALP program has been revised several times over the years, but its overall objective has remained essentially the same: "The SALP process is intended to further NRC's understanding of (1) the way in which the licensee's [nuclear utility's] management guides, directs, evaluates, and provides resources for safe plant operations, and (2) the effectiveness of these actions." [21]

Unlike the resident inspectors and diagnostic evaluations, SALP is not an inspection program. It is a structured process of deliberation by which a seven-member SALP board, mainly composed of senior NRC managers as well as the plant's senior resident inspector, "collect and analyze available Agency insights, data, and other information about a plant." [22] Taking all that into account, the SALP board then writes a report card on the plant's management practices; more particularly, it assigns a numerical performance rating, 1 to 3 (1 being best), in each of seven functional areas—plant operations, engineering and technical support, safety assessment, and quality verification, among others. These ratings, plus supporting documentation, are issued as a SALP report and the whole process is repeated about every eighteen months.[23]

Now let us see what the SALP board looks at. In rating the plant's performance, the board uses six sets of evaluation criteria, including, for example, the set listed in table 3.1. And as this example shows, almost all the criteria speak directly to the issue of management practices—how well management states and disseminates policies, how frequently and effectively corporate management is involved in nuclear plant activities, how effectively corporate management uses safety review committees. And so on. Whatever else we might say about these standards, one thing seems clear: the NRC has come a long way from its pre-TMI regulatory posture of not dealing with management practices.

What is not so clear, however, is how exactly the SALP board judges management practices in light of such standards. For example, ask NRC officials how they distinguish between "effective" and "ineffective" corporate management involvement in nuclear plant activities, and you get answers like these. An assistant regional administrator (who has chaired numerous SALP boards): "There's nothing written or specified. I guess the way I look at management involvement, on a personal level, is that I use the same standards that I use when I assess my own managers. And I think I know what high standards ought to be." A senior resident inspector (who has sat on numerous SALP boards as well, and, as with all senior resident inspectors, is a major source of information in the SALP evaluation): "Well, I can evaluate management involvement based on my past experience, which can't be taught. And I don't think I can put down in words what I look at. But I've been around power plants for a long time, and I've seen a lot of different managements. It's just something you learn with experience."

In any event, it is instructive to note what industry officials think of the SALP process. In a 1989 survey that was concerned with exactly this issue (among others), the NRC questioned a wide variety of officials from thirteen nuclear utilities across the country.[24] Here is part of what the survey found: "Licensees believe that SALP numerical ratings should be eliminated, that the SALP process is being used as an

TABLE 3.1

Assurance of Quality, Including Management Involvement and Control

Category 1	Category 2	Category 3
a. There is consistent evidence of prior planning and assignment of priorities; activities are well stated and explicit	a. There is evidence of prior planning and assignment of priorities; procedures for control of activities are stated and defined	a. There is little evidence of prior planning and assignment of priorities; procedures for control of activities are poorly stated or not well understood
b. Policies are well stated, disseminated, and understandable	b. Policies are adequately stated and understood	b. Policies are poorly stated, poorly understood, or nonexistent
c. Decisionmaking is consistently at a level that ensures adequate management review	c. Decisionmaking is usually at a level that ensures adequate management review	c. Decisionmaking is seldom at a level that ensures adequate management review
d. Corporate management is frequently and effectively involved in site activities	d. Corporate management is usually involved in site activities in an effective manner	d. Corporate management is seldom or ineffectively involved in site activities
e. Engineering evaluations are consistently technically adequate and records and plant performance data are complete, well maintained, and available	e. Engineering evaluations are generally adequate and records and plant performance data are generally complete, well maintained, and available	e. Engineering evaluations are frequently inadequate and records and plant performance data are not complete, well maintained, or available
f. Corrective action is effective as indicated by lack of repetition of events	f. Corrective action is usually taken but may not be effective in correcting the root cause of the problem, as indicated by occasional repetition of events	f. Corrective action is not timely or effective and generally addresses symptoms rather than root causes, as indicated by repetition of events
g. Safety review committees . . . are used to provide critical self-assessments to the corporate management and to improve work activities	g. Root cause analyses and self-assessments are occasionally evident and sometimes result in improvements	g. Corporate management does not appear to rely on self-assessment to ensure quality in activities

Source: U.S. Nuclear Regulatory Commission, *NRC Manual*, chap. 0516, Appendix 0516, p. A-3

improper mechanism to obtain better performance, that it is too subjective, that it is not applied uniformly among NRC's regions."[25] Beyond these particular concerns, the survey also uncovered a more fundamental criticism that went to the heart of the whole SALP enterprise: "Licensees commented that NRC inspectors should not be evaluating licensee management and management systems." The main reason why: "Most NRC inspectors are not trained to evaluate licensee management and management systems."[26]

Now it is hardly surprising that utility officials question the ability of government regulators to evaluate their management practices. What may come as a surprise, though, is the fact that similar doubts can be found within the NRC itself. As one former NRC commissioner tried to explain it:

> There is a recognition within the NRC that management is probably the single most important factor in nuclear safety. But there is a continuing unwillingness on the part of the NRC to get heavily involved in management kinds of issues, and in large part that derives from the fact that *this is a heavy technical agency. And technically trained people are relatively uncomfortable in dealing with management-type issues. It's a lot easier to deal with the hardware issues.* It's a lot easier to deal with an issue of, "Is this procedure written correctly?" "Is this pump designed properly? Is it being maintained properly?" Engineers feel comfortable dealing with hardware and technical kinds of issues. They feel fairly uncomfortable and ill-equipped in dealing with management issues. So I think that management has been a very difficult issue for the NRC to come to grips with. [Emphasis supplied.]

Thus, despite all the NRC's new programs for dealing with management practices, one can detect a certain ambivalence within the agency when it comes to regulating these matters. Which is probably why, although most NRC programs are *solution-forcing* (that is, they prescribe detailed remedies for dealing with particular nuclear plant problems, particularly engineering problems), most of the NRC's regulatory tools for dealing with management problems are *attention-focusing*, and stop short of mandating particular solutions. To cite but one example, consider the SALP program and how the NRC states that the NRC's evaluation of nuclear utility management practices "is not intended to identify proposed resolutions or solutions of problems."[27] Once the NRC draws attention to a management problem, it is left to the utility to come up with the solution. In the words of another former NRC commissioner, there exist "real mixed feelings in the NRC about how deeply involved the agency should become in management kinds of issues." And it is for reasons such as these (among others), I surmise, that time and again the NRC has not been eager to tackle some of the complex issues surrounding the management and operation of nuclear plants, and, what's more, has welcomed the opportunity to delegate those regulatory tasks to INPO.

In March 1990, the *Washington Post* ran a story under the headline, "Is Industry Usurping NRC Functions?" It stated, "Who's in charge here? Has the Nuclear Regulatory Commission turned over some of its responsibilities to a little-known organization . . . the Institute of Nuclear Power Operations, a powerful, publicity-shy organization that supervises the operation of every nuclear power plant in the nation[?]"[28] Consider three examples.

We have already noted how, in 1980, the Kemeny Commission recommended that the NRC "establish and enforce higher organizational and management standards for licensees."[29] In response, the NRC's TMI Action Plan directed the agency to develop regulatory standards for evaluating utility management,[30] which the NRC did in their draft "Guidelines for Utility Management Structure and Technical Resources."[31] But by 1983 the NRC abandoned these efforts. Instead of direct government regulation, the NRC endorsed INPO's regulatory role: "INPO has developed general guidance and criteria for improving the quality of NPP [nuclear power plant] management and organization and has recently initiated an effort to evaluate utility corporate office structures. . . . *NRC can accept INPO's corporate office evaluations as an alternative.*"[32]

Another example involves training. Congress, by passing the Nuclear Waste Policy Act in 1983, directed the NRC to issue regulations for the training and qualifications of nuclear power plant operators, supervisors, technicians, and other operating personnel.[33] In order to meet this directive, in 1985 the NRC published a policy statement that embraced the INPO-run training program: "In recognition of industry initiatives underway to upgrade training programs, the NRC endorses the Institute of Nuclear Power Operations (INPO)-managed Training Accreditation Program . . . [and] will refrain from new rulemaking in the area of training."[34]

When a public interest group sued the NRC for not issuing its own training regulations, the NRC told the U.S. appeals court that a rule was not needed because the existing INPO training program was working. The court ruled against the NRC, however. As *Inside NRC* reported in June 1991, "The [NRC] commission and staff clearly view the rulemaking as a necessary evil, mandated by a court decision, but really unnecessary in the real world." In (reluctantly) complying with the court's mandate, the NRC issued a proposed training rule in January 1992.[35] The net result: the new regulation in effect codifies INPO's training program. Or, to cite the regulation itself, "The proposed rule generally reflects current industry practice."[36]

Still another example concerns the maintenance of nuclear plants. In March 1988 the NRC took the first steps toward developing a comprehensive maintenance rule for the nuclear industry; for, like airliners, nuclear plants require exacting (and costly) maintenance to ensure safe and reliable operation. When it issued a revised policy statement on maintenance in December 1989, however, the NRC's ambivalence (particularly the staff's) became apparent:

> The Commission desires to have in place an industry-wide program that will ensure effective maintenance is achieved and maintained over the life of each plant. . . . The Commission recognizes that . . . the Institute for Nuclear Power Operations (INPO) can contribute, through their leadership, to an industry-wide program for improving and maintaining effective maintenance and encourages such leadership. . . . In view of the progress made to date . . . the Commission has decided to hold rulemaking in abeyance for an 18 month period to monitor industry initiatives and progress.[37]

When the NRC staff reported the results of its eighteen-month evaluation to the commissioners, they recommended that no maintenance rule be issued and that the NRC embrace INPO's maintenance program as an industry standard.[38]

I have only remarked here upon some of the most important ways the NRC has refrained from regulating nuclear industry management practices and has embraced, implicitly if not explicitly, INPO's regulatory regime as an alternative to direct government regulation.[39] And while informed opinions on the merits of all this may differ, there can be little doubt that INPO's existence has influenced the NRC's post-TMI regulatory regime in significant ways. How the nuclear industry should train its workers, how it should collect and analyze industry operating experience,[40] how it should manage the nuclear utility, how it should operate and maintain nuclear plants—the evidence suggests that all these areas (and more) would probably be governed by a much more comprehensive and detailed body of NRC regulatory requirements had it not been for INPO's creation. Thus, we can see now more clearly why Ralph Nader concluded that INPO exercises "quasi-governmental functions." What remains to be explored is how this secretive organization carries out those functions.

4

Institute of Nuclear Power Operations

We must constantly remind ourselves of what INPO's role is," the chairman of INPO's board of directors, Lelan Sillin, told his audience of fellow nuclear utility CEOs. Sillin, a leader in INPO's creation and administrative development, then went on to explain that "INPO was not created to brag on us, do PR for us, or make us feel more comfortable." Rather, INPO was "created as an independent organization" to "point us in the right direction" by calling out "our weaknesses" and by ensuring that "we are overcoming them":

> In establishing INPO, the nuclear utility industry took the un-
> precedented step of embracing the concept of self-improvement
> and self-regulation. In doing so, the industry assumed a major
> responsibility. . . . *We adopted a philosophy by which all of the*
> *nuclear utilities would operate,* and we committed ourselves in-
> dividually and collectively to achieve a standard of excellence
> in the conduct of our nuclear power responsibilities.

In a word, Sillin concludes, "INPO was established as a *conscience* for all of us."[1]

Nuclear power's collective conscience—this is a most instructive analogy for thinking about INPO's regulatory role, as I hope to show in the chapters to come. A dictionary definition of *conscience* tells us that it is "the faculty of recognizing the distinction between right and wrong in regard to one's conduct coupled with a sense that one should act accordingly."[2] Notice how this definition has two parts: a *norma-tive* dimension (the ability to distinguish between right and wrong); and a *motivational* dimension (in addition to making normative dis-tinctions, a person's conscience also brings pressure to bear so that he or she will act accordingly). As for INPO, it also performs both roles.

For the normative part, INPO articulates a new industrial morality for all the nuclear utilities, thus spelling out what conduct is virtuous and what goals are legitimate and desirable. (See chapter 6.) And for the motivational part, INPO distributes praise and shame coupled with peer pressure, thereby inducing nuclear utilities to honor the new morality's industrial principles and practices. (See chapter 7.) The overriding purpose of all this? Like a conscience, it is to promote *responsible* corporate conduct among the nuclear utilities. Now if these considerations suggest that INPO represents the industry's *collective* conscience, they also hint at another aspect of INPO's regulatory role—its communitarian dimension. By striving to unify the industry around a distinctive set of shared values, beliefs, and practices (a common "philosophy," as Sillin puts it), INPO is seeking to build a distinctive kind of community. "INPO represents a unique compact among us, among the members. I don't know anything like it in any industry," a nuclear utility CEO on INPO's board of directors observed. "INPO is in the position of the glue that holds the compact together."[3] INPO is a *unifying* institution, as these comments suggest; and as we shall abundantly see in the chapters to come, this represents one of INPO's most significant contributions to nuclear power's post-TMI regulatory transformation. To fully appreciate the nature and significance of this contribution, however, we must turn first to INPO's origins and administrative development. Why did the nuclear industry create INPO in the first place? And what formative factors have most influenced INPO's subsequent administrative development?

Origins

When utility officials describe the pre-TMI nuclear industry, a collective portrait emerges in which each nuclear utility behaved like an "island unto itself" or an "independent barony." In a word, the industry was *fragmented.* What is more, because the social ties linking individual nuclear utilities were so weak, "the industry had not been able to act on a unified basis in any meaningful way," as one industry official puts it. Consider once again the observation of a prominent nuclear utility CEO, making a similar point in 1983 before a group of fellow nuclear CEOs: "For years, each of us decided on his own marketing strategy, financing program, labor contracts, and power sales contracts. . . . *We ran our business independently, free to give little regard to what our sister utilities did"* (emphasis supplied).[4]

How, then, did this narrowly insular outlook affect nuclear power's pre-TMI system of industry self-regulation? In reading all the TMI accident studies, one will find that they have almost nothing to say about the industry's collective regulatory efforts. Why? True to form, the nuclear utilities "never mobilized an industrywide effort to concentrate on safety-related operational problems," a leading TMI accident study informs us.[5] Then came TMI.

"Three Mile Island had one great effect," a former member of the NRC's predecessor, the Atomic Energy Commission, observed a few short months after the accident. "It pulled the industry together for the first time." Before TMI, nuclear power was a "fragmented industry" composed of "utility fiefdoms," "each operating in its own little sovereign state." But "all of a sudden," he continued, the industry was "pulled together" in trying to cope with "a common problem"—the consequences of TMI.[6] It was a traumatic shock that transformed the industry's traditional habits of thought in fundamental ways by highlighting, as never before, the nuclear utilities' common interests and mutual interdependence. Perhaps no example makes this point more clearly than the industry's response to two fundamental threats—government regulation and problem nuclear utilities—both of which led to INPO's creation.

Responding to widespread criticism triggered by the accident, the NRC prepared to launch a massive regulatory assault on the industry. An action plan was developed, for instance, that can best be described as a "wish list," recalls an NRC official, as it contained "almost every regulatory idea that had been floating around the agency."[7] It should also be noted that the plan was not limited to the owners of TMI, nor to the industry's poorer performers. It applied to all the nuclear utilities.

If industry officials found any one thing especially disturbing about these regulatory developments, it was a significant shift in the NRC's regulatory posture. Prior to TMI, as we saw in the last chapter, most of the NRC's energies were devoted to regulating the *technological hardware* used in nuclear power generation (such as the plant's relief valves and coolant pumps). As for the *institutional arrangements* for using that technology—the nuclear utility's information and management systems, for instance—the NRC had paid relatively little attention to such matters. But TMI changed all that. It taught NRC officials to take institutions far more seriously, and so they began to redirect their regulatory efforts accordingly.

"If the industry had not created INPO," said one of its founding fathers, Middle South Utilities' CEO, Floyd Lewis, "it is my firm conviction that . . . we would today [1981] be in a lot worse shape than we are, perhaps facing . . . even federal operation of nuclear plants."[8] Obviously, nuclear utility officials wanted to curb the NRC's regulatory response to TMI, especially those initiatives directed at their institutional arrangements for managing and operating nuclear plants. And it was with that hope in mind that they joined together and took the unprecedented step of collectively endorsing a program of industry-wide self-regulation. Thus INPO was created. "Our foremost objective is to make the process [of industry self-regulation through INPO] work," said the chairman of INPO's board of directors in 1983, "and thus prevent the further intrusion of government and prescriptive regulation into our management."[9]

Just as the TMI accident mobilized the industry in response to a common *external* threat—government regulation—it also helped to unify the industry in reaction to a mutual *internal* threat, unsafe nuclear utilities. Question industry officials about the TMI accident's single most important lesson, and you typically get some variation on a theme well stated in a 1983 speech to nuclear industry CEOs. The TMI accident demonstrated "the very special nature of nuclear power," and it did so in two closely related ways.

First of all, the industry realized that "a really catastrophic accident" was no longer virtually inconceivable. The probability is "very low" yet "always present" that "thousands of people and hundreds of square miles" may be seriously harmed for "very large spans of time." So when it comes to the consequences of a serious accident, no other industrial technology can match "the very special nature" of nuclear power's destruction. Looked at another way, the TMI accident forcefully demonstrated as never before that "each licensee is to a considerable extent a captive of every other licensee":

> It isn't enough for a CEO to assure that in his own company the
> responsibility for safety has been properly assumed and every
> possible need fulfilled. He must also be certain that every other
> licensee is fulfilling that responsibility satisfactorily because
> the insufficiency and failure of one of them has a potential for
> destroying the credibility of all the others.[10]

Like a chain, then, the nuclear industry is no stronger than its weakest link. If there is another major accident in the United States, according to this logic, with all that would mean for increased public opposition to nuclear power (to say nothing of increased government regulation), it may well break the industry, or so industry officials feared. They were hostages of each other. And because of that life-or-death interdependence, the industry could no longer afford the fragmentation, the narrowly circumscribed and detached way of acting and thinking, that characterized the socioeconomic network linking nuclear utilities prior to TMI. Says an industry official, TMI abruptly moved nuclear utility executives from an "attitude of not my brother's keeper to one that everything my brother does is going to affect me." In the words of another industry official: "We set up INPO after the TMI accident *to protect our very substantial investment in nuclear power.*"[11]

To put this development in more general terms, the bonds of community can be fashioned from various elements, and one of the vital forces that moves people and groups in the direction of community is the experience of interdependence. If members of a group have no need for each other, if nothing is to be gained through a continuing relationship, it is not likely that community will emerge. But if they do share interests in common, and those interests are strong enough to support an ongoing relationship, then the conditions are ripe for a community of interest to emerge. And so it is that the TMI accident, by forging a strong community of interest, resulted in INPO's creation. Today these interests remain a powerful source of integration. Yet it is fundamental to recognize that the emergence of community is a developmental process and that over time the industry has become something more than a bare community organized around a skeletal framework of common interests. Additional sources of integration have been developed as a result of INPO's creation, including, most important, a common framework of unifying norms, purposes, and practices. (See chapter 6.)

So much for INPO's creation. Our task now is to examine INPO's subsequent administrative development, and in the course of doing so, probe an enduring tension that may well represent the single most important factor that set INPO on its distinctive course.

INPO's Enduring Tension

"The mission of the Institute," according to INPO's *Institutional Plan* (the closest thing INPO has to a formal constitution), "is to promote the highest levels of safety and reliability—to promote excellence— in the operation of nuclear electric generating plants."[12] Like so many formal statements of organizational purpose, it is broad and vague. So the question arises as to what exactly it means. Addressing this point in a 1986 speech to nuclear utility chief executive officers (INPO's most important constituency), INPO's president had this to say:

> I have been asked a number of times to describe INPO's mission in more specific terms. Our mission is to promote safe and reliable plant operations, but what does this really mean? Specifically, we want to *prevent core damage,* the physical breaching of the clad with fuel dispersion into the coolant. *If we are successful in doing that in U.S. reactors, we will have carried out our mission in the United States.*[13]

At this point many readers are probably skeptical as to INPO's regulatory role. All this talk of INPO operating as an industry conscience that promotes industry standards of excellence in order to prevent damage to reactor cores sounds well and good, the reader may think, but it probably amounts to little more than self-serving public relations on the part of an industry eager to avoid more government regulation. After all, INPO is an *industry organization,* and so it is difficult to imagine how it can elude co-optation and maintain the autonomy required to carry out its regulatory tasks free from undue industry interference.

Such skepticism must be taken seriously. Not simply because the prevailing social science view cautions us to regard private regulatory organizations like INPO with suspicion, though that is important, but because it points to an enduring tension of far-reaching importance for understanding the evolution of INPO's regulatory role. The nature of that tension? Let us go back to the early years of INPO's operation to find the beginnings of an answer.

INPO's Legitimacy Problem

When asked about the major challenges INPO has faced over the years, an INPO vice president offers this answer: "Establishing credibility—that was our major challenge. It wasn't easy in the beginning, and we still have to work on building credibility." "Obviously," said a member of INPO's board of directors in a 1983 interview, "you can't endow anybody or any organization with credibility. It must be earned." He went on, "You must have credibility with the people you evaluate, and I'm not talking about the CEOs of the company, I'm talking about the operators, the maintenance people, the engineering people and the maintenance supervisors." For INPO, he added, earning that credibility has been "a great big task."[14]

This is puzzling. INPO is an industry organization created and funded by the nuclear utilities; one might expect to find industry officials behaving like proud parents, radiating confidence and support for their new industry offspring. Yet a recurrent theme that emerges from interviews with INPO and industry officials is that INPO lacked such support. Why?

Part of the explanation has to do with the fact that INPO was a new organization, the first of its kind in the nuclear power industry devoted to "self-regulation." What exactly did that mean? How would INPO behave as a regulator? "It wasn't clear what INPO's role was initially," a nuclear industry official recalls, "especially when they started doing plant evaluations and inspections. The industry didn't know what to make of them. Were they a regulator or what?"[15] So industry officials were apprehensive. "We were concerned that INPO was another police force entering the industry," says another industry official. Sounding a similar theme, Detroit Edison CEO Walter J. Mc-Carthy described the industry's outlook this way:

> The immediate reaction from most people was that they didn't need anyone else to observe them. People felt it was all they could do just to run the plant. They just weren't ready for outsiders to come in and study them.
>
> Imagine if you were told that a special review team would be visiting your home to study your family. On the team there would be a specialist in cooking, a specialist in housekeeping and a specialist in childcare. And you're told these specialists will publish a report on what they see.
>
> I think this is the kind of feeling that prevailed in the earlier days. . . . I think a lot of people . . . were supporting INPO, saying, "We really need an organization to look at the other guy, but we don't need to change ourselves."[16]

INPO was an additional burden in an already irritatingly burdensome regulatory environment, as these comments imply. Worse yet, INPO was imposing demands (and costs) that went beyond those already required by NRC regulations. "There was a lot of concern," an industry official observes, "that we would now be dancing to two orchestras—NRC and INPO." While no one seriously challenged the NRC's authority to impose regulatory requirements on the plant, as the government's regulatory regime was suffused with the color of law, the same could not be said of INPO's regulatory requirements. "When INPO started issuing a number of edicts," another industry official recalls, "the utility personnel said, 'Here's more administrative garbage that's being placed on us and we don't really have to live by it because they aren't the law. And what we are going to do is live by the law and not by a lot of edicts that have been put out by some bumbling organization down in Georgia.'"[17]

This last barb, that INPO was a "bumbling organization," brings us to the main explanation of INPO's credibility problem. The ranks of INPO's leadership and staff (for reasons I will get to later) were dominated by ex–nuclear navy personnel with no prior experience in civilian nuclear plants. As to why this fact did not sit well with many in the industry, put yourself in the shoes of a nuclear plant employee. You are confronted with a new organization; it behaves much like a regulator, as it inspects, evaluates, and criticizes how you operate your plant; and it imposes requirements and costs that go beyond what the NRC regulations require. All that was made only worse by the fact that this organization was (and is) dominated by "navy nukes," a term frequently used to describe (and deride) those on INPO's staff with a nuclear navy background. "The reaction of a lot of industry people," as one industry official observes, "was 'Who are you to tell me how to run this plant. You just got off a submarine.'" Because of their nuclear navy background, says another industry official, *"INPO officials did not really understand what was going on in the industry. They had a perception of what it looked like from the navy side, but I don't really think they understood what it looked like from the commercial side. That it is more than running a boat. There's a lot bigger challenges to running a plant than a boat."* (Emphasis supplied.)[18]

At a 1982 workshop for nuclear plant managers, INPO officials asked the following question: "How can INPO evaluation teams be more effective in identifying areas that need improvement?" "Do not waste time telling sea stories," one plant manager answered. "Avoid making utilities think they are being inspected to Navy standards by Navy personnel."[19] Far from being an isolated complaint, such feelings were widespread within the nuclear utility industry. INPO was an organization dominated by outsiders—"navy nukes"—too far removed and thus generally out of touch with the practical realities of nuclear plant operations. "Because INPO had an overabundance of ex-nukes," an industry official recalls, "a lot of people in the utility industry felt that INPO was trying to jam nuclear navy standards down their throat."

INPO's Quest for Legitimacy

In saying that INPO is a *communitarian* regulator, whatever else that may mean, one thing seems clear: there must be a *close integration* between regulator and regulated. The nuclear industry must view INPO as "one of us"—not an outsider like the NRC, but an *industry* organization that closely identifies with, understands, and is responsive to the industry's special needs and concerns. Solidarity is important. For it is the chief way a communitarian regulator like INPO acquires the legitimacy and develops the firm base of industry support so vital to carrying out its distinctive regulatory role. Conclusion: If INPO had done nothing to address its legitimacy problem, INPO's regulatory role would certainly be in very serious trouble today.

That hasn't happened, however. Though it would certainly be an overstatement to suggest that INPO has won the industry's total confidence and complete support, there is wide agreement among industry officials that INPO has in fact made significant progress when it comes to enhancing its legitimacy. How? That question asks us to change our focus and consider one of INPO's most striking features. Its administrative structure—from top to bottom—encourages a level of industry participation that would be unthinkable among governmental regulatory agencies. Industry participation, in short, has been the key ingredient in INPO's quest for legitimacy.

The idea of co-optation is helpful here. Generally defined as "the process of absorbing new elements into the leadership or policy-determining structure of an organization as a means of averting threats to its stability or existence," co-optation is a legitimation strategy.[20] And most important for our purposes is a variant of this process involving the *public* sharing of power by the organization with "outside" persons. (One example is the United Automobile Workers' president sitting on Chrysler's board of directors.) "The coopted participants *legitimate the system of authority in the eyes of their fellows,* and they can serve as channels of communication and control, *thus helping to bridge the gap between rulers and ruled.*"[21] How do INPO's pathways for industry participation—board of directors, industry review groups, and peer regulators, among others—help bridge the gap between regulator and regulated? And if co-optation is a key to understanding INPO's administrative structure, this raises some further questions. To what extent is industry participation a tool by which the industry exercises power over INPO? And to what extent is industry participation a tool of INPO itself? What does INPO gain from industry participation? And what does INPO surrender?

Board of Directors

As INPO's *Institutional Plan* states—and its organization chart illustrates (see figure 4.1)—INPO's "organization is similar in many ways to a typical U.S. corporation. A board of directors, elected by INPO's members, oversees the operations and activities of the Institute. The president of the Institute is elected by and reports to the Board of Directors." [22] Sitting on the board (in 1991) are nine nuclear utility CEOs, one nuclear utility vice president, one nuclear plant manager, and INPO's president. Very senior industry executives thus dominate the board, and have done so ever since the issue of its makeup was settled at the time of INPO's creation. "One of the early questions was the matter of governance," recalls one of INPO's founders, Duke Power CEO William S. Lee. "For credibility, it was argued that *a majority of directors should be from outside the industry.* The counterargument was that *the INPO board must be in a position to commit the industry.*" [23]

One view, then, argued for industry *outsiders* sitting on the board so as to help reassure a skeptical public (especially Congress and the NRC) that INPO was indeed truly independent of the industry. As for the counterargument, that too involved considerations of legitimacy, albeit of a different sort. The board should be drawn from *insiders*, industry executives, to help legitimate INPO's authority in the eyes of industry officials, and, most important, to help bridge the gap between regulator and regulated. The latter argument prevailed—INPO's board of directors should "represent" the industry. [24]

> The industry recognized the success of INPO required a governing body that would be actively involved. . . . Thus, in establishing INPO the industry decided *INPO should have a strong Board of Directors—made up of eleven representatives of the utility industry. . . . The board has been active in charting INPO's course* and intimately involved in reviewing INPO's operations, program and effectiveness. [25]

These words, spoken in 1983 by the chairman of INPO's board, were addressed to an audience of top-level nuclear industry executives won-

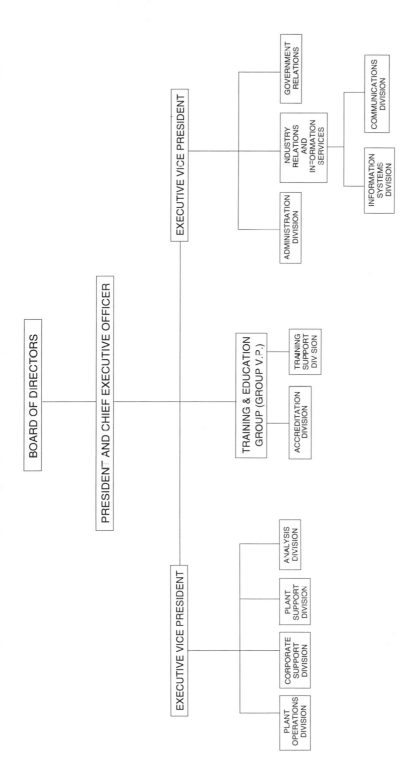

Fig. 4.1 INPO Organization Chart

dering what kind of organization INPO really was, and would become. And the key point to notice in these remarks (and many like them) is how they seek to allay such concerns by saying, in effect, "Not to worry. The board of directors—the industry's elected representatives— is at the helm charting INPO's course. INPO, unlike the NRC, is *our* organization. We, the industry, are INPO's boss."

To what extent does the board actually govern INPO's affairs? Although the precise facts are far from clear, the basic situation seems to be something like this. "Based on my experience I would say that the board doesn't get involved much in the details of running INPO. That's pretty much left up to Zack Pate [INPO's president]. But the board is very involved with the big issues—where they want INPO to go, what programs to get involved with, whether to take on evaluations worldwide or keep it in the U.S., things like that." Comments like this one, made by a former INPO board member, could be heard in a number of interviews. "The board is like any classical board of directors," says an INPO vice president. This means that the board provides a "broad policy-level overview" to help ensure that "INPO focuses on the right things." It also means that the board "very rarely gets involved in detailed issues."

It would appear that the board calls the shots on the big issues, though on closer inspection I was unable to uncover any examples in which the board actually vetoed something that INPO really wanted. One possible explanation, of course, is that INPO and industry officials keep such disagreements well hidden from public view. Another explanation is that the board is extremely supportive of INPO's role, and for good reason, remarks a nuclear utility CEO. No consideration of the board's role should fail to include the lessons of TMI, he explains, and those lessons make it "virtually inconceivable" that the board would oppose INPO on any major issue. "The industry realized after Three Mile Island, and it was reinforced by Chernobyl, that we stand and fall together. So even if you have problems with INPO on this or that issue, you really do want INPO to do a good job. I mean, INPO needs to do a good job in watching those other guys so they don't ruin it for me and everybody else. That's what TMI did. One plant ruined it for everybody." "You've got to realize that the board of directors is looking at the overall industry and the impact any one operator can have on the total industry," as another board member tried to explain it. "From that standpoint, it tends to put a control on the board to require a very high standard of excellence from the operation of all companies or else all companies fail."

Whatever the reality behind the rhetoric may be, the central point remains. Ask nuclear utility officials who governs INPO, and they will point to the industry's spokespersons on the board of directors.

Industry Review Groups

Cut now to another stratum in the industry hierarchy, the vice presidents, plant managers, and other top officials directly responsible for the day-to-day operation of the industry's nuclear plants. They too have a voice in INPO's regulatory affairs, thanks to INPO's two Industry Review Groups (IRGs), formed in 1980. Their charter states: "The Industry Review Groups are intended to complement INPO's in-house technical and operational capability *by providing working-level feedback from personnel involved in day-to-day management of the nuclear industry.*"[26] In providing that feedback, the two IRGs, each with about a dozen industry officials, are more like advisers than policymakers. Yet their advice is taken seriously, for their recommendations and opinions always have the ear of INPO's senior management. "All of the major new initiatives that INPO has undertaken over the years have been supported by the IRGs," says an INPO official:

> That's one set of folks we don't bypass. We look at them as representatives of the industry. And we keep them cut in. I mean we're talking V.P. level folks, and their direct contact here at INPO is a division director or vice president, not some place way down in the organization. So we're talking very senior level contacts.

"This outside review structure," INPO's president once remarked, is "one of the most important parts of INPO's heritage."[27] What makes the IRGs so important? The most obvious answer is responsiveness, keeping INPO programs and practices in touch with the industry's legitimate needs and concerns. "The INPO staff will have an idea they'll want to bounce off our group to get feedback," says a nuclear industry vice president and IRG member. "It's a strictly advisory role, but very valuable to the staff because *the folks on the advisory group have their hands on the day-to-day activities back home. So we can give the staff a good managerial perspective on whatever issues they're dealing with.*"(Emphasis supplied.)[28]

Now consider the symbolic side of the coin. The IRGs are also important because they embody a special message for industry officials concerning INPO's bonds with the industry. Here is a revealing example taken from a speech by a senior vice president, and IRG chairman, whose task was to explain the IRGs' nature and purpose to an audience of senior industry executives. "I think we have a very broad base [of industry representatives] on our IRG, and I think *we speak*, by and large, *for the industry."* (Emphasis supplied.) As if to press the point, he then described in some detail how the IRG speaks for the industry, by actively reviewing INPO programs and by closely evaluating INPO's performance, among other things. Finally, he added, one very important point must be made: Because the IRG speaks for the industry *"do not point your finger at INPO and say, 'They did it to us.' No, we in the industry did it to ourselves."*[29] Who, then, is the regulator? the regulated? The lesson is clear: in some significant respects (particularly when compared to the NRC), INPO and the industry are nearly indivisible.

Peer Regulators

"The conduct of evaluations is one of the most important functions performed by INPO." So states INPO's *Institutional Plan,* and by the end of 1991 INPO had conducted 502 inspections of nuclear plants as well as 141 inspections of their corporate-level support systems.[30] Perhaps the most obvious indicator of an organization's priorities is where it spends its energy and resources, and on this score inspections rank very high, as INPO spends more on this program than on any other regulatory task. So the inspection process is well worth a detailed examination. What are its methods of operation? Its goals? And how does all this fit into the larger context of our inquiry—the development of community and communitarian regulation? We shall return to these questions in chapter 7. Here I wish to look in some detail at one of the most remarkable features of INPO's inspection program—the role of peer regulators—for no other aspect of INPO's regulatory regime more tellingly illustrates INPO's distinctive quest for legitimacy than they do.

For INPO, peer evaluators are a further way to reach out to the industry and harness the involvement of yet another key group—reactor operators, maintenance supervisors, chemistry technicians, and other rank-and-file nuclear plant employees. More precisely, INPO has two different programs for this purpose—peer evaluation and loaned employee—and we begin our discussion with the first.

On the typical INPO inspection team that goes to a nuclear plant, as many as six peer evaluators are among its twenty or so members. Assigned by their utility to INPO for the two-week inspection, plus a week for preparation and training, the peers are normally matched with inspection teams going to a plant of similar design to their own. How did the 257 industry employees who participated in the program in 1990 enhance INPO's legitimacy?[31]

Consider the example of Ralph Gayne, an INPO peer evaluator. Our source is an INPO publication and the account is typical of many that INPO publishes in order to educate industry employees, by way of narrative and example, as to the nature and purpose of its various programs. More than an example, then, Ralph Gayne's experience is meant to be exemplary; a portrait of the peer evaluator's role at its best. An assistant supervisor for operations with seventeen years of nuclear operating experience, Gayne begins by recalling the reaction of plant employees at the inspection's outset: "When we first hit the plant and started on operator rounds . . . *they [plant employees] were cool to us*":

> [Gayne] explains that he was with an auxiliary operator (AO) on plant rounds when a rod control accumulator alarm sounded in the control room.
>
> Gayne accompanied the AO to the accumulator and observed him testing for water leaks and low gas pressure. The AO, Gayne says, found the alarm was caused by a water leak, not low pressure, and drained the accumulator to eliminate the alarm. When they went to the local test panel, the AO cleared the alarm, and the light stayed on. "Which," Gayne explains, "says to him that there was still low pressure."
>
> The AO was prepared to pressurize the accumulator with nitrogen gas. As the two discussed the situation, Gayne commented that the low pressure reading could be the result of a closed valve on a line that sends nitrogen to the pressure detector. If the valve were opened, the alarm light would go off, and the pressure would rise.
>
> *"He asked me, 'How do you know that!'" Gayne recalls. "I told him my plant was similar to his and that I had probably done that 500 times as an AO myself. Once they realized that you know what their job's about, that you've done it yourself, all resistance just evaporated."*

The lesson: "Beyond bringing added technical expertise to the evaluation team . . . the use of industry personnel . . . *increased acceptance of Institute programs and recommendations among its member utilities."*

It is a lesson that goes to the heart of the peer evaluator program's basic purpose. Peer evaluators, as one nuclear plant employee puts it, "give the evaluation process a lot more credibility because they're not talking from a textbook, so to speak":

> If you take a group like INPO, put them in Atlanta, have them evaluate plants full-time, and they don't have any current operating experience, *you tend to look at them more as regulators.* But peer evaluators know what it's like in a power house. So the guys being evaluated naturally feel better about the evaluation because they're being looked at by somebody with a current industry perspective and who's familiar with their type of problems.

It is also worth noting that prior to joining the INPO inspection team, Ralph Gayne "was not a very enthusiastic supporter of INPO." "Unfamiliar with many of the Institute's programs, he felt that INPO was just one more organization trying to tell him how to do his job." But being in the shoes of an INPO inspector for three weeks changed all that. Now, the article happily concludes, "he is more aware of INPO's role in the industry and sees the evaluation process in a positive light." [32]

All in all, another small victory in INPO's quest for legitimacy.

Since this account of Ralph Gayne's experience is meant to have a certain representative significance, as do most of INPO's stories, it provides a revealing glimpse of the values and purposes the program is meant to embody. And what this story (and others like it) pays homage to are the ties that bind and unify. For one thing, peer evaluators are the unifying force in a kind of bonding process that helps bring INPO and the industry closer together in various ways, especially by endowing the inspection team with a practical authority that only comes from many years of hands-on industry experience. For another, they also help bring the industry itself closer together. It may be surprising to learn that most nuclear plant employees, as if marooned on an island, never visit another nuclear plant. So they "tend to feel isolated from the world," in the words of one reactor operator. [33]

Overcoming that isolation is another benefit of the peer evaluation program because it helps to break down those invisible barriers separating nuclear plants. Like Ralph Gayne, for instance, a peer evaluator can share his experience with the plant being inspected (as Gayne did with the auxiliary operator), and, from the inspected plant, the peer evaluator can take good ideas back to his own plant. "The program," says a peer evaluator, "is a great way to encourage cross-fertilization within the industry."[34]

A similar analysis can be made of INPO's loaned employee program. In 1991, about one in every seven INPO employees was a nuclear plant worker on loan to INPO.[35] While the utility pays his or her salary, the loanee spends up to two years working full-time at INPO's Atlanta headquarters in some regulatory capacity—developing standards, inspecting plants, analyzing accident data. And so on.

"When I first got to INPO, I didn't recognize the importance and need for loaned employees," a permanent INPO inspector (and former nuclear plant employee) recalls. "It wasn't until I was there two or three years that I realized once you're away from the utility business, and you're out of the mainstream, you lose the current perspective on what's of real concern to the industry. So what the loaned employees bring to INPO," he adds, "is a current perspective on the issues that are important to the industry now."

Another way of saying this is that the loaned employee program, by establishing a close working relationship between employees from INPO and the industry, widens INPO's frame of reference in a way that makes it less insulated and more responsive to the day-to-day practical realities that confront nuclear plant employees. As another INPO official puts it, "An evaluator sitting in Atlanta that doesn't do anything but go look at plants loses perspective on what it takes to get things done in a plant. Loanees keep that up front. They kind of keep you honest by bringing their utility viewpoint and the practicality of how things get done."

Just as INPO becomes intimately acquainted with the industry's point of view, this process also deepens the loanees' understanding of INPO's cultural orientation. When loaned employees go on an inspection, for example, and most of them go on about a dozen inspections during their stay, they are immersed in the inspection process for many months, in total, not as detached observers, but as full-fledged INPO inspectors. It is a subtle form of socialization, as we shall see in chapter 8, that leads loaned employees to interpret and evaluate the world of nuclear plant operations in a very special way—the INPO way.

It is also instructive to cast a glance at the loaned employees' role in unifying the industry. This is another important aspect of the program, and it is well illustrated by an INPO story that discusses the nature and purpose of the loaned employee program in the context of Consolidated Edison's experience. "We're a relatively small nuclear utility," said Stephen Bram, the company's vice president for nuclear power. "What we get from participating in the [loaned employee] program is an individual who has had the opportunity to *see beyond the boundaries of our plant*, to see what others are doing, and to *learn first hand how standards of excellence are being applied throughout the industry*."[36]

As an example of what he is talking about, consider Eddie Everett, a Consolidated Edison nuclear plant supervisor who (like the company's other two loaned employees) had never journeyed to another nuclear plant before the company sent him to INPO. "When I was out in the plants I was able to meet people and establish points of contact for different subjects. . . . I must know a hundred people on a first-name basis," he continues. "They call me all the time, and I call them. I couldn't have made those contacts any other way." Another loaned employee, John McAvoy, concedes that he was somewhat naive before traveling to other plants. "I thought that with the high caliber of our people and all of our improvement initiatives, we were doing as well as any other plant." As he visited other plants, though, that view changed. "I was impressed with how much other plants had accomplished in some areas. I saw that higher standards of excellence can actually be achieved." He goes on: "You find you're a much more critical thinker. You look at things differently, and you don't accept the things you accepted before." "Every power plant I go to, I learn something," says Consolidated Edison's third loanee, Mike Shannon. In fact, Shannon requested accelerated travel while at INPO so that he could see more plants. He also regularly shares that information with Consolidated Edison. "Once a quarter my company flies me back for a day, and I write up a summary of my activities. I also get together with the entire department and brief them on what I've learned."

All this is rather like an allegory, with the loaned employees personifying some of the program's central aspirations. Like untraveled provincials, they were isolated and unfamiliar with the ways of their industrial world. But not anymore, thanks to the loaned employee program. By journeying to other nuclear plants and INPO's headquarters, the closest thing the industry has to a cultural capitol, the loaned employees have been pulled into a common world and exposed to a new fund of ideas from which they can draw. It "broaden[ed] their knowledge base," says Consolidated Edison's vice president, and it deepened their "insight into *how our activities at the plant relate to initiatives at INPO and in the whole industry*." (Emphasis supplied.)

Now wiser in the ways of the industry, the employees, we might say, have been turned into nuclear industry cosmopolitans.

In rounding out this picture of INPO's participatory framework, two other programs should be mentioned—the reverse loaned employee program and INPO workshops. As the mirror image of the loaned employee program, the reverse loaned employee program has permanent INPO employees—from chemistry technician to vice president—working at a nuclear utility for up to two years. In both cases, moreover, the basic rationale is much the same: to enhance INPO's legitimacy, and strengthen industry support, by narrowing the gap—INPO versus industry perspective—that tends to divide regulator and regulated. In 1991, there were sixteen reverse loaned employees.[37]

As for workshops, between 1980 and 1991 attendance at INPO's 111 workshops totaled 14,825. Of greatest consequence is the annual three-day gathering of all nuclear utility CEOs in Atlanta, where they discuss the major safety-related issues confronting the industry. (See chapter 7.) But there are also a variety of others that focus on a range of more specific topics—emergency preparedness, maintenance, operations, and radiological protection, among others. The single most important function of these meetings? To "pull the industry together," says an INPO official:

> The workshops provide a forum for people with common problems and common ideas to get together and sit down and talk. You know, we have all these fancy presentations, and we have breakfasts and evening receptions, which is all fine and nice. But the biggest thing we do is get people together in Atlanta who have common problems and give them an opportunity to find peers they can talk to.

"Of the whole INPO mission," he adds, "I think that's probably the single biggest thing we've done—just getting the industry talking." "Before we had these workshops," says a nuclear utility vice president, "we had no central meeting place. There was no synergy, no place to get this kind of first-hand information on issues. It was pretty fragmented."[38] Here as elsewhere in our discussion of INPO's participatory mechanisms, we can't help noticing a groping for community, a longing to overcome the fragmentation and get the industry talking.

To summarize: One of the central forces shaping INPO's administrative development has arisen from its dependence on the nuclear utilities, INPO's most important external constituency. Funded by utility contributions, INPO depends on the industry for its very exis-tence.[39] But that is not all, for industry support is also vital to the very success of INPO's core regulatory task. To transform an industry's habits of mind, to infuse its complex organizations with a common framework of regulatory principles, in short, to be an industry con-science, is no easy task. Formidable under the best of circumstances, it becomes doubly difficult when industry support is tenuous. And therein lies INPO's basic problem. For a variety of reasons, not least being INPO's nuclear navy background, garnering strong support from across the industry has been easier said than done. This is not to say, of course, that INPO has no industry support. But it does say that all too often that support has been more grudging than enthusiastic.

Seeing INPO's predicament in this way makes its participation-centered legitimation strategy quite understandable. In order to bol-ster the industry's confidence and support, and enhance the respect-ability of its regulatory regime, INPO has involved nuclear utility executives and employees in most of its regulatory activities, from top-level policy-making (through its board of directors) to the day-to-day implementation of its regulatory programs (through peer evaluators). All this leads industry officials to agree that INPO has made signifi-cant progress in remedying its legitimacy problem. But at what price?

An outside observer might well wonder whether INPO is so open to industry influence as a consequence of all these participatory mech-anisms that it cannot possibly maintain the independence required to be an effective regulator. If we believe that, we will expect to find evi-dence that INPO's close industry ties have in fact weakened its regula-tory role in some noteworthy ways. There is such evidence, and it will be discussed in chapter 7. It must also be said, however, that the total picture is a good deal more complex. For a fuller understanding of INPO's administrative development, we need not only to explore INPO's *external* ties to the industry, but to probe INPO's *internal* com-mitments as well. The nature of these commitments?

THE NUCLEAR NAVY CONNECTION

"When an organization has a culture that is widely shared and warmly endorsed by operators and managers alike," writes James Q. Wilson, "we say that organization has a sense of *mission*."[40] The Forest Ser-vice, the FBI, the Army Corps of Engineers—all good examples of or-ganizations that have (or had) a strong sense of mission—illustrate one of the chief ways an organization acquires a distinctive way of seeing and responding to the world. "This usually occurs during the formative experience of the organization, an experience shaped and interpreted by a founder who imposes his or her will on the first generation of operators in a way that profoundly affects succeeding generations." It is a process of "imprinting," if you will, and the imprint "is deepest and most lasting when the founding executive has a strong personality and a forcefully expressed vision of what the organization should be."[41] Leadership is the key.

In the search for INPO's first chief executive, industry officials looked far and wide before picking, from a list of 107 candidates, retired navy admiral Eugene Wilkinson. "We were not looking specifically for a naval officer," recalls an industry executive actively involved in the search; if anything, "retired senior military officers in industry generally had a poor reputation." Yet despite those misgivings they chose Wilkinson because of his extraordinary qualifications.

For many years Wilkinson served under Admiral Hyman Rickover, the legendary father of the 150-ship U.S. nuclear navy. Indeed, he was one of Rickover's star protégés. Not only had Rickover "hand-picked and -trained Wilkinson," he also chose Wilkinson (then thirty-five years old) as the first commanding officer of the first nuclear submarine (the *Nautilus*) and later the first nuclear surface warship (the *Long Beach*).[42] When Wilkinson joined INPO in 1980, he brought with him as his chief assistant Zack Pate, who in 1984 succeeded Wilkinson as INPO's president. Pate also had a distinguished career in Rickover's nuclear navy; and like Wilkinson's, his professional ties with Rickover were especially close. (Pate served his last three years in the navy as Rickover's special assistant.)[43] Both men thus possess very similar backgrounds and training, and, as one would expect, they also share a similar philosophy of nuclear management—that is, a matrix of values, beliefs, and practices developed by their charismatic leader, Admiral Hyman Rickover. (See chapter 6.) Thus, INPO has always been led by Rickover men.

Arriving at INPO's new Atlanta headquarters in 1980, Wilkinson confronted the challenging task of building a new organization. Above all, he faced two critical decisions: Where should INPO's personnel come from? And how should INPO define its regulatory role?

This was also a time when the nuclear industry was experiencing a severe skilled-labor shortage, and it was quite usual for nuclear utilities to raid one another for experienced personnel. This presented INPO with a major problem. "We tried to staff up with industry people," a top-level INPO official recalls, "but we were just unsuccessful in getting the people to come to INPO. The job market worked against us. And people just didn't know how INPO was going to work or if it was even going to last very long." The force of circumstances thus led INPO to make a critical decision of lasting significance, for the only other labor pool with the nuclear know-how INPO required was the navy's nuclear submarine program. "We had to staff this place up," the same INPO official recalls. "And there were a lot of good people coming out of the navy that were available." So INPO hired them. More by accident than design, INPO thus acquired a remarkably homogeneous leadership and staff during its formative first years, a group of industry outsiders whose prior socialization in the nuclear navy gave them a distinctive way of thinking about nuclear safety.

That way, of course, was the Rickover way of thinking, and here is how a longtime nuclear navy officer describes its basic thrust:

> He [Rickover] infused into the Navy the idea of excellence. He had to. You don't just fool around with nuclear energy. He said that the *standard* would be excellence and he made that happen. . . . In the Navy, Rickover showed we could make the demand of excellence. It's a proud word for us. . . . He was the genius who gave a generation of naval officers the idea that excellence was the standard. . . . If you made a mistake, there would be no bloodletting. But a shortcoming, a failure to work toward the standard of excellence, that was not tolerated. . . . He taught that to a whole generation of naval officers.[44]

The list of navy officers infused with this idea of "excellence" includes INPO's two presidents as well as a wide array of other former naval personnel who later filled INPO's ranks. It is no wonder, then, that the official statement of INPO's mission is "to promote the highest levels of safety and reliability—to promote excellence—in the operation of nuclear electric generating plants."[45] The parallelism is not coincidental. Indeed, Rickover would certainly have applauded this vision of INPO's role, as he was absolutely convinced that the civilian nuclear power industry should adopt the navy's overall approach to nuclear safety. "Although commercial nuclear plants and Naval nuclear plants differ in many ways," he wrote after the TMI accident, "they do not differ in the underlying principles which make for safe operation. These apply equally to both." "It is my hope," he continued, that "those principles will become more widely understood and practiced. . . . *Such attitudes and principles must, in my opinion, become industry's standard.*"[46]

From what has already been said about their background and train-ing, we would expect to find INPO officials sharing Rickover's convic-tion. And they do. "Over the years," as a very senior INPO official puts it, "the navy has developed pretty high standards for operating their nuclear plants. And those of us who came from the navy, obviously, were colored by that. That was our background. Now the utility plants are a lot different, *but the same standards ought to apply.*" (Empha-sis supplied.)

Here we come face-to-face with a core assumption that goes a long way in defining INPO's regulatory role. Like Rickover, INPO officials have been strongly committed to the notion that the commercial nu-clear industry must adopt the nuclear navy's industrial principles. The same general standards ought to apply, they believe, and it is INPO's essential task to help ensure that they do. To forget this, as Secretary of Energy (and retired admiral) James Watkins makes us aware, is to obscure perhaps the most important thing we need to understand about INPO's role in the nuclear industry's post-TMI regulatory trans-formation: "After Three Mile Island, INPO began a program to identify benchmarks of excellence in operations and in so doing paved the way for renewed commitment to safe operations. The utilities you repre-sent have spent the last decade changing your approach to the manage-ment of nuclear plants." And where did those benchmarks of excel-lence for reforming nuclear utility management come from? "Although I do not intend to dwell on Admiral Rickover and his ac-complishments, you should be reminded that for over 30 years he not only created an entire nuclear navy of over 150 ships but was respon-sible for ensuring their safe operation over that same time period. He left us with a tremendous legacy. . . . Almost all of the corrective ac-tions that you have been attempting to incorporate in your own pro-grams since TMI," Watkins concludes, "were hallmarks of his program from day one."[47]

It is always tempting to exaggerate a trend, and what with Watkins being a navy man himself, his observations concerning the nuclear navy's influence may be a bit overdone. Even so, there is a great deal of truth in what he is saying; we shall see abundant evidence of this in the chapters to come.

DILEMMA OF COMMUNITARIAN REGULATION

What does all this add up to? It is now possible to see INPO's adminis-trative development as the product of two very different factors, the pull of industry interests and the tug of nuclear navy aspirations. But I also want to argue that the enduring tension that characterizes INPO's administrative development points to a fundamental dilemma of communitarian regulation.

"To ensure credibility with its members and with the federal government," states INPO's *Institutional Plan*, "*INPO must maintain its independence* with respect to any individual member." "At the same time," however, "*INPO must be responsive* to the collective needs of the nuclear utilities."[48] This complicated stance expresses the tension inherent in INPO's role as a communitarian regulator. As a *communitarian* regulator, it must promote a *close integration* between regulator and regulated. It is essential for the nuclear industry to view INPO as an *industry* organization that is strongly responsive to its special needs and concerns, as we have seen, because this is the principal way INPO acquires the legitimacy and garners the industry support so important to carrying out its distinctive regulatory role. The other side of the coin is no less important. As a communitarian *regulator*, it must promote a *separation* between regulator and regulated. The regulatory system, like the judicial system, requires autonomy to insulate itself from corrupting industry pressures, and, most important, to safeguard INPO's integrity as the industry's collective conscience. INPO must be true to its (nuclear navy) principles.

So it is that INPO's regulatory role involves conflicting imperatives. Institutional arrangements that both enhance integration and safeguard autonomy are essential to its communitarian regulatory strategy. Yet the logic of these two approaches may operate at cross purposes; as integration between regulator and regulated increases, so does the risk of undue industry influence; but as autonomy increases, so does the possibility of insularity and unresponsiveness, thus creating a rift in the communal bonds uniting regulator and regulated, and thus weakening if not undermining vital industry support for its regulatory role. What suffers in either case is INPO's distinctive competence as a communitarian regulator and its ability to promote industry unification around a shared industrial morality.

Part Two

Communitarian Regulation

5
Industrial Morality

You will remember that a well-developed system of communitarian regulation has three defining features—a well-defined *industrial morality* that is backed by enough *communal pressure* to *institutionalize responsibility* among its members. That is the key to understanding INPO's distinctive regulatory role in the nuclear power industry, as I hope to show in the chapters to follow, and I begin by discussing nuclear power's new industrial morality.[1]

Someone aspiring to become a nuclear plant manager today would be well advised to thoroughly study INPO's "The Development of Prospective Nuclear Plant Managers and Middle Managers."[2] For one thing, "the report can be used to develop a checklist that candidates can use to guide and track their progress toward obtaining the knowledge, skills, and experience needed for eventual assignment to the plant manager position." For another thing, the report is authoritative. It was developed in light of "best industry practices," formulated with the help of "utility senior managers and executives who have served as plant managers," and comprehensively reviewed by "senior industry personnel and the INPO staff."[3]

An aspiring manager may well have second thoughts after reading the report, however, because the job is so demanding. "Nuclear plant management must deal with a wide scope of responsibilities . . . if the station is to achieve high standards in operational safety and reliability."[4] This includes an array of broad "functional responsibilities"— including, among others, using quality assurance programs to enhance operational safety; monitoring plant modifications to ensure they accord with company policies, regulatory requirements, and sound safety practices; monitoring document control and storage to ensure that appropriate historical records are maintained; directing plant operations to achieve safe and reliable performance; using plant and industry operating experience to improve operational safety and reliability. The report also includes a very long list (about four hundred elements) that itemizes the specific managerial, technical, and moral capabilities required "for excellent performance in these challenging management positions."[5] All in all, the report thus formulates a well-defined and very demanding image of what it means to be a *good* nuclear plant manager. Although some may have doubts about tackling such a role, there can be little doubt as to what the role requires.

It was not always thus. We learned in chapter 2 that before TMI the nuclear industry's normative system did not take institutions seriously; the vast majority of safety standards (governmental and nongovernmental) concentrated on hardware-related issues while neglecting the institutional arrangements and processes for managing, operating, and maintaining nuclear plants. We also learned that the system embodied a rudimentary industrial ethic; bare compliance with minimum NRC regulations was more than adequate for ensuring safety, on the prevailing view, and private industry standards were silent on matters of operational excellence.[6] As a nuclear utility official quoted earlier suggests, all this left an aspiring nuclear plant manager in search of excellence without a moral compass: "You didn't have definitive standards you were striving to attain. You had minimum NRC regulations you could aspire to, which was just meeting the minimum regulatory needs. But standards of excellence were not available."

Today, the situation is altogether different. As a result of the post-TMI regulatory transformation led by INPO, the nuclear industry has a well-defined industrial morality that covers a wide array of industry officials, including aspiring nuclear plant managers. In fact, developing such standards has always been a core regulatory activity at INPO, as we shall see. But first we must ask where this new industrial morality came from.

Nuclear Navy's Industrial Principles

The obvious place to begin looking for an answer is the nuclear navy's industrial principles. Like Admiral Rickover, as we saw in the last chapter, INPO's nuclear navy–trained leadership was convinced that the commercial nuclear industry had a great deal to learn from the navy's approach to nuclear safety. And, what's more, it was INPO's job to see that they did. So some understanding of the nuclear navy's industrial principles and practices is essential for understanding the nature and purpose of nuclear power's new industrial morality.

In some respects the navy's approach to nuclear safety was similar to that of the NRC's prior to the TMI accident. Both stressed the central importance of *engineering* safety.[7] Like the NRC, for example, the submarine's nuclear plant was designed with wide margins for error so that it could withstand the worst "credible" accident. In both safety programs, moreover, redundancies were built into the reactor in case a system or component failed. Now the all-important difference: Rickover's nuclear navy has always taken institutions seriously, unlike the NRC's pre-TMI regulatory regime, and has always considered *institutionalized* safety as important as *engineering* safety.[8]

To illustrate, let's consider the principles listed in table 5.1. Written by Rickover himself, they are a prime example of the nuclear navy's industrial morality.[9]

> I am often asked how I ran the Naval Reactors Program, sometimes by people hoping to find methods for use in their own work. Frequently there seems to be an expectation that I could tell them about some simple, easy procedure which made the Naval program function. Unfortunately there is none. Any successful program functions as an integrated whole of many factors. Trying to select one as the key will not work. Each element depends on all the other elements. . . . Attaining competence and reliability in a nuclear operation is difficult, but recognizing them is not. In fact, with experience in operation, *it is possible to lay down certain principles which are essential to safety.* . . .
>
> While the physical aspects of commercial nuclear power stations differ substantially from Navy nuclear propulsion plants, the same underlying precepts must govern the operation of both.

These precepts, Rickover added, represent "tested 'principles of operation' which are fundamental to all nuclear power activities."[10]

Notice first that these principles of operation are just that—principles—and not mechanical rules or specific procedures.

> I have mentioned the principles of operation which I used in building the Naval Reactor Program. *I emphasize that these are principles, not procedures or practices.* Procedures or practices must be changed as circumstances change. Principles are constant and can be applied now and in the future. If a management is imbued with these principles and accustomed to using

TABLE 5.1

The Nuclear Navy's Industrial Principles

Rising standards of excellence:

"Excellence in operating nuclear power plants cannot be achieved merely by meeting a set of minimum standards." "A technology having inherent public risk, a technology which is still new and still evolving, must be built upon rising standards of excellence." By "raising standards and goals when lower thresholds of competence have been met," utility managers "should be expected and encouraged to do more than merely meet regulatory requirements. They should be expected and encouraged to achieve levels of performance which meet their own professional standards of excellence, and which equal or exceed the best practices in the industry." "The degree to which a management understands and applies this principle is one measure of its competence and reliability."

Technical self-sufficiency:

"Nuclear power is a technology whose complexity far exceeds that of other common methods of generating electricity. . . . It is essential that decision-making managers not only have extensive technical training themselves, but that they also have *expert analytical and engineering resources readily available within their own organization.* It is insufficient to rely solely, or even primarily, on outside contractors or consultants for technical support, a practice which is commonly used. A nuclear utility must have its own broad-based technical staff capable of all but the most specialized services." (Emphasis supplied.)

Respect for radiation:

"One criterion for judging the quality of management of a nuclear plant is the degree to which radiation control . . . is given prominence in organizational level, in staffing, and in the demand for high standards of performance in this area. This attitude of management is not always found because radiation problems are new even to experienced managers in non-nuclear plants and are generally underrated. Radiation sources are elusive and the effects of poor radiation control are not easy to see. There is a tendency to look on the control requirements as overdone and, in any case, to be within the capability of the normal work force to carry out."

Facing facts:

"Facing up to difficulties, regularly informing higher levels of management of problems and determining and correcting their root causes involve attitudes and practices which are essential to operating competence. Unfortunately, there is a disposition in all operating organizations to minimize the potential consequences of problems and to try to solve them with the limited resources available at the level where they are first recognized. The practice of forcing problems up to higher levels where greater resources can be applied must be assiduously fostered by top-level managers."

Importance of training:

"The selection and training of operators is at least as important as any other element of safe reactor operation. It is vital that mental abilities, qualities of

TABLE 5.1 continued

The Nuclear Navy's Industrial Principles

judgment, and level of training be commensurate with the responsibility involved in operating a nuclear station. A management's attitude toward excellence in operation and its understanding of how to achieve excellence are both revealed in the quality of training provided."

Concept of total responsibility:

"Operating nuclear plants safely requires adherence to a concept wherein all elements are recognized as important and each is constantly reinforced. Training, equipment maintenance, technical support, radiological control, and quality control are essential elements, but safety is achieved through integrating them effectively in operation decisions. Management's understanding of this principle at the corporate and plant levels is a valid measure of competence. The organizational structure gives some indication of management's awareness, but is less important than understanding and applying the principle."

Capacity to learn from experience:

"Since we are dealing with persons and machines which cannot be made perfect, it is important to recognize that mistakes will be made. We must do our best to design machines having tolerance for mistakes and to continue to improve them through experience. This process of evolutionary improvement . . . depends on a capacity to acknowledge mistakes and to determine and correct their underlying causes, whatever the cost. An inability or unwillingness to learn from experience is intolerable in nuclear operations."

Source: Hyman G. Rickover, "An Assessment of the GPU Nuclear Corporation and Senior Management and Its Competence to Operate TMI-1" (19 November 1983).

them, it will adapt to change. . . . If management has chosen such a course, it will lead to a competent and dependable operation.[11]

As a set of guiding principles, an industrial morality does not specify or dictate (at least within broad limits) particular policies or procedures. It does, however, ask fidelity to principles that define and uphold a special competence—the fitness to operate nuclear reactors safely and reliably.

Second, notice how an industrial morality articulates standards of excellence that embody a conception of the institution at its best. In each case, for instance, the nuclear navy's principles define an appropriate excellence (a "criterion of competence" in Rickover's terms)—facing the facts, respect for radiation, learning from experience, and so on—that is only variably achieved and that must be honored to ensure a nuclear plant's "fitness to operate" in a "competent," "dependable," and "safe" manner.[12] "Excellence in operating nuclear power plants" is the polestar.[13]

Third, some industrial moralities are more (or less) well defined than others, more (or less) complex than others, and more (or less) demanding than others. As for the nuclear navy's, it is quite well defined (especially when compared to the nuclear industry's pre-TMI fossil fuel–oriented industrial morality) and very demanding as well. "Although easily stated and readily defined," as Rickover puts it, "*these principles are exceedingly demanding of a management which chooses to adopt them.*"[14]

Finally, we should take this chance to notice the industrial morality's distinctively moral dimension. It is not difficult to imagine Rickover using these principles to assess a nuclear utility's technical competence when it comes to, say, minimizing a nuclear plant worker's exposure to radiation. Yet he also viewed these principles from another angle. They can and should be used to assess a nuclear utility's moral competence as well, especially management's integrity or inner commitment to responsible behavior.

> These principles express attitudes and beliefs. They acknowledge the complex technology. They recognize that safe nuclear operations requires painstaking care. They declare that a management must be responsible—all the time. . . . I believe that *our criteria,* and the principles on which they are based, *measure more than the structural or technical adequacy of an organization.* If used knowledgeably, *they can expose a management's motivation to act responsibly, which we call integrity.* A lack of integrity would be incompatible with conformance to these criteria.[15]

By involving attitudes, beliefs, and motivations of this sort, the nuclear navy's industrial morality cannot be fully accounted for by merely technical criteria. It also extols a distinctive moral posture— always mindful of nuclear technology's grave risks, always committed to thorough and painstaking care, always motivated by a keen sense of responsibility for the technology's tested principles of operation. In a word, it asks for integrity. "If a management is imbued with these principles," Rickover wrote, "it will lead to a competent and dependable operation."[16]

At the very least, then, we may observe that the nuclear navy possesses a distinctive industrial morality. We have only to look at Rickover's articulation of its guiding principles to see that—and more. It is a well-defined and demanding set of principles, most important, that stands in stark contrast to the rudimentary industrial ethic (the fossil fuel mentality) that held sway over the pre-TMI civilian nuclear industry. But that is not all: from the evidence we have concerning the nuclear navy background of INPO's leadership, there are also good grounds for thinking that these principles are vitally important for understanding INPO's regulatory role. Now we must explore further, first, by asking how INPO has used these principles as authoritative starting points from which to develop a large body of more detailed rules, and second, by asking how INPO has used these nuclear navy standards as foundational principles for the development of community and communitarian regulation in the nuclear power industry.

STANDARDS

Like many industry organizations, INPO is in the business of writing industry-wide regulatory standards, an enterprise that typically raises many doubts and questions among outside observers. Although we know very little about the inner workings of the Society of Automotive Engineers, the Aerospace Industry Association, or the great many other nongovernmental code-writing organizations that have produced an estimated 32,000 standards,[17] the conventional wisdom counsels strong skepticism. "Private standards-setting is widely thought to be controlled by those who want the least done. Most private standards are 'consensus' standards. . . . This process seems practically designed to ensure that standards-setting follows the path of least resistance. The need for consensus . . . leads to a 'watering down' of many standards."[18] In this way of thinking, when firms throughout the automotive industry send technical representatives to a safety standards writing committee organized under the auspices of the Society of Automotive Engineers, we can expect to find a search for consensus among all the parties involved; and because that consensus must include the least safety-conscious, we can also expect to find a search for lowest-common-denominator standards. That, distilled to its essence, is the conventional view of private standards-making.

What about INPO standards? Are they watered down by those who want the least done?

To find the beginnings of an answer, we must go back to Rickover's very first principle of nuclear power operations. "Excellence in operating nuclear power plants cannot be achieved merely by meeting a set of minimum standards. A technology having inherent public risk, a technology which is still new and evolving, *must be built upon rising standards of excellence which substantially exceed those [NRC regulations] used for licensing purposes."*

What is true of the nuclear navy's cultural orientation—that nuclear power operations must be guided by rising standards of excellence—is also true of INPO's overall approach to nuclear safety.

> The nuclear utility industry recognized that all nuclear power facilities are affected by the performance at any one facility. This understanding encouraged all U.S. nuclear utilities . . . to join together and commit themselves *to strive for standards of excellence as determined by INPO. . . .* INPO's role is to promote excellence in the management and operation of its members' nuclear power plants and the attainment by all nuclear utilities of the best possible performance.[19]

These remarks, coauthored by Rickover's former protégé and INPO's first president, Admiral Dennis Wilkinson, clearly suggest a strong nuclear navy influence. More to the point, they also epitomize the basic character of INPO's normative system. In myriad ways, but with extraordinary singleness of purpose, INPO's regulatory norms articulate what is worth striving for. Which is also why, like Rickover, INPO draws a clear distinction between standards of excellence and NRC standards. "Basic differences exist . . . between NRC regulations and INPO evaluation criteria. An NRC regulation is a condition that must be met to obtain or retain a license, while INPO criteria are . . . based on standards of excellence."[20] While the NRC "stresses compliance with regulatory requirements," in other words, INPO "stresses assistance in achieving excellence." "Both of these functions are necessary—indeed are complementary. Each, however, serves a different purpose."[21]

We might think of the difference this way. To get a driver's license, we must comply with state regulations, just as every nuclear utility must comply with NRC regulations for a license to operate nuclear plants. Now it is one thing to demonstrate a basic level of competence by passing a driving test, and quite another to be the best possible driver one can be. Likewise for nuclear plant operators: "Compliance with [NRC] regulations, while meeting government safety requirements, does not alone produce the best possible performance."[22] Something more than government standards is needed, which brings us to the fundamental rationale for INPO's normative framework. By establishing "benchmarks of excellence" (INPO's phrase), INPO maps out the route by which nuclear utilities can surpass lowest-common-denominator standards, surpass basic NRC requirements, and strive for the best possible performance. Or, to put the essential difference in broader terms, NRC regulations establish a "baseline morality"[23] (by specifying the nuclear utilities' *minimum* obligations or *basic* duties), whereas INPO norms generate a "morality of aspiration"[24] (by spelling out the best standards realized so far).

All right, one may say, but does all this talk about benchmarks of excellence really amount to anything more than watered-down standards dressed up in self-serving industry rhetoric? That is an important question, and it is one that requires us to take a closer look at INPO's regulatory norms, of which there are four types: performance objectives, criteria, guidelines, and good practices.

THE ELEMENTS

In order to operate safely and reliably, an INPO inspector once told me, a nuclear plant must have the "elements." Asked to explain, he offered this example:

> If you look at problem plants that have been shut down by the NRC, and somebody's taken the reins and the plant has risen from the ashes, typically they've done four things. They've given clear directions; they made sure that the direction is understood and implemented the way they want it to be understood and implemented; if it's not, they found out why it's not; and they hold people accountable for meeting that direction or expectation.

These are some of the elements or institutional building blocks (by no means all) that support a well-operating nuclear plant, and these elements are what INPO's *framework* of general standards is all about. I emphasize framework because INPO does not demand exacting compliance to a highly detailed body of prescriptive rules, unlike the NRC, but rather institutes a more open-textured system of *general* standards within which nuclear utility officials make their own decisions as to specific objectives, internal arrangements, and the allocation of resources.

A case in point: INPO's *Performance Objectives and Criteria for Operating and Near-Term Operating License Plants*. For INPO inspectors and utility officials, this is INPO's regulatory bible, and it provides them with the following guidance for interpreting the major elements of INPO's normative system (performance objectives, criteria, guide-lines, good practices):

> The purpose of this document is to provide a working reference for INPO evaluators and for member utilities' use in self-evaluation. *INPO emphasizes achievement of the performance objectives.* . . . The criteria in this document are result-oriented. The *methods for achieving the desired results are gen-erally not stated. Thus, considerable judgment is required in applying the criteria.*
>
> INPO has developed guidelines and good practices to assist member utilities in meeting the performance objectives and cri-teria. Guidelines describe methods for addressing one or more performance objectives. It is anticipated that *utilities may use different approaches or methods* than those described in INPO guidelines, but *stations [nuclear plants] are expected to meet the intent of the guidelines.* INPO good practices . . . provide as-sistance as needed. It is anticipated that *other methods and pro-cedures in use may be as effective as those described in good practices.*[25]

If this passage makes one thing clear, it is that INPO strongly discour-ages a rule-bound and compliance-oriented approach; what really mat-ters are results—above all, the achievement of performance objectives. Said one INPO inspector, "The performance objectives are what I'm actually measuring against. That's what I use; that's the guidance. I keep asking myself, 'Does this behavior relate to the performance ob-jectives?' If it doesn't relate, then I don't deal with it." The performance objectives, by articulating the elements of a well-run nuclear plant, are the system's foundational principles. (See tables 5.2 and 5.3 for examples.)[26] As for the influence of Rickover's nuclear navy prin-ciples—facing facts, technical competence, vital importance of train-ing, capacity to learn from experience, and so on—all these are embod-ied in INPO's performance objectives.[27]

As a concrete example, let us consider the second performance ob-jective listed in table 5.3: "Operations organization and administra-tion should ensure effective implementation and control of operation's activities." Another way of saying this is that control room operators, those directly in charge of pulling the levers and pressing the buttons that control the nuclear reactor, should faithfully and effectively carry out company policies and procedures, just as a nuclear submarine or

TABLE 5.2

Examples of INPO Corporate Performance Objectives

On the corporate utility's organizational structure:

"The corporate organization is established in such a manner that the functions, assignments, responsibilities, and reporting relationships of individuals are clearly defined, understood, and effectively implemented. All major aspects of the nuclear operation are encompassed, with emphasis on line management control of safety and reliability."

On the organization and administration of the operations department:

"Operations organization and administration should ensure effective implementation and control of operations activities."

"The corporate organization effectively supports the station(s) and minimizes the assignment of duties to the station staff(s) not directly related to day-to-day plant management."

On management involvement and commitment:

"Corporate management directs, monitors, and assesses nuclear station operations and provides support, guidance, and assistance to attain and enhance safe and reliable operation. Corporate managers assigned responsibilities for nuclear matters have direct involvement in significant decisions that could affect their responsibilities. Management commitment to the operation of the nuclear station(s) in a safe and proper manner is evident from personal involvement, interest, and knowledge."

On maintenance of nuclear plants:

"Corporate management ensures maintenance activities at the nuclear station(s) are effective in maintaining equipment in a high state of readiness and in good material condition to support safe and reliable plant operation."

Source: INPO, "Performance Objectives and Criteria for Corporate Evaluations" (December 1987).

Boeing 747 crew must scrupulously follow the captain's orders to ensure safe and reliable operations. All this matters, as we shall see in chapter 8, for in recent years INPO has uncovered a number of alarming (and in some cases potentially catastrophic) incidents caused by operators who behaved more like reckless stunt pilots than conscientious airline captains in their disregard for such procedures.

What is a nuclear utility executive to do? How can he advance upon this performance objective and make certain that his control room operators are scrupulously following established policies and procedures? The short answer is revise the plant's organizational practices in light of INPO's criteria, guidelines, and good practices. Take the criteria first.

TABLE 5.3

Examples of INPO Plant Performance Objectives

On nuclear plant organization and administration:

"Station organization and administration should ensure effective implementation of policies and the planning and control of station activities."

On the organization and administration of the operations department:

"Operations organization and administration should ensure effective implementation and control of operation's activities."

On learning from industry operating experience:

"Significant industry operating experiences should be evaluated, and appropriate actions should be undertaken to improve safety and reliability."

On plant performance monitoring:

"Performance monitoring activities should optimize plant reliability and efficiency."

On the conduct of nuclear plant operations:

"Operational activities should be conducted in a manner that ensures safe and reliable plant operation. Reactor safety should be a foremost consideration in plant operations. Management policies and actions should actively support this operating philosophy."

On operating procedures and documentation:

"Operations procedures and documents should provide appropriate direction and should be effectively used to support safe operation of the plant."

On maintenance:

"The maintenance organization and administration should ensure effective implementation and control of maintenance activities."

Source: INPO, "Performance Objectives and Criteria for Operating and Near-Term Operating License Plants" (Atlanta: INPO, April 1987).

For each performance objective, INPO develops supporting "criteria" that outline the various tasks normally required to achieve a given performance objective. On controlling operations personnel, for example, the criteria instruct our nuclear utility executive to define the plant's organizational structure clearly, provide resources and staffing sufficient to accomplish all tasks, define and explain the responsibilities and authority of each position, and so on. (See table 5.4.) Note that INPO does not prescribe the precise methods for performing these tasks. How management defines the organizational structure is not important; what matters is that management does in fact define the structure, and does so clearly. So the criteria, as with the performance objectives, focus on results—whether or not the organization struc-

TABLE 5.4

INPO Criteria for Operations Department Organization and
Administration

(1) The organizational structure is clearly defined.

(2) Staffing and resources are sufficient to accomplish all tasks.

(3) Responsibilities, and authority of each management, supervisory, and
professional position are clearly defined and understood.

(4) Interfaces with supporting groups are clearly defined and understood.

(5) Administrative controls are employed for operations activities that affect safe
and reliable plant operation. Examples of such activities include equipment
isolation, use of jumpers and lifted leads, posted operator aids, and shift
turnover.

(6) Performance appraisals are effectively used to enhance individual
performance.

(7) Operations personnel are actively encouraged to develop improved methods
of meeting safety, quality, and productivity goals.

(8) Performance indicators are established and used to improve operation's
performance.

Source: INPO, "Performance Objectives and Criteria for Operating and Near-Term Operating
License Plants" (April 1987), p. 15.

ture is "clearly defined"—which also means that they require considerable judgment in their application.

In theory, the criteria are not mandatory. If the utility meets the
performance objective in question, INPO policy maintains that not
every supporting criterion has to be met. In practice, however, a very
strong presumption prevails among INPO inspectors, albeit rebut-
table, that a nuclear plant should embody all the elements spelled out
in the criteria. "If you're meeting the performance objectives without
meeting some of the criteria, that's considered okay," an INPO inspector explains. "But it's uncommon. A lot of experience has gone into
putting the criteria together, and they're very closely linked to the performance objectives. That makes it pretty tough to stray from them
and still meet the objective."

A great deal of experience has also gone into the INPO guidelines.
Elaborating on the criteria, the guidelines offer our nuclear utility executive a fuller picture of the various tasks ordinarily required to meet
the performance objective. To ensure that the operations department
effectively implements all established policies, for example, utility officials must define operating objectives, establish expected performance levels, closely monitor performance, hold department personnel accountable, and so on. (See table 5.5.) Again, the standards are

TABLE 5.5

Guidelines for Operations Department Organization and Administration

On establishing operations department policies:

"Procedures or other definitive documentation should specify policies that are to be applied within the operations department. These documents should also provide for the types of controls necessary to implement policies as discussed in this and other chapters of these guidelines. Operations department procedures should support corporate and plant guidance in plant operations. Responsibilities for implementing these policies, including the responsibility of shift personnel, should be clearly defined. Operations personnel should clearly understand their authority, responsibility, accountability, and interfaces with other groups.

"It is a primary responsibility of the operations superintendent to ensure implementation of utility and plant policies that affect the operations department."

On providing sufficient resources:

"The operations superintendent should be provided with sufficient resources to accomplish assigned tasks. These resources should include technical personnel needed to support plant operations."

On monitoring plant operating performance:

"Operating problems should be documented and evaluated. Based on assessments of these problems, corrective actions should be taken to improve operations department performance. Additionally, frequent direct observation of operations activities by supervisors and managers is essential to monitoring operations performance.

"Operating goals should be used as a management tool for involving cognizant plant groups in improving operating performance and for measuring operating effectiveness. . . .

"Inspections, audits, reviews, investigations, and self-assessment are a part of the checks and balances needed in a plant operating program. Line managers and supervisors should perform routine activities. Deficiencies identified should be documented and trended. Also, other groups, such as quality assurance personnel, should periodically review and assess operational performance. These reviews can assist line managers and supervisors in identifying and correcting problems."

On ensuring accountability:

"Workers and their supervisors should be held accountable for operating performance. Personnel involved in significant or frequent violations of operating practices should be counseled; provided with remedial training, or both; or disciplined when necessary. Supervisor performance appraisals and promotions should include an assessment of operating performance."

On teaching management skills:

"There should be a formalized management training program incorporated into the plant training programs. This is especially important to the first-line supervisors on shift to aid them in managing shift activities."

Source: INPO, *Guidelines for the Conduct of Operations at Nuclear Power Stations* (June 1985), pp. 1–2.

general; a utility may deviate from the specific approaches or methods defined in the guidelines as long as it meets the "intent" of the guidelines.[28] Within INPO's normative world, then, the guidelines are authoritative role models for implementing the performance objectives and criteria.

The INPO "good practices" are another kind of authoritative role model for implementing the performance objectives and criteria. Suppose that our utility executive, determined to improve the operations department's performance, has made a variety of administrative changes in light of INPO's performance objectives, criteria, and guidelines. Yet with the latest INPO inspection report he learns that the department's performance, when compared to the rest of the industry, is merely average. Perplexed, he might wonder how the very best performers are managing their departments. He does not have to look far for an answer.

INPO's good practice on the conduct of operations, based upon the industry's most successful nuclear plant programs as well as INPO's collective experience,[29] describes an exemplary program for managing the operations department and meeting the performance objective.[30] By reading its twenty-three pages, our industry official can learn, among other things, how a model program defines the responsibilities of all key positions (including the department head, shift supervisor, supervisor, and reactor operator) and how it delineates the procedures for operating the plant (including those designed to make certain that control room personnel comply with established operating procedures; see table 5.6). All this is but one example of the 131 good practices, covering the gamut of nuclear plant operations, that INPO has produced.[31]

The good practices are not compulsory.[32] "We do not evaluate against the good practices," says an INPO inspector. "Typically, we use the good practices by saying, 'Here's this problem you have, here's what we think the causes of it are, this good practice may help you in improving your program.'"[33] So in the eyes of industry officials, whatever authority the good practices possess largely depends, not on sanctions, but on a belief that they are capable of generating effective action. "There's been a lot of thought and a lot of effort going into preparing those good practices," says a nuclear utility vice president. "So it's kind of foolish not to take advantage of them. Really, they're an institutionalized benchmark that enables me to learn a lot more than I could by trying to go around and visit every other plant and see for myself better ways of doing things."

TABLE 5.6

INPO Good Practice: Conduct of Operations

On ensuring compliance with procedures:

(1) Plant equipment shall be operated in accordance with written approved procedures.

(2) If the individual actually performing the activity cannot or believes he should not follow the procedure governing that activity as written, he shall place the system/component into a stable and safe condition and inform the responsible supervisor. Situations such as this could occur if the procedure is found to be inadequate for the intended task, if unexpected results occur, or if two or more procedures governing the activity conflict. The supervisor shall resolve the discrepancy in the procedure by either one of the following:

  (a) determining the methods by which the activity can be performed using the procedure as written and conveying this to the individual performing the activity

  (b) submitting a procedure change, either temporary or permanent, depending on the actual situation (no further procedural steps shall be accomplished until the procedure change is approved).

(3) In cases of emergency when procedures are inadequate for the situation, plant operations personnel are directed to take such action as necessary to minimize personnel injury and damage to the plant; to return the plant to a stable, safe condition; and to protect the health and safety of the general public and of the personnel on site. These actions shall be documented and, if appropriate, incorporated into a revision of the affected procedure.

On implementing procedures:

(1) Procedures that control operations where reliance on memory cannot be trusted and where operations must be performed in a specified sequence shall be followed step-by-step with the procedure present. . . . If there is any doubt as to the procedural action by the individual performing the job, the procedure must be present. . . .

(2) Controlled copies of appropriate system operating procedures and temporary procedures shall be available to operations department personnel for in-plant use at important local/manual stations.

Signing off on procedures:

(1) Procedures sign-off lists are used as an aid in confirming the completion of steps in proper sequence as required. In addition, it provides formal documentation of the completion of critical steps in the procedure and thus aids in any subsequent determination of equipment or system status. Sign-off lists are executed when specified by the associated procedure or when included as an integral part of the procedure. After the completion of each item on the sign-off list, the operator completing the step initials the item.

(2) The completed sign-off list is inserted in the control room system status file. The previously completed sign-off list is removed from the file and forwarded to the operations department head.

Source: INPO Good Practice, *Conduct of Operations* (July 1984), pp. 18–19.

QUEST FOR THE BEST

Given the oft-remarked penchant for watered-down standards among rulemaking industry associations, there is every reason to have expected adulterated standards from INPO as well. Yet nothing we have learned so far warrants such a conclusion. To the contrary, "INPO's standards continue to improve each year so that if you get an outstanding grade from INPO this year, and you don't make improvements in your processes or your programs, then you won't get that same high score next year from INPO because their standards have gone up in the meantime." Comments like this one, made by a nuclear plant quality control manager, could be heard from one interview to the next. Far from a downward push toward lowest-common-denominator standards, the basic thrust of INPO's rulemaking process is continual upward mobility. To illustrate, consider the process by which INPO revised its guidelines for the maintenance of nuclear plants, here described by INPO's president:

> [INPO] put together maintenance assistance and review teams to visit a plant and take a focused look just on maintenance. To do that, we formed a special team that included . . . three or four maintenance people from INPO and a team manager from INPO. We asked EPRI [Electric Power Research Institute] to designate a member who could accompany our team. We also asked the cognizant NSSS [nuclear reactor] supplier. If the plant was a Westinghouse plant, we asked Westinghouse to identify a knowledgeable maintenance person to accompany this team. We also added to the team a maintenance peer from a utility where we knew the maintenance program was working pretty well. So the team was a mixture of people, but all with a great deal of expertise in maintenance and all with a common cause.

"With these teams," he continued, "we first conducted four visits to plants that we thought had good maintenance—as good as there is in the industry. That was to see how to do it and to let our teams be *calibrated to the highest standards that we could find in the industry.* . . . We're incorporating the feedback gained from this process into a revision to the maintenance guidelines that we hope to publish soon."[34]

We have here a paradigm example of how INPO calibrates (and continually recalibrates) its own standards in light of the industry's highest standards. That is INPO's defining orientation, at base, and that is what gives the whole process its upwardly mobile trajectory. By starting from the best standards realized so far, INPO thus links the standards-making process, not to those who want the least done, but to those who most closely approximate, in one program or another (including maintenance), the industry at its best.[35] And that defining orientation, another INPO official explains, is what truly distinguishes INPO's approach from the much-criticized aspects of traditional industry standards-making.

> When you say industry standards, most people think in terms of ANSI consensus requirements. Our standards are different. They're not minimum requirements because we don't go out and try to get a vote from everybody on whether they would commit to it or not. That's what results in low standards. As we initially draft those standards we have a lot of utility input. And we frequently refine them based on our experience, again with utility input.

"But the way INPO is structured," he continued, "and our charter and institutional plan requires, if we at INPO feel that we need to improve performance in an area and write tougher criteria, or new criteria, then we do it. We certainly get a lot of industry input, but we don't go out and get a vote. Basically, we have a process with a lot of industry involvement, but the final decision is ours to make. We tell the utilities, 'Okay, we're going to do this, and as a member of INPO you're now obligated to strive to meet this criterion and we're going to hold you to it.' It's just a different concept and process from how consensus standards are made."

What does all this add up to? While much remains to be clarified, there can be little doubt that INPO's standards-making role has transformed the nuclear industry's normative landscape. "Before INPO, there weren't any standards from an excellence perspective," an INPO official recalls. "There was nothing on how to organize your technical services department, or how to best set up management control systems. There was nothing. What you had was fifty-four utilities that operated like fifty-four independent fiefdoms." How things have changed. A nuclear utility vice president crystallized the comments of many industry officials interviewed when he said that INPO's normative order "sets the example for the industry and gives the industry a way of objectively looking at each plant to determine areas in which its performance falls short of *industry expectations*." (Emphasis supplied.) What INPO norms really do, says another industry official, "is communicate an ideal standard of behavior to everybody." Or, as yet another industry executive observes, INPO's normative order has become "the source of collective practices in the industry."

Notice how these comments presume a collective "we"—what the "industry" expects and what the "industry" practices—that would have been unimaginable when the fifty-four utilities operated like fifty-four independent fiefdoms. Or so it seemed until INPO's normative order, by promoting a unified vision of the industry's aspirations and a unified language of self-understanding ("we the industry"), established a plane of collective industry expectations that transformed nuclear power's moral universe in a subtle yet decisive way.[36]

Another fundamental point about INPO's normative system ought to be mentioned. It also promotes an *ethic of responsibility*. What the industry expects and what it considers obligatory are two sides of the same coin to a significant degree. Hence, the emphasis on industry expectations is also a way of underscoring the myriad responsibilities of industry membership. "INPO is very strong on fixing responsibility," as a nuclear plant superintendent explains it. "That's a big issue in all of their programs across all areas—ensuring that accountability and responsibility [are] clearly defined."

Indeed, to overlook how INPO's normative order stresses the responsibilities of industry membership is to ignore perhaps the most important thing we need to understand about INPO's standards-making role as a form of communitarian regulation.

To illustrate, consider how INPO's normative order promotes an ethic of responsibility in the case of the nuclear utility's senior nuclear manager (typically a vice president for nuclear operations). Since the performance objectives are the touchstones of INPO's normative order, it is especially revealing to note how the senior nuclear manager's performance objective stresses one aim above all—"carrying out his responsibilities." (See table 5.7.) And of all of his responsibilities, none are more important than those outlined in the criteria—directing nuclear operational matters within the corporation, supporting the nuclear plant through active personal involvement, reviewing violations of plant procedures and taking corrective action, monitoring nuclear plant performance against established goals and objectives, ensuring that nuclear plant personnel are assigned appropriate tasks by corporate personnel. All this (and much more) is what one's role requires as

TABLE 5.7

Senior Nuclear Executive

Performance Objective

The senior nuclear executive receives appropriate support and has the authority and control necessary to carry out his responsibilities.

Criteria

1. The senior nuclear executive has the safe and reliable operation of the utility's nuclear station(s) as his primary responsibility and is not assigned responsibilities other than nuclear plant operations and support.

2. The senior nuclear executive directs nuclear operational matters within the corporation. He makes or concurs in final decisions regarding significant nuclear safety matters.

3. The senior nuclear executive clearly communicates management principles and expectations guiding the overall management of nuclear operations and the professional conduct required of all nuclear employees.

4. The senior nuclear executive is actively and personally involved in nuclear station direction and support. Examples of functions related to safety and reliability in which the senior nuclear executive is actively involved include the following:

   a. approving qualification and staffing requirements for key station and corporate management positions, including all positions that can directly affect plant safety

   b. concurring with corporate policies governing each functional support area for nuclear activities

   c. visiting the nuclear station(s) periodically to appraise plant conditions and practices

   d. interacting with the corporate-level safety review group performing independent reviews of matters affecting nuclear safety

   e. reviewing timeliness and effectiveness of implementation of in-house and industry operating experience

   f. reviewing effects of new regulations on plant operations

   g. reviewing station operating status and current problems and reviewing reports of unanticipated and unusual occurrences at the station(s)

   h. reviewing selected data and trends in the functional support areas for nuclear activities and monitoring station performance against established goals and objectives

   i. reviewing preparations for and progress of major outages

   j. monitoring station modification status

   k. monitoring radiation reduction activities to verify proper implementation of corporate radiation exposure policies

   l. assessing the effectiveness of root cause determinations for recurring problems and unanticipated and unusual occurrences

5. The senior nuclear executive (in addition to line managers and appropriate staff personnel) is personally involved in monitoring and assessing nuclear activities.

TABLE 5.7 continued

Senior Nuclear Executive

6. The senior nuclear executive receives regular updates covering those activities that are delegated to other corporate managers related to nuclear activities.

7. The senior nuclear executive ensures that station personnel are not assigned inappropriate work or tasks by corporate personnel. He controls assignments and requests that divert the station manager's attention from safe and reliable station operation.

8. The senior nuclear executive has sufficient control over those areas assigned to managers who do not report to him to ensure safe and reliable operations of the station(s).

Source: INPO, *Performance Objectives and Criteria for Corporate Evaluations* (December 1987), pp. 5–6.

a senior nuclear manager, according to INPO's normative system. So what the system expects (and considers obligatory) is the performance of certain tasks or functions generated by one's role in the industry and essential to achieving one's mission. As to the choice of means for accomplishing these tasks—specific objectives, internal organization, allocation of resources, and so on—such implementing details are a matter of nuclear utility prerogative.

Here we begin to see an underlying pattern that has special relevance for understanding the larger significance of INPO's normative system. Whether someone is a nuclear utility CEO or control room operator, a nuclear plant manager or maintenance superintendent, each position (like the senior manager's) embodies a distinctive cluster of responsibilities *from the standpoint of INPO's normative system*. It is all part of seeing the nuclear industry as a social landscape of responsibility-generating institutional roles. And therein lies the real point: by constructing the social world of nuclear power operations in this way, INPO's normative system integrates the industry around a common language of self-understanding, an industry-wide interpretive framework for construing what it means to occupy a particular role and what it means to behave in a manner appropriate to that position. In this way, in short, INPO's normative system institutes *obligations of role*. So from one perspective INPO's performance objectives and criteria, guidelines and good practices, can be viewed as an elaborate body of interrelated rules. Yet looked at another way, that system of rules also articulates a constellation of institutional roles, each of which spells out in considerable detail what it means to be a responsible member of nuclear power's industrial community.[37]

THE QUESTION OF COSTS

A fundamental tension marks the history of INPO's administrative development, as you may recall from the last chapter. There we saw factors that encourage a close integration between INPO and the industry (most notably, INPO's need to garner industry respect and support), just as we saw factors that bolster INPO's independence of the industry (most notably, the nuclear navy–inspired professional commitments and aspirations of INPO officials). Hence, INPO is both an industry organization *and* a professional organization, a combination of opposing qualities that sometimes creates fundamental tensions in INPO-industry relations. Perhaps no example makes this point more clearly than industry's mounting concerns over the new industrial morality's costs.

"A growing number of utilities . . . are questioning whether the Institute of Nuclear Power Operations (INPO), in its zeal to push nuclear plant operators to 'strive for excellence,' is contributing to escalating production costs and shoving the nuclear industry toward noncompetitiveness," a nuclear industry trade journal reported in 1990.[38] The article then goes on to quote Leon Russell, former manager of Calvert Cliffs nuclear plant and now manager of nuclear safety and planning at Baltimore Gas and Electric Company:

> "INPO sees a good practice at one plant and by inference wants every plant to adopt it." "If you try to adopt every good practice that exists in the industry, your costs are going to be pretty significant. . . . Up through 1988 costs continue to rise on the order of 10% a year," he said. "It's very unsettling. . . . It just can't continue on and on without us (nuclear) becoming more expensive than fossil fuel plants."

INPO's role in escalating costs, Russell added, "is going to be a question in utilities' minds more and more as costs continue to escalate."[39]

Concern over rising costs is a theme sounded by many industry officials, and, what's more, they attribute much of the problem to INPO's nuclear navy roots. "I think there is a basic weakness with INPO," complains an industry official. "INPO does not concern itself at all with economics. And part of the reason for that, I think, is that INPO, its organization and culture, is pretty much that of the naval nuclear program." "In the navy you don't think first and foremost from the standpoint of business profit and loss," as another industry official complains. Adding, "INPO's the same way."[40]

INPO's response to such concerns? Typically, you get an answer like this one:

> We do not worry a lot about cost-effectiveness. The word we fo-
> cus on a lot is safety—that's paramount, of course—and then
> there's reliability. In other words, we see a strong connection be-
> tween the two. A reliable plant, one where the equipment oper-
> ates as designed, is going to be a safer plant. That also means it
> will be a more cost-effective plant. I mean safety and reliability
> and cost-effectiveness are not exclusive in that sense.

These comments, by a top-level INPO official (and former nuclear navy officer), exemplify the basic INPO line on costs: *in the long run,* increasing safety and increasing cost-effectiveness go hand in hand. Safety pays, in short, which also summarizes how the nuclear navy's cultural orientation views the matter. Admiral Rickover's former as-sistant (and current Secretary of Energy), retired admiral James D. Watkins:

> My training and experience began in the early days of nuclear
> energy, where I learned firsthand from Admiral Rickover the im-
> portant principles of safe and reliable application of nuclear
> technology. . . . *Achieving safety is expensive, but those who
> seek to obtain the benefits of atomic power need to realize that
> there are no shortcuts, no easy fixes and no viable alternatives
> to safe operations if the nuclear industry is to survive.*

The lesson for commercial nuclear utilities?

> Although many utilities believe that they have reached a high
> level of performance and safety, and perhaps they have, now is
> not the time to relax. *Maintaining safety is a costly endeavor
> that requires sustained corporate commitment.* . . . I know how
> expensive that can be, and I know how many companies are
> pressured by the bottom line. But in order to ensure that the
> commitment to safety and excellent plant performance is not
> threatened, *it is imperative that the utilities resist the natural
> business tendency to reduce the resources dedicated to foster-
> ing safe and excellent practices.*[41]

The lesson is not just that maintaining safety is a costly endeavor. It is that the principles of nuclear safety Rickover articulated (and INPO champions) are especially *precarious* values, partly because they in-volve relatively subtle and fragile institutional practices (for instance, learning from experience), and partly because they must compete directly with the more immediate and pressing realities nuclear utility officials constantly confront (for instance, budgetary pressures to go with the shortcut and easy fix).[42]

This goes a long way toward explaining why INPO's cultural orientation does not assign a high priority to the whole issue of cost-effectiveness. Though it would be foolish to ignore the cost issue completely, INPO officials will tell you, it would be even riskier to overreact to utility concerns. Generally motivated by the pursuit of short-run economic advantage, time and again such concerns are inimical to the precarious values that nurture and sustain high levels of nuclear safety. So these natural business tendencies must be resisted, they say. Otherwise, if they are permitted to run their natural course, unchecked, all this talk about "pursuing excellence" will be just that—wishful thinking and idle rhetoric. For INPO, as for the nuclear navy, achieving safety is a demanding and expensive quest that must be pursued for the sake of the industry's long-term survival.

All very well and good, skeptics might say, but it is by no means clear that nuclear utilities will in fact take these demanding (and costly) ideals seriously—any more than it is obvious that individuals will always act on their ideals. Which brings us to the next chapter's basic question: what *motivates* nuclear utilities to strive for these industrial principles despite escalating costs and other competing organizational demands. From where, to state the issue in broader terms, does this new system of communitarian regulation draw its force?

6

Communal Pressure

In 1987 Senate hearings, INPO's vice president, William Conway, was asked to explain the nature of INPO's enforcement powers.

> Senator Breaux: You do not have, as I understand it, any enforcement mechanism to enforce those recommendations in the form of any civil penalties . . . to place on a utility . . . that just said, "We don't agree at all with what you are telling us. We are just not listening to what you have to say."

> Mr. Conway: That is factually accurate. . . . However, I think one of the more important things that we are able to do is *bring a considerable amount of peer pressure, if necessary, to gain the interest of the people who may not be totally reactive to what we would suggest and what we would recommend.*[1]

It has long been understood that the force of peer expectations can be a potent source of motivation, even in the face of almost certain death. An unusual but instructive example: "At the battle of Waterloo, soldiers who flinched in the face of the enemy were reproved by other soldiers. This was facilitated by deploying the troops in formations that made each man constantly aware of the men on either side of him. To desert meant to disgrace oneself in the eyes of a comrade." What kept the officers fighting? "They were not drawn up in tight formations, and there were no pistols at their backs. At Waterloo, *the answer was honor. "Officers . . . were most concerned about the figure they cut in their brother officers' eye. Honor was paramount."*[2]

One moral we can draw from this experience is that the force of peer expectations works best in small face-to-face groups which stay together for long periods of time. If this means that group solidarity (and therefore peer pressure) is most likely to flourish under intimate

91

conditions, it also seems to follow that as the size of the group increases, and relations become more and more depersonalized, the force of peer expectations will diminish accordingly. Can peer pressure effectively encourage (or discourage) conduct that is esteemed (or frowned upon) in a large and relatively impersonal social setting, such as the nuclear industry, where more than 100,000 people work at 111 plants operating at 70 sites around the country? Size and fragmentation would seem to preclude that possibility, yet the evidence we will be considering suggests otherwise. The ordering force of peer expectations can be quite effective in large industrial settings, provided that the right institutional conditions exist, and in this chapter we seek an understanding of what those conditions are in the nuclear industry's case.

THE EARLY YEARS

When Admiral Eugene Wilkinson began his job as INPO's first president in 1980, he expressed complete confidence in the nuclear utilities' willingness to respond to INPO's recommendations thanks to the power of peer pressure. "There is *great pressure* on any responsible management when a question of plant, personnel, and public safety is involved and our recommendations will be based on improving safety." "In my opinion," he concluded, "*responsive action by each utility will not be a problem* when these principles are used to promote safety."[3]

Reality turned out differently, however. By 1983, after completing two rounds of plant inspections, INPO officials were dismayed over the "wide variation among utilities in following up recommendations from INPO evaluations."[4] And by 1985, with the problem showing few signs of improvement, troubled industry officials commissioned a thorough evaluation of the industry's self-regulation activities. This resulted in a widely circulated and very influential study commonly referred to as the "Sillin report," after one of its coauthors.[5] "It has become evident," their report stated, "that not all U.S. nuclear utilities are meeting their commitment to excellence in operations; indeed some are still only marginally meeting regulatory requirements and some utilities have experienced operational events [an industry euphemism for accidents] at their plants demonstrating unsatisfactory performance."

The root of the problem: INPO's powers of peer pressure were not terribly effective in dealing with certain nuclear utilities. For at least implicitly, and to some extent explicitly, the report's authors distinguished between two groups of nuclear utilities, those that are generally responsible and safety-conscious and those that are not. Although INPO may be reasonably effective in dealing with the former group, the report suggested, experience with the latter category, the industry laggards, necessitated increased powers of peer pressure for INPO.[6]

But that was not all. Quite apart from the laggards, something also had to be done about most other nuclear utilities, owing to the fact that their performance, when compared to their foreign counterparts', also cast serious doubt on the industry's self-regulation effort.

> While some nuclear units in this country have performance records that rank with the best in the world, overall performance of the U.S. nuclear utility industry, despite the commitment to excellence, has not compared favorably to the performance shown by light water nuclear power plants being operated in such comparable industrialized countries as the Federal Republic of Germany, France, Japan, and Switzerland.[7]

What is to be done? As a "first priority" INPO and the industry must "take additional aggressive self-improvement steps."[8] As one of the report's coauthors recalls, "We devoted much of our attention to encourage INPO to take a more aggressive role." "We wanted to enhance the quality of peer pressure," he adds. "That was the purpose of our recommendations." Just how these highly influential recommendations enhanced INPO's powers of peer pressure will be discussed in a moment, for at this point an inquisitive reader may well ask: What happened to Admiral Wilkinson's confident prediction? What happened to the "great pressure" that would make each utility responsive to INPO's recommendations? A brief look at the fate of two regulatory tools—insurance and inspection reports—sheds some light on these questions.

Although we seldom think of insurance as a regulatory tool, in some industrial settings it has been a significant motivating force when it comes to promoting regulatory goals.[9] But not within the nuclear industry. The connection between insurance and nuclear safety was almost established after the TMI accident, yet it wasn't, and to see why it wasn't is to understand something important about the fate of peer pressure during INPO's early administrative development.

Soon after the TMI accident the nuclear utility industry created a mutual insurance organization—Nuclear Electric Insurers Ltd. (NEIL)—to shield individual nuclear utilities against the cost of replacement energy when a plant is shut down by an accident, thereby avoiding a repeat of the crippling financial burdens experienced by TMI's parent company.

Meanwhile, in their discussions leading up to INPO's creation, INPO's architects planned to use NEIL as a regulatory tool. As one of INPO's principal architects recalls, "We intended to tie together the INPO evaluations and insurance as an enforcement tool. The idea was that would be the iron hand behind the velvet glove."[10] Under this scheme, if a nuclear utility failed to respond satisfactorily to INPO recommendations, the iron hand could revoke the recalcitrant utility's insurance. The plan was never implemented. "There was a great resistance to using insurance as a weapon because of the enormous financial impact this would have on a utility," another industry official explains. "You see, what the withdrawal of insurance would do to any utility, it would immediately affect their bond rating, their Wall Street situation. It could very well be financially catastrophic. It would be kind of like having a nuclear bomb in your arsenal." Those who argued for using insurance as INPO's major regulatory weapon were thus overruled. For many industry officials, apparently, that was too much clout to place in the hands of this new and unfamiliar organization.[11]

Our second example involves the wording and distribution of INPO inspection reports and once again illustrates how nuclear utility officials constrained INPO's enforcement powers. At the outset, those reports were circulated among all the nuclear utilities on the theory that, by exposing problem plants to industry scrutiny—and most important, industry reproach—the force of peer pressure unleashed in the process would surely move them to address their problems. Things turned out quite differently, however.

After reading dozens of these reports, one can't help noticing their carefully restrained wording and their tactfully diplomatic tone. Nor can one avoid the sense that, for some reason, INPO officials were extremely reluctant to use bluntly candid language in their written assessment of a nuclear plant's performance. They were pulling their punches, and the reason why is not hard to uncover. As an industry organization, INPO was responding to the concerns of its most powerful constituency—the nuclear utility CEOs—who were understandably nervous about the risks associated with such reports. "We have to be careful not to give ammunition to intervenors [outside industry critics] out of the INPO reports," a nuclear utility CEO cautioned INPO officials at a 1981 meeting.[12] INPO heard similar warnings from other CEOs, including one of its leading industry boosters, Carolina Power and Light CEO Sherwood Smith:

> As has been stated by others [nuclear utility CEOs], these [INPO inspection] reports, in being made public, reach many audiences. Those audiences are not always friendly. Their attitude is not always constructive, and they use great pressure on public service commissions to look for excuses to deny utilities very badly needed rate relief. *We would hope that it would be possible for the narrative in the INPO report to take into account those audiences who will study the report very carefully so that an effort is made "to talk about the glass being half full as well as the fact that the glass seems to be, in some areas, half empty."* We think that the INPO report can serve a very valuable and useful function for the industry in that regard.[13]

The message to INPO was clear: sanitize your inspection reports so that you don't get us into trouble with the public. And INPO, by muting its criticisms and picturing the glass half full, did just that.

How did all this affect INPO's powers? By 1985, even relatively sympathetic industry observers, such as former NRC chairman John Ahearne, questioned INPO's "apparent inability to find any plant that is significantly weak." "INPO has made a motto of standards of excellence," he went on. "But there has never been a plant that has failed to meet these standards." "INPO appears unable to say that a certain plant just doesn't meet the standards for good operating practices. . . . This is not believable."[14] More interesting, still, we find leading nuclear utility officials raising similar concerns about those sanitized inspection reports. Cleansed of harsh judgments and filled with "comforting words," such reports made it too easy for nuclear utility officials to brush aside INPO's criticisms. "Part of the difficulty that some utilities have experienced has been in the nature of INPO's reports," the chairman of INPO's board of directors explained to an audience of fellow nuclear utility CEOs:

> While there have been areas needing improvement identified and responses called for, because of concern for the sensitive nature of the reports and their possible misuse, comforting words have been included. . . . *We find that oftentimes, the comforting words . . . resulted in management's placing too much em-*

phasis on them rather than giving needed attention to the
areas requiring improvement.[15]

So as a tool of peer pressure INPO inspection reports had some serious weaknesses. They were supposed to communicate to nuclear utility officials that their performance was not up to industry standards, and motivate them accordingly, yet oftentimes they didn't. They were supposed to focus the industry's attention on the deviant nuclear plants among them, but generally failed to draw such invidious distinctions, thereby shielding problem utilities from industry-wide visibility and scorn. All in all, then, by insisting that INPO sanitize its reports for public consumption, the industry sapped those reports of their motivational force.

Given these shortcomings and given INPO's stress on peer pressure, one might expect INPO to take steps to make their inspection reports less restrained and more blunt. They did. But with this change INPO officials also made another revealing change, announced by the chairman of INPO's board in these terms: "There will be greater attention given to whether the comfort words can be included justifiably in the report to the utility. The INPO staff will be endeavoring to make the reports clearer and more to the point." In view of this change, he continued, INPO would no longer encourage industry-wide distribution of the reports.

This is a puzzling development for an organization that claims peer pressure as its primary enforcement tool. Why not make the reports clearer and more to the point and also continue their distribution to the other utilities? "You have to think about the institutional infrastructure and the culture of the industry," a top-level industry official explains.

> It's one thing to urge an organization such as INPO to move in
> and take dramatic steps. But it had to build its credibility in the
> industry. *If INPO had moved too fast, the price could have
> been the destruction of the whole INPO concept.* You need to
> understand that the INPO ethic—self-regulation through peer
> pressure—is a very fragile thing because the industry had not
> subjected itself to that kind of discipline before. [Emphasis supplied.]

In this way of thinking, then, INPO's powers of peer pressure are best understood from a developmental perspective. As a new and unfamiliar organization in the eyes of many industry officials, INPO first had to strengthen its tenuous and insecure social base within the industry so as to avoid threats to its stability and existence. If this meant that the early years of INPO's administrative development were conditioned above all by external pressures arising from its dependence on the utilities, it also meant that INPO was in no position to take the dramatic steps required to effectively mobilize the industry's powers of peer pressure. Conclusion: INPO was a cautious if not timid regulator.

PEER PRESSURE REFORMED

How things have changed in a short six or seven years. Now ask industry officials about INPO's powers of peer pressure and you get an answer like this one from a nuclear utility vice president: "The peer pressure INPO exerts is enormous. It is there. It operates. And I will tell you, it has a tremendous impact on the utilities because it's really a compelling force." Just talk? Or are there good grounds for concluding that a once weak and timid regulator has now become a compelling industry force?

Let's start by returning to the Sillin report's principal conclusion: if nuclear industry self-regulation is to succeed, INPO must become much more aggressive. INPO must enhance its powers of peer pressure, to be more precise, and it must do so mainly by targeting the nuclear industry's most senior executives—above all, the chief executive officers. Why single out the CEOs? In response to just that question, a Sillin report coauthor responded, "It's the CEO that sets the tone":

> Unless he's involved, unless he shows his commitment, unless he shows his attention, unless he follows up and shows he's following up on problems that INPO identifies, it's not going to be an effective operation. I can't stress that enough—the importance of commitment from the top. Now some utility leaders perceive these things as important, and others, well, let me say they perceive them as less important. And that's where we come in. We wanted to make *everybody* perceive them as important. And to bring that about, we recommended that INPO increase the level of peer pressure.

The problem of CEOs not paying serious attention to how their nuclear plants are performing comes out most clearly in the way some CEOs first responded to INPO inspection reports. "The problem we found is that some CEOs were not looking at the INPO evaluation report," recalls another Sillin report coauthor. "And obviously, if the chief executive officer is not getting that information, it's pretty hard for him to have a judgment of the quality of effort his people are putting out." Think here of the nuclear industry's pre-TMI cultural orientation, the fossil fuel mentality, and how it downplayed the CEO's involvement in nuclear plant operations. In the case of some nuclear utilities, it would seem that those old managerial habits persisted well beyond the TMI accident. In any event, the Sillin report coauthor goes on:

> We found too great a tendency among some utility CEOs (who may have a legal or financial background) to let the vice president for nuclear handle all the responsibility for technical operations, including the INPO evaluation. But what happens if the report is critical of the person in charge, the nuclear v.p.? There's nobody there to look over his shoulder, and the likelihood is that we're not going to see the effective response we want. But if you get the CEO involved, that's when you start seeing the improvements take place. So the belief on our part is that the CEO of the utility, whatever his background, has to be directly involved because he's so critical to an effective operation.[16]

Performance Indicators

This way of thinking about the CEO's pivotal role motivated a number of Sillin report recommendations. Now INPO insists that the CEOs review the INPO inspection reports as well as the utility's responses to the problems identified by the inspection.[17] INPO also insists, again following the Sillin report, that the CEOs make all this information known to their board of directors.[18]

Why the utility's governing board? "Bad news has a hard time making its way up the organization. That's why we did it," says a Sillin report coauthor. "A lot of the CEOs weren't communicating the INPO findings to their boards. As a matter of fact, it was a minority of CEOs that were communicating that information upstream to their board."

Intensifying this pressure, INPO established industry-wide performance indicators during this period, the mid-1980s, thus adding a new dimension of industry self-awareness. "Ten years ago, if your president, CEO, or board member asked you 'How are you doing compared with the rest of the industry?' you had a lot of wiggle room," recalls a nuclear utility vice president. "It's very different today," he goes on, "because we're all sitting there looking at the INPO indicators which tell you where you stand with other plants of the same vintage and other plants of the same type." [19] As an example of what he is talking about, consider California's Rancho Seco nuclear plant. (See figure 6.1.) Notice how each indicator's performance is plotted on a graph and compared with the rest of the industry; notice further that on nearly every measure Rancho Seco's performance conspicuously stands among the industry's "worst quartile." Is Rancho Seco a good or bad performing plant? If the answer seems obvious, that's just the point: with these performance indicators, nuclear utility officials now had an industry-wide normative benchmark for judging "good" and "bad" nuclear plant performance. Public Service Electric and Gas CEO James Ferland:

> Even in the early 1980s, we had access to information on performance of our nuclear and fossil units, including financial data of various types. . . . *What we needed, but did not then have, was information allowing us to quantitatively compare performance of individual nuclear units with performance of the entire nuclear industry. . . .* This program [INPO performance indicators] has allowed us to monitor performance of our units on a consistent, quantified basis and compare that performance to the entire nuclear industry. [Emphasis supplied.]

What real difference has all this made? "Some of us found that, even in areas where we thought our performance was pretty good, others were doing much better. That stimulated many of us to improve the performance of our units." [20]

Another way of saying this is that the INPO indicators led utility officials to interpret their nuclear plants' performance in a more objective and impersonal light, not how each stands alone, but where they stand *relative to* an industry-wide field of performance. Each nuclear plant thus became related to the others in a new way, a new context of shared experience rather like a hundred once-solitary joggers grouped into a single race. For like a race, according to INPO, the performance indicators "provide a basis for healthy competition between nuclear stations and between utilities in the industry-wide quest for improved performance." [21]

Is there any reason to believe industry officials take such comparisons seriously? Consider these comments by a vice president for nuclear power:

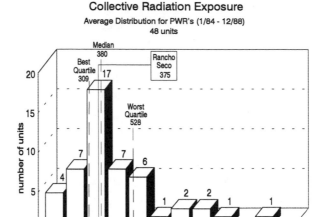

Fig. 6.1 Performance Indicators for Nuclear Plants *(cont. pp. 101–3)*

We track our performance against the INPO indicators to see how we're doing performance-wise compared to the rest of the industry. I review those indicators with my management team once a month to see where we stand, and I also give a report to my president once a month on how we're doing on the indicators. Then there's our CEO and board of directors. Three times

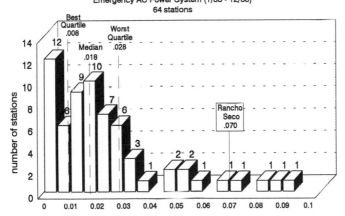

Volume of Low-Level Solid Radioactive Waste

Safety System Performance

a year I give a presentation in which I show them where we stand in the industry in terms of the ten indicators. Obviously, they're very interested in how we stack up relative to everybody else.

Since comments like this one could be heard in a number of interviews, and more important, given the fact that all the indicators have shown significant improvement, industry-wide, it seems reasonable to conclude that industry executives take these comparisons quite seriously. Which is hardly surprising, students of organizational behavior

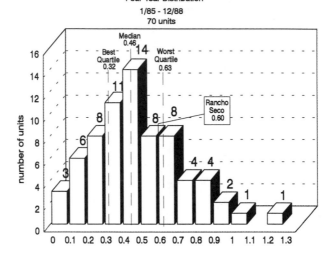

Unplanned Automatic Scrams Per 1000 Hours Critical
Four Year Distribution
1/85 - 12/88
70 units

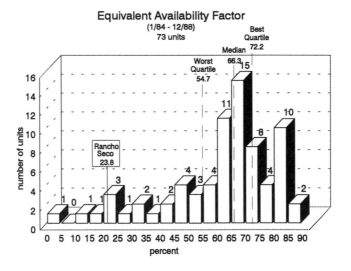

Equivalent Availability Factor
(1/84 - 12/88)
73 units

tell us, as institutions generally devote more attention "to activities that are failing to meet targets than to activities that are meeting them."[22] And if the performance indicator program does anything, it establishes conspicuous industry-wide goals or targets that no utility official can easily ignore.[23]

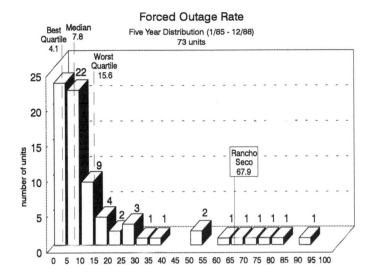

Forced Outage Rate
Five Year Distribution (1/85 - 12/88)
73 units

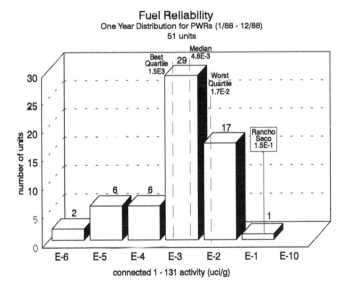

Fuel Reliability
One Year Distribution for PWRs (1/88 - 12/88)
51 units

Management by Embarrassment

A nuclear utility CEO crystallized the comments of many industry officials interviewed when he said, "Peer pressure is just visibility throughout the industry. There's a strong sense now that if any utility is in trouble we're all in trouble. If anybody has another accident like TMI it's going to have dire results for everybody. That's what brings the peer pressure. *You get the whole top level of the utility industry focused on the poor performer."* (Emphasis supplied.)

He is sounding some now-familiar themes, but his last remark is worth stressing because it brings to light a new and critically important point, that peer pressure is mainly a matter of industry leaders directing their gaze at poorly performing plants. To see what this means, we can best begin with the Sillin report's two most significant recommendations: INPO should (1) grade the performance of each utility and (2) publicize the results. "INPO already had an informal system for grading nuclear plants that they used internally," explains a Sillin report coauthor. "We wanted to give it greater precision and visibility because *there's nothing more compelling than to be identified as a laggard among your peers."* (Emphasis supplied.)[24] And so, having adopted both recommendations, in October 1987 INPO offered its first ranking of all nuclear plants:

Category 1 (Excellent) .... 8 plants
Category 2 .... 22 plants
Category 3 .... 28 plants
Category 4 .... 7 plants
Category 5 (Marginal) .... 3 plants[25]

As for publicizing these grades, each year all the CEOs and their senior nuclear officers, among others, attend an INPO-sponsored conference in Atlanta. Meeting in executive session, the CEOs and INPO's president all participate in a remarkable ritual. "Some people call it management by embarrassment," explains a CEO:

All the CEOs are gathered in a big room with Zack Pate [INPO's president], and he flashes up the most recent evaluation numbers for each of the utilities by name. That's the only time we learn how our peers are ranked, and it kind of hits you right between the eyeballs. The first slide has all the number ones, the best-rated utilities. Lots of praise from Zack, and all those CEOs kind of puff up and get a big smile on their face. [They also receive a plaque.] Then come the number twos, and those guys also feel pretty good about it. And then come the number threes, and they just kind of sit there passive. Then you get down to the fours and the fives. And after some pretty frank discussion of their problems, those guys are feeling rather uneasy to say the least. I guess you could say it's a sense of pride or ego. All CEOs are pretty egotistical. I mean these are people who have worked their way up to managing a major utility, and our societal cultural aim is to strive to be the best and get to the top of the pyramid. I think that's really the driver here. We all want to be a one, and none of us want to be viewed as a poor performer among our peers.

And so, with the industry's chief executives gathered in a single room for this formal occasion, INPO classifies their social world of nuclear power in a distinctive way—hierarchically—as each nuclear plant is embodied with an official status (ranging from the "excellent" 1 to the "marginal" 5), a status publicly proclaimed before everyone's eyes. "When the ratings all began to come out at the CEO meetings," as one CEO puts it, "suddenly we weren't all equal anymore."

And when those ratings came out, observes another CEO, that was when "the peer pressure really started taking hold":

> The industry learned one profound lesson from Three Mile Island, that no one operating these plants is an island unto himself. He can be the best goddamned operator in the world, but if the guy on the bottom of the list gets into trouble, the whole industry is in trouble. It doesn't matter whether you're Commonwealth Edison and you're 70 or 80 percent nuclear or whether you're Florida Power Corporation and you're only a fraction nuclear, you've still got a tremendous investment in nuclear and you're still relying on those plants to make electricity. And if anything upsets that, it's going to hurt your business. That's clear from the TMI accident. We're all in the same boat here—that's the bottom line. One guy goes down and it has a tremendous impact on all the utilities—on their operations, on their resources, on their ability to earn money.

"And that's the reason the peer pressure can be effective," he goes on. "Because the industry guys in that room start looking at you, and people are uncomfortable with being held up to opprobrium if not worse amongst their peers." As the chairman of INPO's board of directors (and Duke Power CEO) said at one of these CEO-filled meetings:

> The future of your own organization, the future of the nuclear industry and indeed the utility industry as we know it today rests with you. Each of you personally has a great potential impact on the future of everyone of us in this room and thousands and thousands of other people—employees of ours—who do not even know you. . . . *But, look around this room. One group*

of you in this room operates plants that perform better, safer, and more reliably. Another group of you operates your plants in an average manner. And then, there is the other group.[26]

Communitarian Social Control

"The whole INPO exercise has a curiously American feeling about it, a touch of the earnest chat in the locker room to sort out, man to man, the reasons why the quarterback is letting the team down."[27] Comments like this one, by a reporter with the *Financial Times* of London, could also be heard on occasion from industry officials. As one nuclear utility vice president tried to explain INPO's power of peer pressure: "The basketball team at Carolina doesn't want to be number two in the national rankings just like North Carolina State or Duke don't want to be number two. They all want to be a number one. It's exactly the same for the CEOs. That's the driving force behind those rankings, really, just like a big sports competition." The sports analogy is a fruitful way of thinking about the motivations of CEOs and other top-level industry officials, but I also want to suggest a quite different context for envisioning INPO's institutional mechanisms for allocating praise and distributing shame, what John Braithwaite terms the "family model" of social control.[28]

In the theoretical perspective Braithwaite has developed, the main idea is "reintegrative shaming," and the most obvious place to see it at work is in family life. Think of it this way: when my five-year-old daughter throws a rock at her little brother, I express my disappointment with a stern look, she lowers her head in shame, repents, and, in the end, I give her a warm hug. Here we have, in its simplest form, a prime example of how reintegrative shaming works.[29]

Now take an example central to our discussion. It involves a meeting of all the nuclear industry's senior nuclear officers, and it takes place at the very time their CEOs meet nearby in executive session to discuss nuclear plant rankings. Superficially, the meeting might be called an example of information exchange, as the typical format involves three vice presidents, one after another, standing before their peers in order to reflect upon a recent "event" at their nuclear plant. But "information exchange" is too bland a description for what actually goes on. More than a detailed explanation of an accident, it also involves "baring your soul and telling all your peers (people that you know) that you screwed up," explains an INPO official. "You know, I'm not a Catholic, but it's probably like going to confession. In the end you'll feel better, but when you're there it's pretty difficult." And so, as they stand before a congregation of their peers, these utility vice presidents, like penitents, show regret for their misdeeds, as in this brief excerpt from a videotape of one of these meetings:

It's not particularly easy to come up here and talk about an event at a plant in which you have a lot of pride, a lot of pride in the performance, in the operators. . . . It's also tough going through the agonizing thinking of what it is you want to say. How do you want to confess? How do you want to couch it in a way that, even though you did something wrong, you're still okay? You get a chance to talk to Ken Strahm and Terry Sullivan [INPO vice presidents] and you go over what your plans are, and they tell you, "No, Fred, you've got to really bare your soul." . . . It's a painful thing to do.

Different as these two examples are, among family members and nuclear industry executives one can detect a generally similar process at work. Within an ongoing relationship sustained by close ties (whether a family or occupational community), wrongdoing arouses the disapproval of a significant other (whether a parent or professional peer), thus invoking a sense of remorse and repentance in the wrongdoer, which leads to reacceptance (reintegration) by the significant other. Wrongdoing, shame, and reintegration—that, distilled to its essence, is the family model of social control.[30]

Four aspects of this process deserve special comment.

Communitarian social control. Reintegrative shaming is a distinctively communitarian strategy of social control, as it requires a large measure of "interdependence" and a "clearly majoritarian morality" if it is to be effective.[31] Likewise, from what has already been said in preceding chapters—about the widely shared notion that nuclear utilities are hostages of one another and about the emergence of a well-defined industrial morality—peer pressure is also closely related to the development of community in the nuclear industry.

Moral education. Moral education, not only of the wrongdoer, but also of other community members who witness or hear about the shaming spectacle, is a principal aim of reintegrative shaming.[32] So too for peer pressure in the nuclear industry. To cite but one example, return to the senior nuclear officers' meeting, where another utility vice president said this to a roomful of his peers: "I stand before you to confess my sins because I strongly suspect that if you spend a couple of hours with your nuclear engineer, that you'll find that these events can happen in your plant also." Then, after detailing the causes of the problem, including his culpability in the matter, he ended on this note: "I hope that I have given you the benefit of my newly found knowledge. . . . *Learn it well, my friends. If you don't, you'll be invited to serve on this panel next year and tell us about it."* (Emphasis supplied.) Learn it well, in other words, or you will be invited to suffer through the community's public disapproval of your misdeed. "If there's ever motivation to go back to your plant and make sure those conditions do not exist at your plant, well, I can't think of a better way to get it across," says a nuclear utility vice president. "When that guy is standing up there, he's coming from a real life experience that we all participate in. It's empathy, I guess, because I really feel the emotion that this guy's going through."[33]

Emulation. If social disapproval of unwanted behavior is a defining feature of reintegrative shaming, so is praising exemplary conduct. This is not just because the community should honor its good citizens; it is much more because the community needs alternatives to the shamed behaviors, role models, for all its members to emulate.[34] The same point can be made about INPO when it publicizes the good practices uncovered at nuclear plants, and also when INPO's president publicly praises the number-one-rated plants and awards them plaques commending their performance. As an INPO official explains it, this is all part of INPO's principle of emulation: "One of INPO's basic principles is the concept of emulation. We want to identify those plants that are achieving a large measure of success in what they're doing so they can become a role model for everybody to emulate and to try to improve their performance."

Targeting CEOs. One of the best ways to use reintegrative shaming to regulate corporate business behavior, counsels Braithwaite, is "to choose chief executives as targets for shame" because they have a "special responsibility for setting the tone of . . . corporate cultures."[35] That INPO officials would wholly agree is now quite clear. Indeed, from what has already been said about INPO's mechanisms for allocating praise and distributing shame (especially after the reforms triggered by the Sillin report), it would be hard to find a clearer case of communal pressure aimed directly at CEOs. "The whole process is CEO-driven," in the words of a vice president for nuclear power. "If I let INPO know that I don't particularly like something they're doing, then I'll probably have my CEO calling me up to ask me why Zack Pate was calling him up telling him I'm one of the least cooperative of all the utilities in the country. That's how the process works. Zack Pate does not hesitate to use his direct contacts with the CEOs to put the pressure on us." Why are CEOs so willing to oblige INPO's president? Though the answer is complex, it would certainly include the threat of invidious comparisons ("management by embarrassment") at the annual CEO meeting. It would also include the "special procedure" INPO follows "in the event a member is not responsive to INPO programs" or is "unwilling to take action to resolve a significant safety issue":

> The procedure calls for INPO and the member's management to work to resolve any issues in contention. Should resolution not be satisfactory, the procedure calls for specific interactions between INPO's chief executive officer and the [utility's] chief executive officer and, ultimately, the board of directors of the member. The procedure gives INPO the authority to suspend the organization from membership if it continues to be unresponsive.[36]

I shall have lots more to say about this special procedure in the next section, so for now it is enough to note some of its main features as described by a top-level INPO official:

> If a utility is not responsive, the peer pressure we can bring to bear starts at the CEO level. Now it's very unusual when INPO's president can't arm-twist or talk the CEO into following what INPO wants them to do. But if he can't then he [INPO's president] goes to the [INPO] board of directors, which is made up of CEOs from various utilities, usually with well-performing plants. So they're well-respected CEOs. . . . What will happen is that a subcommittee of CEOs will be designated to contact the CEO and basically tell him to get his act together and shape up. And if they need to, they'll make direct contact with outside board members of the company.

So here again we are in the presence of the ordering forces of communal pressure, as well-respected CEOs representing their industry personally rebuke one of their peers. And here as elsewhere we find INPO's tools of peer pressure aimed, first and foremost, at the nuclear utility's CEO.[37]

It is time to take stock. We began this chapter by asking whether the ordering force of peer expectations can effectively encourage (or discourage) conduct that is esteemed (or frowned upon) in a large and relatively impersonal social setting, like the nuclear industry, where more than 100,000 people work at 111 plants operating at 70 sites around the country. The simple answer is yes, provided that the right conditions exist. So what does the nuclear industry's experience tell us about those conditions?

The first point to recognize is that a well-developed capacity for exerting peer pressure presumes a context of shared interests and values; not that 100,000 nuclear industry employees are somehow united in this way, but that the industry's leadership, particularly its fifty-four CEOs, hold significant interests and values in common. Think here of the way industry elites picture themselves as hostages of every other utility and how they judge deviant and exemplary conduct in terms of a common framework of industry-wide standards.

But a context of community is not all. For all the talk about peer pressure during the early years of INPO's administrative development, INPO was a relatively cautious and timid regulator. Then came the critical turning point that eventually transformed INPO's powers of peer pressure into a potent regulatory force—the institutional reforms generated by the 1986 Sillin report. And if any lesson attaches to this transformation, it is that a well-developed capacity for exerting peer pressure vitally depends on well-designed institutional mechanisms for allocating praise and distributing shame. I say "well-designed" because those institutional arrangements must orchestrate those forces in a finely tuned way, as in the case of the annual CEO meeting's "management by embarrassment," where INPO mobilizes, amplifies, and channels those communal pressures in a movingly dramatic display of public acclaim and censure. In that and other ways INPO's institutional mechanisms thus cultivate social settings where the ordering force of peer expectations can flourish in the midst of a large and otherwise impersonal industry.

PEACH BOTTOM

Now it is time to consider a detailed example of how INPO exercises peer pressure. The case of Philadelphia Electric's Peach Bottom nuclear plant merits close examination as an especially important example of INPO's powers of peer pressure at work—important because no other plant has been subjected to such intense industry pressure through INPO, before or since, as Peach Bottom was a most vexing problem plant, the first ever to be shut down by the NRC for nonme-chanical reasons. Important, too, because today the Peach Bottom case has become something of a myth, an industry-wide symbol of INPO's coming of age as a potent regulatory force. With Peach Bottom, finally, we get a rare glimpse of INPO in action behind the scenes, thanks to several years of previously confidential correspondence from INPO to Peach Bottom officials.

On March 31, 1987, NRC officials ordered Philadelphia Electric Company to shut down Peach Bottom once they had discovered that night-shift control room operators were playing video games and sleeping on the job. It later came out in fact that *all* the operators had fallen asleep on several occasions, thus leaving the operating reactor unattended, and that control room horseplay (rubber band and paper ball fights) was also a problem.[38] All this (and much more) added up to one of the nuclear industry's most embarrassing revelations in re-cent years.

What role did INPO play in all this? Our story begins in December 1984 when INPO had completed Peach Bottom's fourth plant evalua-tion. In reviewing their findings with Philadelphia Electric executives, INPO officials listed several basic problems. These included:

— "a pervasive unwillingness by managers and supervisors to con-front, correct, counsel, or take other appropriate actions to stress and enforce standards of expected performance."
— a "perception of lack of corporate support in implementing needed changes has resulted in a reluctance by plant management to ad-dress some issues, including setting higher standards and holding people accountable in many areas. Plant management perceives that strong action to enforce higher standards may be overturned or otherwise undermined by higher authority."
— "Long standing company practices (or company tradition) . . . is an impediment to change or improvement. . . . The tendency not to take action if it goes against long standing practice (or perceived practice) is widespread. It appears to us that this is often used as a crutch to maintain the status quo."[39]

Because of these deep-seated problems the next INPO inspection was scheduled earlier than normal, December 1985, twelve months after the preceding INPO inspection. Once again INPO identified seri-ous problems at Peach Bottom. "The observations and findings from this evaluation," INPO told Philadelphia Electric executives, "indi-cates that management actions to overcome institutional barriers and instill higher performance standards have been ineffective." As INPO's president observed in a letter to Philadelphia Electric's CEO, the INPO inspection "indicates that long-standing problems in operations, maintenance, and radiological protection continue to exist. The lack of progress in these key areas is disturbing."[40] So disturbing, in fact, that INPO's President Zack Pate requested a meeting with Philadelphia Electric's CEO.

The meeting did not go well, at least from Pate's perspective. Less than a week later he again wrote to Philadelphia Electric's chief executive: "Your organization is using its knowledge to defend the status quo—to demonstrate to you that things are okay—rather than using its extensive experience to analyze INPO material with the goal of upgrading the station's performance." What's more, he added, this "is a recurring pattern over the past several INPO evaluations."

Pressing the point further, INPO's president then highlighted Peach Bottom's failings from a comparative perspective: "Since the previous evaluation at Peach Bottom in December 1984, we have evaluated 44 plants, and only 3 have been assessed in the lowest category. Peach Bottom's performance *is* marginal." (Emphasis in original.) Given that, and given the fact that this level of performance "has been consistent throughout the past three evaluations," it is "vitally important" that you get "personally involved" in correcting these problems, Pate wrote Philadelphia Electric's chief executive.[41]

Yet fundamental problems persisted. Just four months after the December 1985 inspection, INPO sent a small evaluation team to Peach Bottom for a "progress check."[42] But there was no progress. Which again prompted INPO's president to write Philadelphia Electric's chief executive,[43] and again travel to Philadelphia for a private meeting with company executives. All to no benefit, though, for when INPO conducted yet another inspection of Peach Bottom, in October 1986, the report sounded a distressingly familiar theme: Peach Bottom's large number of problems "are indicative of a need for more effective management and supervisory oversight of plant operations."[44]

All this raises an obvious question. In spite of several INPO inspections, and despite numerous letters and several personal meetings between INPO's president and Philadelphia Electric's CEO, why had Peach Bottom made so little progress in addressing these long-standing problems? After all, such arm-twisting is one of the industry's most direct and forceful expressions of peer pressure, say industry officials, and yet, for all the twisting, Peach Bottom officials didn't budge. If the story ended here, it would be difficult not to conclude that INPO's powers of peer pressure were too feeble to overcome the resistance of a recalcitrant utility. That is true, with two caveats. First, all this occurred in the early years of INPO's administrative development, prior to the Sillin report reforms. (Indeed, INPO's frustrations with Peach Bottom probably go a long way toward explaining why the Sillin report was written and why its authors recommended a variety of reforms aimed at bolstering INPO's powers of peer pressure—in short, to deter future Peach Bottoms.) Second, the Peach Bottom case does not end here.

Before pressing forward, though, it is best to explain why INPO was having so much difficulty in getting Peach Bottom to change its ways. Although the total answer is complex, the root of the difficulty was plain enough. As the relevant portion of the official diagnosis by Philadelphia Electric's outside consultants reads: "The organizational structure and management philosophy used to operate the [Peach Bottom] units were typical of those in the fossil plants."[45] What this means, an INPO official explains, is that Peach Bottom's cultural orientation, particularly that of its corporate leadership, clung to the outmoded ways of thinking and acting traditionally found within coal and oil-burning power plants:

> The people at Peach Bottom and Philadelphia Electric thought that "By God, we've done it this way for years, and it's worked for us. So we don't see any need to change." It was a fossil fuel mentality. They had never really joined the nuclear era. The people that they had running their plants were not nuclear trained people. Initially, *they came from the fossil world; they were ex-fossil people. And I think the standards they were espousing didn't keep current with the modern nuclear technology and the change in standards that was going on in the rest of the industry.* They had blinders on that said, "We've done it this way all our lives. And by God we aren't going to change." In a few cases they had people who wanted to change, but they were shouted down by the old-timers who said, "No, we aren't going to do it that way." Or management didn't give them the support they needed in key areas. So they just gave up and management had their way. *So it was a culture problem of long standing that was just too much for any one individual to overcome.* And if the CEO wasn't going to change things, it wasn't going to get done. Because the CEO and the president and the next guy down all had that old culture. There wasn't anybody

down below them that was going to change them. [Emphasis supplied.]

"The bottom line," he adds, "was that Peach Bottom and Philadelphia Electric ended up doing what INPO wanted. But in the process it hurt a lot of feelings and embarrassed a lot of people." To see what Philadelphia Electric eventually did (and why), let's return to our chronology of events.

Soon after Peach Bottom's shutdown in March of 1987, INPO formed a five-member industry panel to further mobilize the industry's collective response to the Peach Bottom problem. Composed of three nuclear utility vice presidents, one nuclear plant manager, and an INPO official, the panel investigated the circumstances surrounding Peach Bottom's shutdown and evaluated Philadelphia Electric's plans to restart the plant.

They were harsh critics. When Philadelphia Electric submitted a recovery plan to the NRC on August 7, 1987, the industry panel condemned it as seriously flawed. Twice they met with Philadelphia Electric's senior management, including the chief executive officer and chief operating officer, and each time they strongly criticized Philadelphia Electric's senior management for dodging personal responsibility for the Peach Bottom fiasco.[46] INPO's president did likewise. He argued that the restart plan failed to attack the fundamental cause of Peach Bottom's problems—poor corporate leadership—and on August 28, 1987, he brought those charges before a meeting of Philadelphia Electric's board of directors: "The fundamental approach to nuclear operational management at Philadelphia Electric Company has not changed and is unlikely to change noticeably in the foreseeable future. The underlying problems at Peach Bottom will be slow to change *because of the absence of fundamental changes at corporate.*"[47] If Peach Bottom's restart plan is to be successful, he went on to explain, it must address "the real root causes of the situation at Peach Bottom"—namely, "leadership and management practices from the highest levels in the company to the plant manager."[48]

The INPO-led industry campaign against Philadelphia Electric's corporate leaders took a curious turn on September 11, 1987, when a member of the INPO-created review panel had a phone conversation with a senior NRC official. They discussed the Peach Bottom restart plan, particularly its overall tone, which seemed to be saying, "Don't blame senior management for Peach Bottom—it's all the fault of the plant operators." Three days after the phone call, NRC Chairman

Lando Zech strongly criticized the Peach Bottom restart plan at a commission meeting with Philadelphia Electric's top management. What's more, his remarks were strikingly similar to those INPO's president had delivered only weeks earlier to Philadelphia Electric's board of directors. "If there is any difference in the operators, it has been my experience it is because of management," the NRC chairman observed: "The operators reflect management. You are here today; you have told us about your problems 'at the plant.' I understand that. But I would submit that your corporate management problems are just as serious. . . . Part of the problem, as far as I can see, is leadership, right from the top down. I mean that."[49]

What should one make of this? Specifics are hard to come by, but it is interesting to speculate whether INPO and the NRC were collaborating behind the scenes and whether INPO was using the NRC as a way of further escalating industry pressure. In any event, over the next three months INPO continued to criticize Philadelphia Electric's plans to restart Peach Bottom, a campaign of mounting industry pressure that culminated in a letter from INPO's president to Philadelphia Electric's board of directors.

The letter—twelve pages, plus seventeen attachments—was a thorough indictment of the utility's management at Peach Bottom. Among the more pointed passages in the letter's conclusions and recommendations are the following. On Peach Bottom prior to the shutdown: "The grossly unprofessional behavior by a wide range of shift personnel . . . reflects a major breakdown in the management of a nuclear facility. It is an embarrassment to the industry and to the nation." On how Peach Bottom got that way: "A corporate culture has been allowed to develop, from the top down, that down played, rejected, or ignored problems. Management was defensive from the top down. Problems frequently were not reported up the line organization, and those that were often were not dealt with effectively. The climate of this organizational behavior was set from the highest levels of corporate management." On Peach Bottom since the shutdown: "Through virtually the end of 1987, some eight months after the shutdown, INPO continues to find widespread performance problems at virtually every level at Peach Bottom and in the corporate nuclear organization." On accountability: "The shift superintendents, shift supervisors, control room operators, operations supervisors, plant manager, and some others at Peach Bottom have been held accountable through relief from their jobs and other measures. . . . By contrast, however, no one in the corporate organization appears to have been held accountable." On Peach

Bottom's organizational culture: "It is clear to us that the problems at Peach Bottom are the direct result of the low standards and lack of accountability accepted by corporate, and, in fact, fostered on the plant by a lethargic and defensive organization. This situation existed over a long period of time, and became a way of life—a culture—in the PECo corporate nuclear organization and at Peach Bottom."

In the letter INPO's president also made several recommendations for addressing these problems. Most significant, he expressed a vote of no confidence in Philadelphia Electric's corporate leadership and their ability to bring about the needed changes required for a safe restart of the plant:

> Major changes in the corporate culture at PECo [Philadelphia Electric Company] are required. The recently announced reorganization will not achieve this. Experience shows that the same managers, placed in a different organizational arrangement, are usually unable (or unwilling) to effect major changes in standards, accountability, etc.

The message was plain: Philadelphia Electric's top corporate management should be fired. INPO's president also made this request, that copies of his letter and supporting attachments be sent to Philadelphia Electric's insurance company, to each co-owner of Peach Bottom, and to the NRC's senior management.

If anyone got the message, Philadelphia Electric's board of directors certainly did. They met to discuss Peach Bottom and the INPO letter on February 1, and what emerged from that meeting was the "early retirement" of Philadelphia Electric's chief operating officer, followed six days later by the "retirement" of Philadelphia Electric's chief executive officer. With the toppling of Philadelphia Electric's leadership, the nuclear organization's old guard (and its fossil fuel–oriented habits of mind) was soon swept away as part of the new leadership's program of total institutional reform. And with those reforms in place, in March 1989 Peach Bottom, after a twenty-five-month hiatus, finally resumed operation.

What is the meaning and significance of the Peach Bottom story? What does it tell us about the nature of INPO's influence and the effectiveness of peer pressure as an enforcement tool? Surely the parable of the blind man and the elephant is relevant here, as these events can be described in multiple ways, each leading to a quite different impression of what happened and how to make sense of INPO's role. But of all the perspectives, none is so important for our purposes as the industry point of view and how its officials understand what transpired between Philadelphia Electric and INPO.

Consistently, industry officials would say something very much like the following, from a vice president for nuclear power: "You're probably familiar with the Peach Bottom situation. Up there the CEO got a letter from the INPO president pointing out the problems of Peach Bottom. It really brought their unit down to zero. Kept them off line. And it resulted in significant management changes, and also significant capital expenditures." The moral is plain: "INPO has a great deal of clout. . . . The utility executives take it very very seriously." For this industry official, then, as for many people interviewed, Peach Bottom is a symbol of INPO's new power. Or, what amounts to the same thing, Peach Bottom represents what can happen to powerful nuclear utility executives when they stubbornly resist INPO's advice. For example, another industry official attaches this lesson to the Peach Bottom story: "The peer pressure that was exerted on Philadelphia Electric bore results. And the publicity that inevitably follows has a tremendous impact because *there's nothing more sobering to utility executives than to see other utility executives lose their jobs.* And that's what happened at Peach Bottom." (Emphasis supplied.)

For nuclear industry officials, as these comments imply, Peach Bottom has come to signify an important change in INPO's authority, a kind of rite of passage signaling a major breakthrough in the organization's development. A definition of authority once offered by the German historian Mommsen helps illuminate the point. Authority, he said, is "more than advice and less than a command, an advice which one may not safely ignore."[50] With that in mind, put yourself in the shoes of a nuclear utility executive. You've just received your March 1988 issue of *Nuclear News* (the industry's largest-circulation monthly trade magazine). You read its story on Peach Bottom and learn that both its chief executive officer and chief operating officer have been fired. You read further, pausing to reflect on this passage: "[The Peach Bottom] matter suggests some details about the relationship of INPO to its members. . . . INPO appears to be tough. . . . INPO has influence. . . . INPO's voice is evidently recognized as authoritative, and . . . could be heard clearly all the way up at the top of the corporate ladder."[51] Because of what happened at Peach Bottom, you think to yourself, you cannot safely ignore INPO's advice. Now, much more so than ever before, you must take INPO seriously. The Peach Bottom affair, according to still another industry official, represents "the moment of truth where INPO's character had to really be tested":

> What happened during the Philadelphia Electric situation is
> that the chief executive of that operation, for reasons of person-
> ality, background, whatever, just would not pay any attention to
> INPO's recommendations. What happened is that INPO, to-
> gether with the NRC, forced Philadelphia Electric to change its
> management. INPO played a very strong role in that. . . . What
> this has done, of course, is have a salutary effect on all other
> chief executives. They now pay more attention to INPO than
> they ever did before.

And how might INPO further enhance its powers of peer pressure?

SECRECY

On March 22, 1993, the Supreme Court ended Ralph Nader's nine-
year legal battle to make INPO documents public.[52] The court in effect
upheld INPO's secretive ways, and that secretiveness, more than anything else, is what nuclear power critics have found most troubling
about INPO. "Our biggest beef with INPO is that everything is so se-
cret," says a critic with the (antinuclear) Nuclear Information and Resource Service. Citing Peach Bottom as a prime example, and how
INPO had identified serious problems at the plant before the NRC did,
he adds: "We believe that the public has a right to know about those
problems, and the industry just doesn't have the right to cover up,
which is what they're doing by refusing to release the INPO documents." All this raises some simple—albeit difficult to resolve—questions. To what extent (if at all) is INPO's penchant for secrecy justified? Should INPO's findings, particularly its nuclear plant inspection
reports, be a matter of public record?

INPO (among others) says no. A longtime industry observer (and
former NRC chairman) puts the matter as follows:

> One of the real advantages INPO has is to be able to sit down
> with the utility and tell them, "Look, you're doing this wrong."
> The INPO people are really given complete access. People talk
> to them extremely candidly. Now if that kind of information
> were to be automatically published, it wouldn't happen. People
> wouldn't talk to them that candidly, and the reports would not
> be anywhere near as critical. So I think you have to go back to
> what is the fundamental advantage INPO has. The fundamental
> advantage is INPO's credibility and its ability to deal with the
> utilities in a very open manner. If INPO's process was made

completely open, then there would be no real value of having them over the NRC, and one might as well eliminate INPO.

This line of reasoning—confidentiality is vital to INPO's regulatory effectiveness—goes a long way toward explaining why INPO keeps its activities hidden from public view.[53] Critics aren't convinced, however—including one who crystallized the comments of others interviewed when he said, "If these utility executives are not honest enough to be forthcoming, then they have no business operating nuclear plants and their licenses should be revoked."[54]

Ideally, we would like to know how more public visibility—and public accountability—would actually influence INPO's regulatory effectiveness. Are there ways of accommodating the critics' legitimate concerns while at the same time maintaining INPO's effectiveness? The answer is far from clear, and as matters now stand (especially since the recent court ruling), it is hard to imagine INPO changing its secretive ways. Then again, maybe not. Consider the following:

> INPO should report the number of plants performing at or above the industry's standard of acceptable performance and the number evaluated as below that standard of performance.
> Those plants evaluated as achieving excellent performance in their operations should be identified by name, and those evaluated as requiring special attention and assistance also should be identified by name.[55]

So said the nuclear industry's very own Sillin report, which also recommended that all this information be made public in order to enhance INPO's powers of peer pressure. "To make the peer pressure really effective requires visibility, among your peers, and even more so the NRC and the public at large. That was the basis of our recommendation," says one of the report's coauthors. And all this triggered a "very extensive" debate among industry officials, he continues, "because the consequences of public identification can be rather severe, including economic consequences—the price of the stock—as well as the future careers of the management involved." Which is why, although every other Sillin report recommendation was adopted by the industry, the proposal to make those rankings public was not. At least for now, he hastens to add, because "publicizing the rankings is probably only a matter of time."

Peering ahead, then, it is possible (maybe probable) that INPO will modify its secretive posture, at least to some extent, if only to strengthen its hand with recalcitrant utilities. It is also worth noting that the National Research Council recently (1992) made a similar recommendation—that INPO should publicly identify chronic poor performers[56]—and did so, like the Sillin report, with the idea of enhancing INPO's powers of peer pressure. As one of the report's lead authors tried to explain it: "Until INPO is willing to publicize who exactly are the biggest problem plants in the industry, the real recalcitrants, it will not have realized its full potential impact on the industry."[57]

This chapter's main question has been: What motivates nuclear utilities to live up to the demanding and often costly industrial principles and practices articulated by INPO's normative system? The main answer seems to be: peer pressure among nuclear utility CEOs and other top-level industry officials, generated by INPO's industry-wide institutional mechanisms for allocating praise and distributing shame. That this is so, that INPO is well on its way to having a well-developed capacity for exerting peer pressure on member utilities, emerges from the above discussion. Now our stage is set for the next critical question. How exactly does INPO use this well-defined industrial morality, backed by a well-developed capacity for exerting peer pressure, in order to *institutionalize responsibility* among the member utilities? I will take up this question in the next two chapters through a close look at two major INPO programs—learning from industry experience and the professionalism project.

Part Three

**Institutionalizing
Responsibility**

7
Learning from Experience

According to the NRC's nearly two-hundred-page investigation report, the worst nuclear accident of 1990 began at 9:17 A.M., March 20. That was when a nuclear plant truck driver, by smashing into a utility pole, brought down transmission lines supplying off-site electricity to the Vogtle nuclear plant, located about twenty-five miles southeast of Augusta, Georgia. The collision set off a chain of events that left all vital safety systems at the plant without any electrical power for about thirty-six minutes. And as the reactor's coolant system temperature began to rise, the plant manager declared a "site area emergency," thus placing local, state, and federal officials on alert. Though disaster was averted the NRC nevertheless conducted a detailed investigation. Its conclusion: The whole episode could have (and should have) been prevented.

"The incident at Vogtle was neither unique nor without precedent. . . . Precursor events during cold shutdown conditions at other plants involving loss of offsite power occurred 74 times between 1965 and 1989." And, what's more, forty-four operating experience reports containing the lessons learned from those previous incidents (lessons that could have prevented the Vogtle accident, according to the NRC) had been disseminated to all the nuclear utilities, including the Vogtle plant. Despite the wealth of historical data, the accident nevertheless happened. And the fundamental reason why is that "Vogtle personnel had not assimilated this experience into the operating standards for the plant."[1] They had failed to learn from industry experience.

In this episode we have a good example of the significant—yet uneven—progress the nuclear industry has made in learning from experience. You may recall (from chapter 2) that TMI's operators had also failed to learn from industry experience, not because of any stubborn unwillingness to learn, but because there was no effective industry-wide network for sharing such information. Consequently, they had no advance warning whatsoever concerning the faulty relief valve they confronted, nor any way of knowing about the remedies that had been devised for dealing with such problems. By 1990 the situation was very different. Information sharing was no longer the serious problem it once was, thanks in large part to the development of an industry-wide mechanism for learning from industry experience. This explains why the Vogtle plant had received no fewer than forty-four operating experience reports concerning similar events at other plants; TMI operators none. And yet, even with that stream of accident information flowing into the plant, including recommendations for preventive measures, there was an accident because Vogtle officials did not implement those lessons effectively.

One conclusion to follow from this is that it is a mistake to equate *learning about* industry accidents with actually *learning from* that information. Although the Vogtle plant had information about those prior accidents, it lacked the organizational wherewithal to effectively receive, analyze, and act upon that information. And so, long after the TMI accident studies criticized TMI's (and the industry's) inability to learn from experience, impediments remain. In this chapter we seek an understanding of what those impediments are, and, most important, what INPO is doing to overcome them.[2]

In the course of doing so, I shall also be trying to show you INPO's strategy for institutionalizing responsibility. No one will be surprised to know that some corporate actors, like some individuals, are more "responsible" than others. This can mean a variety of things, of course, since we use the word *responsibility* in a variety of senses. But especially relevant for our purposes is the sense of responsibility associated with "competence" or "being fit," for this way of thinking about responsibility is at the heart of INPO's nuclear navy–inspired industrial ethic. As Rickover explained: "I believe our criteria, and the principles on which they are based . . . can expose a management's *motivation to act responsibly,* which we call integrity. A lack of integrity would be incompatible with conformance to these criteria. . . . *If a management is imbued with these principles it will lead to a competent and dependable operation.*"[3]

Thus conceived, being responsible means the ability to measure up to the demands of one's situation. For example, most of us are insufficiently responsible for high and mighty offices because we lack certain competencies, either of intellect, character, or both, required for exercising sound judgment in those roles.[4] Likewise, because most of us lack the special competencies objectively required to measure up to the demands of being, say, a heart surgeon or an aerospace engineer, most of us are not adequately responsible for those roles either. To see how this way of thinking about individual responsibility extends to complex organizations, consider the following newspaper story about the U.S. space program:

> The rules of spacecraft construction may not be etched in stone like the Ten Commandments, but the penalties for ignoring them are generally more swift and more violent.
>
> The dictums are based on decades of experience and are widely disseminated. They cover things such as how to establish clear lines of authority, how to turn blueprints into specifications for thousands of minuscule parts and how to test rigorously on the ground to uncover flaws and increase the odds of orbital success. They go under the unassuming title of system engineering.
>
> Alarmingly, *these rules have been repeatedly and consciously broken during the past decade,* throwing the U.S. space program into a tailspin. Sensor troubles in a $1.7 billion series of weather satellites, the flawed mirror in the $1.5 billion Hubble space telescope, catastrophic faults in the $25 billion space shuttle fleet and design defects in the planned $30 billion space station have all been linked, one way or another, to sidestepping the elementary principles of aerospace engineering. [Emphasis supplied.][5]

So we learn that just as engineers or heart surgeons must honor distinctive technical and moral principles to be capable practitioners of their professions, the U.S. space program must also honor certain principles that define and uphold its distinctive competence; and just as an engineer or heart surgeon is judged to be insufficiently responsible when he or she compromises those principles, so too is the U.S. space program. Of course, what counts as responsible conduct will be different for the engineer and the surgeon, as well as for different types of institutions, since each involves special functions and values. Yet one thing seems clear. In a vital sense, *being responsible involves an inner commitment to principles and principled conduct that define and uphold a special competence.* Institutionalizing responsibility, in turn, is a matter of building those principles or values into the basic premises governing the operation of an institution (like NASA), so that the enterprise embodies a strong and effective commitment to those standards of appropriate conduct (such as the principles of systems engineering) essential to competent and dependable operation.

The same logic applies to nuclear utilities, according to Rickover. Being responsible also involves an inner commitment to competence-defining principles, as the utility must embody a distinctive culture or character, a combination of qualities and attributes rooted in a strong and effective commitment to nuclear power's internal morality and its foundational principles—management involvement, technical self-sufficiency, facing facts, respect for radiation, and so forth. Each represents an excellence of organizational character, and, taken as a whole, they establish an effective and controlling environment of decision within the utility that makes it, in Rickover's phrase, "fit for operation."

As he also argues, one essential element of being fit for operation is the ability to learn from experience. "An inability or unwillingness to learn from experience is intolerable in nuclear operations."[6] And as one would expect, INPO has made this one of the core values (performance objectives) that all nuclear utilities must strive for: "Significant industry operating experiences should be evaluated, and appropriate actions should be undertaken to improve safety and reliability."[7]

The critical question then: If being responsible involves an inner commitment to principles and principled conduct that define and uphold a special competence, including learning from industry experience, how has INPO sought to infuse those principles into the basic premises governing the nuclear plant's day-to-day operation? The question is important, not only because it is essential to understanding how INPO has responded to one of TMI's major lessons (the nuclear industry's inability to learn from experience), but also because it illuminates how INPO performs one of its most important tasks as a communitarian regulator—institutionalizing responsibility.

SHARING EXPERIENCE

"The structure of the nuclear industry has not been conducive to the effective sharing and integration of operating data. The utilities that operate the plants have never mobilized an industrywide effort to concentrate on safety-related problems." So stated a leading TMI accident study.[8] "Every utility was its own little island," as one longtime industry official explained it. "They just felt like they had been operating power plants for many years and they knew what they needed to know about power plants." Then came TMI, and INPO mobilized an

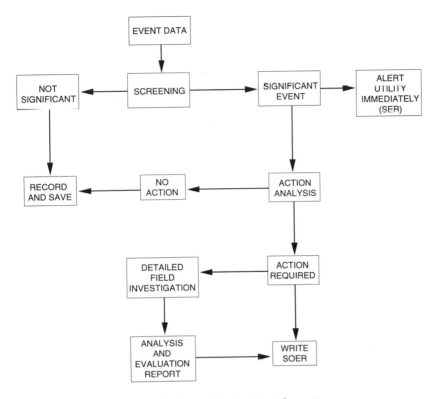

Fig. 7.1 Information Network for Evaluating Significant Events

industry-wide effort to systematically collect, analyze, and share the industry's experience with safety-related problems. It is called the Significant Event Evaluation-Information Network (SEE-IN).[9]

As figure 7.1 illustrates, the SEE-IN program involves a multistage screening process in which between six and seven thousand documents flow through INPO's Events Analysis Department annually.[10] Coming from a variety of sources—utilities, the NRC, reactor suppliers—the reports of abnormal operating experience are first entered into a computerized document tracking system before they are sent to the Events Analysis Department staff members for review. Each staff member is assigned several plants as his or her responsibility, and all events from those plants are funneled to that person. In reviewing the event, the staff person uses INPO guidelines to determine whether an event is significant to nuclear safety or plant reliability. Events judged not to be significant are sent to a second staff member for review, and if that person agrees that the event is not significant, it is stored in the data base. Reviewers are most concerned with the significant ones, of course, and when they discover one, the staff member becomes as familiar with the event as he or she can, which usually means calling the plant for more details. The event is then discussed at the Friday morning meeting of the events screening committee, composed of department managers from all of INPO's technical departments. They assess whether the event is in fact significant, and if it is, INPO alerts the utilities by transmitting a Significant Event Notification (SEN) on Nuclear Network, a computerized teleconferencing system for contacting every nuclear plant simultaneously. If, upon further analysis, INPO uncovers a truly significant problem, one that urgently requires additional action by the utilities, it issues a Significant Operating Experience Report (SOER) together with a list of (mandatory) "recommendations."[11]

Take INPO's SOER regarding control rods as an example. In the early 1980s INPO uncovered twelve "significant events" involving the operation of control rods, which are like a car's gas pedal and brakes combined, as they are used to increase or decrease the speed of the nuclear reaction. So INPO issued four Significant Experience Reports on Nuclear Network, and, upon further analysis, SOER 84–2.[12] "A significant number of control rod mispositioning events have occurred in the last year," the SOER states by way of introduction. Then, after describing the circumstances surrounding these accidents, and noting how procedural errors were their primary causes, the SOER goes on to stress the need to "reemphasize, to personnel at all levels, the critical nature of activities involving direct changes to reactivity since errors can lead to local core damage."[13] Finally the SOER concludes with a list of "recommendations" that, in effect, mandate a variety of changes in plant operating procedures and training methods (see table 7.1).

This is but one example of the hundreds of SOER recommendations INPO has issued over the years so that all nuclear utilities could benefit from the experience of each. No easy task. "When we got started after TMI there was a tremendous volume of information that hadn't been analyzed properly," a top INPO official recalls. "The big problem was determining what was important and what wasn't important. We had to look at everything because we didn't want to miss some key lessons and lead the utilities down the path that says, 'You're safe because you've done all that we told you, and the rest of this is not important.'" At the same time, he adds, "we didn't want to completely snow the industry with paper." Which was a real possibility, given the

TABLE 7.1

Selected Recommendations from SOER 84–2

Procedures should address the actions to be taken during recovery from a mispositioned rod. Procedures should include the following:

    a. prompt notification of nuclear engineering personnel and appropriate plant management prior to recovery

    b. determination of how long the rod has been misaligned

    c. power level at which recovery is performed

    d. rate of control rod movement during recovery

    e. movement of other control rods to support recovery. . . .

Review the operator training program and ensure that it includes the following elements:

    a. procedures governing the movement of control rods and the potential adverse consequences of improper movements

    b. a discussion of the adverse consequences of operating with a mispositioned rod and procedures governing realignment, including how withdrawal of a rod can affect local power peaking

    c. industry operating experience related to incorrect control rod movements, including the use of case studies of actual events. . . .

Source: INPO, SOER 84–2, pp. 5–7.

vast amount of data INPO has screened over the years, more than 75,000 "off-normal plant events" as of 1990.[14]

THE WEAK LINK

In a 1981 speech to fellow nuclear utility executives, an industry official posed the following question: "Has the potential of SEE-IN for increasing safety . . . been realized?" "My answer," he continued, is a "definite No! Experience is not much of a teacher if the lessons learned are not applied. The weak link in the SEE-IN chain is today the slowness or failure of the utilities to implement remedial actions."[15] That was the SEE-IN program's weak link at the outset, and it remained so throughout most of the 1980s.[16] "What we are not seeing," said INPO's president in a 1988 speech to nuclear utility CEOs, "is sufficient success in applying those lessons or recommendations":

> It is sad for us to see—it gives me personally a knot in my stomach—when I see an event at one of our plants where the proper application of an SOER recommendation would surely have prevented it. . . . Gentlemen, we need to do a better job in

applying the lessons learned from experience as captured in SOER recommendations, both with respect to timeliness and with respect to the quality of implementation.[17]

Certainly some nuclear plants do a better job of learning from industry experience than others, say industry officials. And for a clue as to why, listen to how a nuclear plant experience review official explains the variation. "Ultimately, the quality of an experience review program comes down to *the level of management attention given to operating experience,* the desire to have a good strong program and to put good people on it and back them up. *The level of management support is crucial.*" (Emphasis supplied.) Another experience review program official put it this way: "When you see a plant with a large number of open SOER recommendations, most likely the problem is a lack of management support. The two usually go together. You get the large numbers because management doesn't give a damn, and since management doesn't give a damn nobody else pays any attention to you. *So it really boils down to management commitment to the program.*" (Emphasis supplied.)

Management commitment is the key. Yet it remains unclear why some managers are more committed to their experience review programs than others. "I think the biggest problem here is management's lack of understanding of the importance of what's there," a top INPO official explains:

> A lot of senior people will tell you, "Yeah, we really believe the operating experience program is important." But when push comes to shove, and they've got to pay for it, it doesn't get paid for at the level it takes to really support it. That's really been a big problem at some utilities, *a lack of appreciation for what an experience review program can do for them.*[18] [Emphasis supplied.]

Another way of saying this is that certain functions or tasks are considered inherently critical to achieving the nuclear plant's basic objectives while others are not.[19] Take the control room operator's job, a critical task by all accounts, for one cannot operate a nuclear plant without the operators any more than one can fly a plane without a pilot. Both are indispensable. Most important, control room operators are essential to producing electricity, and if one thing is sure, utility officials consider electricity production their real business.

As for the status of nuclear plant operating experience review officials, that is a very different matter. And a major reason why, as they explain it, is that their actual contribution to the nuclear plant's main function, producing electricity, is much more ambiguous. "One of the biggest concerns I have is how do you measure effectiveness," in the words of a nuclear plant operating experience review official:

> In fact, we really haven't figured out how to do it yet because it's something that's very difficult to put your finger on. Ideally, if we're effective in doing our job in the OE [operating experience] area, then we'll avoid having repeat events at our plant. But it's very difficult to measure the event that didn't occur. You just can't tell because the event that doesn't occur you never know about.

Trying to spot the experience review program's contribution to electricity production is like listening to the dog that doesn't bark. And yet, he goes on, "you need to be able to sell your management that this is a worthwhile process":

> Every utility manager wants to avoid events, and if you can somehow show them that this process contributes to that, then they will support it. *But it's very hard to make that connection. Very hard.* You have to understand that most utilities are becoming much more competitive than they have been in the past, and so there's a lot more emphasis on limiting the number of people and the amount of money you spend for projects *where you can't see a direct cost-benefit ratio.* So here I am, an OE manager, asking my station to commit resources to solve problems that haven't even occurred yet. And those are the same resources other managers are asking for to deal with problems that have occurred. [Emphasis supplied.]

To put what he is saying into a long-term historical perspective, learning from industry experience has always been a tenuous and insecure value within the nuclear industry. That was true of the industry's dominant cultural orientation before TMI (the fossil fuel mentality), when maximizing the output of electricity meant fixing the reactor *after* it breaks, not before, contrary to the essential rationale for learning from industry experience. And it remains true to this day, particularly at some utilities, which is not surprising given that organizations characteristically resist new tasks that seem incompatible with their traditional cultural orientation. All this matters, say industry officials, because the level of management commitment can actually impede (or enhance) a nuclear plant's ability to learn from industry experience in at least four significant ways.

(1) Fragmented Responsibility

"You can't have this guy and this guy and that guy all responsible for handling experience review," observes an INPO official. "Somebody has got to make sure it's all getting done in a coherent fashion. *That was a basic problem at a lot of utilities, especially in the early years of the [SEE-IN] program.*" (Emphasis supplied.) It was a basic problem, he goes on to explain, because management did not place much value on learning from industry experience and therefore did not assign clear responsibilities for carrying out those tasks. In most cases, for example, the task of reviewing industry operating experience was a collateral duty assigned to (say) the maintenance department, which usually meant that those responsibilities were subordinated to other more pressing obligations. "We didn't have any full-time people at the site to look at OE," as one nuclear utility executive recalls. "They all had other responsibilities. So it was like pulling teeth to get them to work on experience review. It was a battle because experience review was not their top priority." As a result, learning from industry experience "usually ended up getting a low priority because there was no one really dedicated to look at the stuff and process it." "It's just a matter of priority," he adds. "Basically, no one took on the responsibility of evaluating these things."

(2) "It Can't Happen Here"

"'It doesn't apply.' 'It can't happen here'—over the years I've heard that quite a bit from the utility people," observes another INPO official who has evaluated many nuclear plant experience review programs. "When we write an operating experience report about a boiling water reactor many people with pressurized water reactors would look at that and say, 'Well, that's in a boiling water reactor.' They don't look at what the underlying message is. They just assume that it doesn't apply."

Ask nuclear plant officials about this, and they typically stress two factors. One is a sense of complacency or smugness. "You're always tempted to think that they weren't smart enough to avoid making that mistake, and that we're smarter than that, or we're better than that, or we maintain our equipment better, or whatever," says a nuclear plant experience review official. "There's lots of ways to lull yourself into the belief that the event will not happen to us." The other has to do with the fact that learning from industry experience can be a very demanding and time-consuming task. "You have to appreciate that making that link between your own station and some of those industry lessons is far from obvious," another operating experience review official explains:

> You have to force yourself to be very systematic in the way you review the industry events and recommendations so that you don't do just a surface look. Typically, there are three or more contributors to a major event. So you really need to analyze all those individual contributors, go back to your in-house data base to look at the kinds of problems that you're having at your own plant, and see if there are similar problems that caused the big one. You basically need to sit back and look at the details very closely and ask yourself "What if?" It's really a matter of attitude—a questioning attitude where you don't just look at the top level and say, "This particular event can't happen to us." [Emphasis supplied.]

At the very least, he goes on, making that link requires time and well-trained personnel, among other things. "You can't develop an understanding of what's really happened and how it happened *unless you have the ability and the time to do the research so that you can develop the kind of understanding that demonstrates our susceptibility to the various risks.*" (Emphasis supplied.) "Obviously," he adds, "you won't get that unless you've got management backing you."

(3) Authority

Recall the SOER on control rod mispositioning and how it required various changes in nuclear plant operating procedures and training methods. Here the critical thing to notice is the basic pattern of dependency—who needs whom within the nuclear plant to actually implement those changes. If the SOER recommends changes in training, ordinarily the training department makes the changes; if it recommends changes in plant maintenance procedures, the maintenance department makes the changes. To generalize: the money, personnel, and technical expertise required to implement SOER recommendations are usually controlled by departments other than the experience review program. In the words of one experience review program manager, "I don't have any real clout or real control over getting actions taken": "Once we decide what the corrective actions are going to be, and who's going to do them, then it gets into a scheduling and control program. Now we can bug people and stuff like that in order to try to get these things done. But we really don't have any control." In this way, then, the experience review department is vitally dependent on other organizational units to carry out the experience review program's basic task. Or, to quote an INPO official, "OE [operating experience] people don't have a budget to make any changes and they don't have the authority to go and make any of the changes themselves. *So if the plant manager is not super supportive of that program, then probably it doesn't get the kind of attention it needs.*" (Emphasis supplied.) Management commitment is the key.

(4) Resources

By now it should be obvious that one leading indicator of weak management commitment is inadequate resources—not enough money and manpower to effectively analyze and implement the lessons of industry experience. "It all comes down to being a resource issue," as one experience review official told me. "Even though we're a regulated monopoly dollars come into play very very heavily. Oh, let me tell you about dollars and budgets! You can only do so much." He goes on:

> It's kind of like the beast that may bite me later as opposed to the one at the front of the cave right now. A lot of our resources are aimed at real time fixes; things that have to be done now. So people at the plant are fighting the immediate fire drills, which means that some of the SEE-IN items aren't a high priority and they go out further on the chain of where you can work on it because it's something that may affect you someday, but not today.

We may summarize. With the SEE-IN program INPO has enhanced the nuclear utilities' capacity to learn from industry experience in a most important way. By reducing the fragmentation of industry experience—by creating an industry-wide mechanism to collect, analyze, and disseminate the lessons of history—INPO created significant educational opportunities that never existed before TMI. However, as the Vogtle plant accident vividly illustrates, it is one thing to create new educational opportunities, and quite another to take full advantage of them. Like students, organizations must be committed and motivated to learn. And by reason of their traditional cultural orientation (among other factors), many nuclear utilities lacked those qualities of organizational character—the "motivation to act responsibly" in Rickover's phrase—so vital to the SEE-IN program's success.

BUILDING A STRUCTURE OF RESPONSIBILITY

It's putting it too strongly to say, "Until INPO there was no operating experience review," as does a longtime nuclear plant experience review program manager, but there is a lot of truth in it. For INPO's creation injected into the nuclear power industry a group of persons whose prior socialization in the nuclear navy made them professionally committed to learning from experience as a goal worth striving for. Thus, for the first time ever, learning from industry experience had a committed core constituency, a firm if narrow base of social support within an otherwise inhospitable social environment. And from that point on INPO has been promoting this value within the industry in a variety of ways. To see how, we can best begin by considering what INPO's normative framework says about learning from industry experience.

The Normative Framework

Of INPO's chief tasks, none is more important than the creation, promotion, and diffusion of a distinctive set of unifying values within the nuclear industry. Thus, although experience review programs "can be structured in any number of ways," INPO states, they must all include "certain basic elements." These include screening of operating experience reports to determine their applicability and relative importance to the plant; feedback of applicable industry operating experience to affected departments in a timely manner; evaluation of applicable SOERs to determine corrective actions; a process that ensures the necessary review, approval, and implementation of identified corrective actions; a system to track the status of industry operating experience reports until all actions have been completed and closed; and periodic reports to plant and corporate management on the status of operating experience report screening, evaluation, and corrective actions.[20] Here we see how INPO's normative system spells out a large array of tasks that, taken together, establish industry-wide normative benchmarks that define what is worth striving for and what is accounted as good reason for action.[21]

But that is not all. Turning to INPO's performance objectives and criteria (see tables 7.2 and 7.3), one also learns that these competence-defining principles speak to management's role in supporting the experience review program. Nuclear utility officials must ensure that the organization's structure is clearly defined, that staffing and resources are sufficient, that responsibilities are clearly defined and un-

TABLE 7.2

Operating Experience Review Organization and Administration

Performance Objective

Operating experience review organization and administration should ensure effective implementation and control of the operating experience review process.

Criteria

A. The organizational structure is clearly defined.

B. Staffing and resources are sufficient to accomplish assigned tasks.

C. Responsibilities and authority of each management, supervisory, and professional position involved in the program are clearly defined and understood.

D. Interfaces with in-house and industry supporting groups are clearly defined and understood.

E. Operating experience review personnel have the technical experience and training to perform assigned job functions.

F. Action items resulting from operating experience review receive appropriate approval and are tracked to completion.

G. An effectiveness evaluation is performed periodically to apprise management of how well the operating experience program is functioning and attaining desired results. This assessment examines the following areas:

  1. distribution of operating experience information to appropriate personnel

  2. technical reviews of significant industry operating experience

  3. implementation of action items resulting from the review of operating experience

  4. use of data from in-house events to improve plant safety and reliability

H. Management is appropriately involved in operating experience review activities to ensure adherence to station policies and procedures and to identify and correct problems.

Source: INPO, "Performance Objectives and Criteria for Operating and Near-Term Operating License Plants" (INPO 85–001, April 1987), p. 101.

derstood, that personnel have the needed training and experience, that effectiveness reviews are performed, that management is appropriately involved. And so on. Then (and most likely only then) will the nuclear utility possess the management commitment and support that we now know is essential to learning from industry experience.

But more is at stake than defining tasks, as we saw in chapter 5. INPO's normative system also speaks to the myriad responsibilities of industry membership—what it means to occupy a particular role and what it means to behave in a manner appropriate to that position—including the obligations that run to learning from industry experience. "Responsibilities . . . of each management, supervisor, and pro-

TABLE 7.3

Industry Operating Experience Review

Performance Objective

Significant industry operating experiences should be evaluated, and appropriate actions should be undertaken to improve safety and reliability.

Criteria

A. A comprehensive evaluation is performed on applicable, significant industry operating experience, and appropriate corrective action is completed in a timely manner.

B. Sources of significant industry operating experience information reviewed for applicability include the following:

1. INPO Significant Operating Experience Reports (SOERs)

2. Significant Event Reports (SERs)

3. Significant By Others (SO) notifications

4. INPO Significant Event Notifications (SENs)

5. NRC letters, bulletins, and information notices

6. supplier and architect/engineer reports

C. Appropriate checks are performed to verify that industry operating experience information is being properly classified for applicability.

D. Applicable significant industry operating experience information is distributed to appropriate personnel and departments in a timely manner.

E. Distribution of conflicting or extraneous industry operating experience information to operators and other personnel is minimized.

F. Other applicable industry operating experience information from sources such as the following is disseminated to operations, maintenance, or other personnel for review and training purposes:

1. INPO Operations and Maintenance Reminders (O&MRs)

2. NUCLEAR NETWORK information pertaining to plant operating experience, e.g., selected plant experience entries and daily plant status.

Source: INPO, "Performance Objectives" (see source for table 7.2), p. 103.

fessional position involved in the [operating experience review] program are clearly defined and understood."[22] That is how INPO characterizes one of the bedrock principles of its normative system; and starting from there, the guidelines and good practices go on to detail the substantive content of those responsibilities. Turning to table 7.4, for example, notice how the idea of fixing responsibility is treated as a fundamental aim guiding the formation of policy at all levels. What does it mean to be a top nuclear utility executive, a nuclear plant manager, or an experience review program manager? From the standpoint of INPO's normative system, it means carrying out the

TABLE 7.4

Selections from INPO Guidelines on Learning from Industry Experience

On the responsibilities of top utility management:

* "utility management should establish corporate and station policies to describe the purpose and expected results to be achieved in the assessment of operating experience"

* utility management should establish corporate and station policies regarding "the identification and implementation of corrective actions to address lessons learned"

* utility management should establish timeliness goals for reviewing operating experience information and for implementing corrective actions

* senior utility management "should monitor and ensure timely implementation of corrective actions identified during effectiveness reviews"

On the responsibilities of station line management:

* "station line management has responsibility for the use of operating experience at their station. The operating experience function usually involves a number of organizations. Examples of the organizations typically having operating experience review responsibilities are the independent safety review, operations, engineering, technical support, training, and licensing groups. *The effectiveness of this program depends on strong support by utility and station line management and clearly defined responsibilities and duties.*" (Emphasis supplied.)

* Identification of the lines of authority and responsibility among organizations is an essential element of the operating experience program.

* Responsible functional or area managers should be held accountable for effective application of lessons learned.

On the responsibilities of the operating experience program manager:

* An essential part of a successful operating experience program is a single point of responsibility for overall program administration and effectiveness.

* Responsibility for overall program performance should be assigned to a single manager with sufficient authority to administer the program functions and to ensure the program's effectiveness.

* The dissemination and use of operating experience at the station is the day-to-day responsibility of the operating experience program manager. He is responsible for ensuring that established priorities and due dates are met for the review of in-house and industry operating experience and that corrective actions to address station-specific weaknesses are implemented.

* "the operating experience manager is . . . responsible for maintaining the procedures that define the function and conduct of the program. In addition, he is responsible for reporting the day-to-day status of the program, initiating periodic effectiveness reviews of the program, and recommending and ensuring implementation of corrective actions to address weaknesses identified during reviews. . . . The effectiveness review should include a detailed assessment of the dissemination of operating experience to station personnel and their knowledge and understanding to the material provided, as well as an assessment of the effectiveness of translating operating experience into station corrective actions."

Source: INPO, "Guidelines for the Use of Operating Experience" (February 1989).

cluster of learning-related tasks associated with your role. And how those roles have changed since TMI. In the past, learning from experience was a vague and undemanding idea that made it easy for industry officials to overlook such matters. No longer. As a result of INPO's efforts, it has now become a complex and rigorous industrial practice, one that embraces a wide array of interacting organizational tasks as it spells out what conduct is appropriate and what goals are legitimate and desirable.[23]

Inspections

Now it is time to see how INPO inspectors use this body of task-defining and responsibility-fixing regulatory norms to evaluate and reform nuclear utility practices. And I will do so by discussing a composite INPO evaluation report that combines excerpts from four different INPO reports (three plant and one corporate), limiting our attention to the issue of learning from industry experience. Call the inspected plant Seapoint Ranch. Its conclusion: The plant's performance "is significantly below the industry average" in implementing SOER recommendations and has therefore "not benefitted from many important lessons learned from industry operating experience." Thus "significant improvements are needed in the station's implementation of lessons learned from industry operating experience."

In explaining why Seapoint Ranch's performance was significantly below average, the eighty-five-page inspection report makes its case in two ways. First, a major feature of INPO's results-oriented inspection methodology is to catalog actual performance problems resulting from the plant's failure to translate industry lessons learned into corrective actions. Some examples:

> * Some events have occurred at the station that could have been prevented by improved application of industry operating experience. . . . For example, on two occasions within three months in 1988, the unit scrammed because of a loss of feedwater. In both cases, the loss of feedwater was attributed to valve mispositioning involving operator error [and addressed by SOER recommendations]. Other human performance problems noted that are addressed by SOER recommendations include. . . .
> * Job incumbents are not provided with sufficient training on lessons learned from significant operating experience reports. . . . Lessons learned from five SOER recommendations re-

viewed have not been incorporated into appropriate training materials. For example, SOER 85–2, "Valve Mispositioning Event," recommends that operations, maintenance, and supervisory personnel be trained in procedures used to position and verify valve positions. On five occasions from July 1988 through September 1989, water from the refueling water storage tank . . . was inadvertently transferred due to mispositioned valves.
* Corrective actions taken in response to 118 SOER recommendations were reviewed during the evaluation. Of these, 25 station responses were determined to be not satisfactory due to either insufficient progress being made, or the actions taken not being implemented completely or effectively.

Table 7.5 illustrates another characteristic feature of all INPO inspection reports, the SOER status report, a numerical report card of sorts that summarizes how many of the 417 SOER recommendations Seapoint Ranch has (and has not) satisfactorily implemented. As for those not satisfactorily implemented ("unsats" in industry jargon), the

TABLE 7.5

SOER Status

The status of Significant Operating Experience Report (SOER) recommendations is as follows:

Total number of recommendations issued to date	417
Number previously evaluated as satisfactorily implemented or not applicable	311
Number reviewed this evaluation (including 32 previously reviewed and evaluated as satisfactorily implemented or not applicable)	135
*Number satisfactorily implemented	88
*Number not satisfactorily implemented (7 red tab)	28
*Number not applicable	0
*Number pending—awaiting decision (7 red tab)	17
*Number pending—awaiting implementation (1 red tab)	2

[The report also lists several recommendations and notes that they] have not been satisfactorily implemented, and further actions are needed. Four of these recommendations, previously considered by INPO to have been satisfactorily addressed, have been reopened because subsequent review has determined that the action taken was not effective; e.g., subsequent actions removed procedural requirements or deleted necessary training or the action intended was not completed.

report goes on to detail what further steps are needed in order to comply with each recommendation.

Identifying and documenting performance problems like these is a major undertaking. First the inspection team's approximately twenty members spend a week at INPO's Atlanta headquarters preparing an evaluation plan. Led by a manager and assistant team manager, the team is typically composed of two or three specialists in eight functional areas (operations, maintenance, chemistry, and so on) and, within their respective specialties, they all pay particular attention to the plant's record on learning from experience. This they do in two principal ways during the preparatory phase, by examining the plant's current status (on paper) as to which SOER recommendations it has and has not implemented,[24] and by analyzing all the trouble reports the plant has issued since the previous INPO inspection. For example, when developing an evaluation plan for Seapoint Ranch, INPO inspectors learned how mispositioned valves and a loss of feedwater had recently caused two emergency shutdowns. Probing further, they also learned that Seapoint Ranch officials laid the blame, in both cases, on the plant operators' failure to follow plant operating procedures. This was not supposed to happen, given that similar accidents had occurred before at other plants, and given that INPO's SOER had instructed all utilities on how to guard against such accidents.

"We review all this paperwork up front for leads to pursue," explains an INPO inspector. And to pursue those leads, the inspection team next goes to the nuclear plant. "You go to a plant for two weeks and do nothing but watch what is going on at the plant," another INPO inspector explains:

> You have to collect just a tremendous amount of data in doing the field observations. So the days are very long. You may be in the plant for twelve hours that day, then that night you have to sift through and analyze that data and decide what's important and what's not important. You have to sit back and ask yourself, "Well, what are these things showing me as far as whether they're meeting INPO's performance objectives?" It's a great physical and mental effort and at the end of two weeks I'm just exhausted.

Notice in these comments how the inspection process involves two key tasks: *observing* operational activities at the plant and *interpreting* their significance. "After two weeks you're going to see a heck of a lot," another INPO inspector explains:

> And to try to put some rhyme or reason, some order and some structure, to what you saw really is a skill. Bottom line is you can have all kinds of facts. But trying to decipher what it all means is an art. For instance, you might have some fact that says a procedure missed a couple of critical steps. As a result, somebody tripped the unit by accident. As an evaluator I have to ask why those steps weren't in that procedure. And how come nobody ever caught this before, especially a procedure that's been run many times? And how come the procedure review process didn't pick this up? *Bottom line is you can have all kinds of facts, but facts do not necessarily answer the question "Why?" And it's that question "Why?" that the whole evaluation process is trying to answer.* [Emphasis supplied.]

As INPO officials explain it, then, the most important (and challenging) aim of the inspection process is to translate all those facts into what they call "management issues." Why, for example, did Seapoint Ranch fail to prevent several accidents that could have been avoided, if only they had effectively implemented their SOER recommendations? And why did the plant have far more unimplemented SOER recommendations than the industry average? "Contributing to this problem is a *lack of station management monitoring and follow-up* to ensure corrective actions are appropriately identified and implemented. Also, station personnel responsible for implementing the corrective actions are *not held accountable* for timely and effective completion." (Emphasis supplied.)

Note, first, how INPO traces Seapoint Ranch's learning problems to management's failure to properly monitor corrective actions and ensure accountability, for it is a good example of how INPO inspectors translate particular performance problems into management issues. Note, second, the unstated assumptions about what management should be doing and how INPO's normative system makes those assumptions more explicit. Management should be "appropriately involved in operating experience review activities to ensure adherence to station policies and procedures and to identify and correct problems." And what does "appropriately involved" mean? The idea (or ideal) entails a variety of functional responsibilities according to INPO's normative framework:

Management involvement includes establishing responsibilities, expectations, goals, and monitoring program performance. Items to be monitored include the type and scope of information processed by the program, timeliness of reviews and assessments, and timeliness and effectiveness of corrective actions implemented. Specific indicators of program effectiveness include items such as average screening and assessment times; oldest items in the screening process; the number, average age, and oldest corrective actions not yet implemented; and the number, severity, and recurrence rate of events.[25]

In this way, INPO's normative system establishes a structured way of thinking about nuclear plant operations, one that translates these matters into the language of responsibility (that is, management responsibility) as it spells out what it means to occupy a particular role and what it means to behave in a manner appropriate to that position.[26] As one INPO inspector tried to explain it, the INPO criteria and guidelines "help guide your thoughts to where the real problem is": "If I determine there is a deficiency in performance (and my job is to evaluate their performance against the performance objectives) then the next question is why. Where is it breaking down. That's where the criteria and guidelines come in. They have the basic elements this program should include, and I use them to help me look at the program to see where the links are weak." In the words of another INPO inspector, "Everything I'm going to talk about is in the criteria and guidelines. They give you the whys—why you didn't achieve the performance objective."

A similar analysis can be made of INPO's strategy for inspecting Seapoint Ranch's *corporate* management. "During the recent Seapoint Ranch evaluation several significant weaknesses were identified in the operating experience program," the INPO corporate evaluation states, including "weaknesses in the application of industry operating experience."[27] Once again the fact that Seapoint Ranch had not satisfactorily implemented twenty-five SOER recommendations is the basic performance problem; and once again INPO inspectors translated that basic fact into a management issue, in this case a *corporate* management problem. "Timely action has not been taken by the corporate organization to address and resolve some important problem areas that could affect station operation." Although corporate managers "were aware of weaknesses in the operating experience program," the report continues, they "have not implemented effective corrective action." The fundamental reason why: "Corporate and station managers are often *not held accountable* for timely completion of assigned actions or improvements to the station." (Emphasis supplied.)[28] The aim, as always, is to explain performance problems in terms of management issues, or, more precisely, management responsibilities.[29]

Another point ought to be mentioned. In translating performance problems into management issues, the whole process goes through a surprisingly elaborate review. At the end of every inspection day, for example, the team meets for one to three hours (sometimes more) to discuss their observations and interpret their significance. "This is where the question 'Why?' comes up frequently," an INPO inspector explains. "If I say, 'Hey, the preventative maintenance program isn't working well,' they'll say, 'Okay, that's nice. But why? Why isn't it working well?'" He continues:

> These facts are trying to tell us something, and what we have to do, what the challenge is, is to put the facts together and get to the root of the problem that really needs to be fixed. That's why we have team meetings every day, to get the synergism of people working together, because of the twenty-member team that goes to a station, it's nothing to have three or four hundred man-years of experience in reactors. So one of the things we carry with us is a current summary of industry experience, what really works (and doesn't work) in terms of current industry practices.

After the peer review comes the management review. In the case of operating experience problems, for example, the inspection team's findings (plus the supporting "observation package" that contains the inspectors' raw field notes) are reviewed, first by members of INPO's operating experience department, then by the department's manager, and then by the division's manager. After that comes the "pre-exit meeting" in which the inspection team manager and a senior INPO official (the "exit representative") present the inspection team's case before INPO's president and vice presidents for their comments and approval. Why such an elaborate review process? "Because of INPO's continual need for credibility," an INPO official explains:

> We realize that anything we put out in writing to the industry has an impact. Regardless of how minor it may appear to us, someone in the industry is going to react. It's going to involve resources. And very frequently it's going to involve money. The

slightest finding can have that impact. So this is a way of protecting our credibility. It's a sanity check if you will, right up through the top layers of INPO management. Is the issue valid? Is there enough evidence to support the finding? Is the focus right? Do the words convey the proper perspective on the issue? It's a continual quality check on what we're providing to the industry because we just can't afford to send something out on the street that's going to hurt our credibility.

Legitimacy is important, in other words, because here as elsewhere INPO can't afford to alienate that base of social support—industry officials—so vital to carrying out its distinctive regulatory role.

Upon completing the review, there is an "exit meeting" at the utility's headquarters. The inspection team manager and the exit representative (typically an INPO vice president) meet with top utility officials—the CEO and senior corporate executives involved in nuclear operations, as well as the plant manager—to discuss the inspection's results. Then, meeting privately with the CEO for an "assessment meeting," the INPO vice president emphasizes INPO's concerns and informs him of the plant's final grade—1 (excellent) to 5 (marginal).

We turn now to INPO's recommendations for addressing Seapoint Ranch's learning disabilities as well as the utility's response. As the excerpt listed in table 7.6 illustrates, INPO's recommendation is very brief and avoids detailed prescriptions, while the utility's action plan is relatively detailed. "That's intentional," an INPO official explains:

> The recommendation you see in print has been discussed over and over with plant officials. So the philosophy is that you've already told them in detail what the problem is and you don't need to provide them with all the details in writing. But more importantly, *we don't want to be overly prescriptive on how the plant should fix problems.* We want to bring the problems to their attention and everything we know about it. But *how they fix it is up to them as long as they meet the performance objectives and criteria.* [Emphasis supplied.]

But that is only part of the story. For INPO's nonprescriptive approach to problem solving, insofar as it reduces the risk of alienation, also serves INPO's basic need for legitimacy. "INPO can't go and dictate how you do something," in the words of a nuclear plant supervisor:

TABLE 7.6

Example of INPO Recommendation and Utility Action Plan

INPO Recommendation: "Take action to address important problem areas, including those identified above. Monitor the effectiveness of the corrective actions implemented [in response to SOER recommendations] to verify that improved performance is achieved. The guidance in INPO 89–005, *Guidelines for the Use of Operating Experience*, should be of assistance in this effort."

Utility Action Plan: "Nuclear Inc. [a pseudonym] has initiated formal reviews to identify open issues and problem areas to be addressed. . . . Each issue will be reviewed by Nuclear Inc. senior management, assigned a completion schedule, and tracked until closure. This review will be performed by December 1989. For the longer term, senior management is meeting with employees on a weekly basis to obtain feedback regarding operational or organizational issues, and to provide additional monitoring of the effectiveness of corrective actions implemented.

The Operating Experience Program will be strengthened to assure effective and timely implementation. Action plans have been developed for the 25 significant operating experience report recommendations that have not been resolved. A goal has been established for new SOERs issued in 1990 to assure timely implementation of industry operating experience. . . . These actions will be complete by February 1990. . . . INPO 89–005, *Guidelines for the Use of Operating Experience*, will be utilized in this procedure revision."

Our upper management really gets bent out of shape when INPO starts getting into specifics—"You need to do this; you need to have a separate group to do this." "Wait a minute! You're managing my resources! Get out of my business. I'll take care of it. I'll meet your requirements, but we'll figure out how to do it." *So INPO passes on their expectations—what they expect to be done—and leaves it to the utilities to figure out how they're going to implement it.* [Emphasis supplied.][30]

This gets to the heart of how INPO's inspection system institutionalizes responsibility. For what INPO officials expect to be done (and look for), above all else, is what they call the "internalization of operating experience." An INPO inspector explains: "Do the people (not just in the plant but the whole utility) really pay attention to operating experience? Is it something that's ingrained in them? Is it something that they live with on a day-to-day basis? Basically, you want to find out whether they really take learning from experience seriously, regardless of how small or how minor those lessons may be."

To put his observation in our terms, INPO expects these officials to behave in a manner appropriate to their role so that the utility will embody a sustained and effective inner commitment to learning from industry experience. This is evident in the way INPO's normative system establishes an industry-wide interpretive framework for construing what it means to occupy a particular role and what it means to behave in a manner appropriate to that position, including the role obligations that run to learning from experience. It is also evident in the way INPO inspectors—always asking the "Why?" question—translate particular instances of learning disabilities into broader issues of management responsibility. In this way, as Rickover would have put it, INPO's normative framework "can expose a management's motivation to act responsibly, which we call integrity. . . . *If a management is imbued with these principles it will lead to a competent and dependable operation.*" [31] Indeed, to forget this is to overlook perhaps the most important thing we need to understand about the INPO inspection process. It is a way of imbuing management with those principles that define and uphold a special competence, including the ability to learn from industry experience. In short, it is a way of promoting principled self-regulation.

Peer Pressure

If these observations are correct, there remains the question of whether nuclear plant officials pay much attention to INPO's inspection results. "There's a real incentive to get the INPO findings resolved as quickly as possible because they have such a high visibility." So says a nuclear plant experience review official, and we can begin to see what he means by returning to the annual CEO conference. When INPO's president formally announces each nuclear plant's relative standing within the industry, he also gives each CEO a packet of supporting materials to justify these rankings. "INPO gives my CEO a report card (that's what I call it) that compares our program to other utilities as far as implementing SOER recommendations," observes another experience review program official.

The report card is brief (a one-page graph) and to the point, as it ranks from top to bottom the performance of all nuclear plant experience review programs in terms of unimplemented SOER recommendations. "It lets our CEO know how we're doing compared to everybody else, whether we're doing a great job or a lousy one," yet another nuclear plant experience review program official explains. Which is to say, it establishes a comparative normative framework to distinguish "bad" and "good" performance. [32] "Executives tend to want to compare their plant to other plants and want to be better than the next guy," he continues. "And our management is no different. We want to be, at worst, equal to the average of other plants and to improve on that."[33] "You know," another experience review official at another plant explains, "when a CEO starts asking questions about the operating experience program, it rattles chains all up and down the organization."

Here as elsewhere, we see INPO's powers of peer pressure aimed first and foremost at the nuclear industry's CEOs. It is as though they are nuclear power's commanding officers, from INPO's military-minded perspective, and wherever the commander leads the rest of the troops are sure to follow. Maybe so, but it is by no means a foregone conclusion that all the nuclear utilities will in fact implement all of INPO's SOER recommendations. Consider these remarks by a nuclear plant experience review program official:

> We're moving into an era now where all the utilities are getting
> into such serious financial constraints. Two years ago if an
> SOER came out with a recommendation that said you need to
> do this, and it was going to result in a design change, we would
> usually implement that design change during the next outage.
> But we're moving into a time frame now where we really have
> to assess all this more closely. Is implementing this design
> change going to improve me safety-wise for the money I'm
> spending on it? Is this something that's really going to benefit
> us? It's a nice recommendation, it may be something nice to do,
> but is it really necessary given our resource limitations?

Comments like this one could be heard in a number of interviews, and it remains to be seen how this growing tension over costs will be resolved.

In any event, we must end this discussion of learning from industry experience by noting the measurable results of INPO's efforts. Although the data are fairly crude and we should not press interpretation too hard, consider the numbers. In 1982 INPO found that "20 percent of the plants evaluated had satisfactorily implemented less than 30 percent of all the [SOER] recommendations published at the time of their evaluation visits."[34] By 1984, according to INPO, with 337 SOER recommendations issued thus far, "industrywide 76 percent of those [recommendations] have been implemented."[35] All in all, a sure sign of progress according to INPO.

But INPO officials soon tempered their optimism, as they began to realize the importance of distinguishing short-term and long-term learning in a complex and dynamic organizational context. For example, at each nuclear plant the process of upgrading procedures is

ongoing, as approximately one third of a plant's procedures are reviewed every year. If this means that all the procedures are reviewed
about every three years, it also means that they are constantly changing. And there lies the difficulty: what organizations learn through
procedural changes can also be unlearned through procedural
changes.[36]

"What we found," said INPO's president, "was that hardware
changes were implemented and had remained implemented." But
what they also found "is that some places a recommendation in training, although it had been put in the training program, somehow it got
lost. Or change in a procedure got put in a procedure, but later on it
got taken out." There was "enough of that," in Pate's words, that the
implementation of SOER recommendations became a major source of
concern.[37] In a 1988 speech INPO's president therefore admonished
the nuclear industry's CEOs to scrutinize their operating experience
review programs, evaluate their effectiveness, and remedy their shortcomings.

A personal letter to all the CEOs soon followed. In it Pate noted all
the utility-based learning impediments discussed earlier in this chapter, listed their utility's unimplemented SOER recommendations, and
insisted once again that each CEO thoroughly review their operating
experience programs. He also required a detailed response from each
CEO within six months—what they found and how they planned to
fix it. Perhaps this was INPO's way of addressing the industry's mounting concern over costs. As industry and INPO officials explain it, both
the speech and the letter were part of a major INPO initiative, a con-
sciousness-raising campaign of sorts, aimed at increasing the CEOs'
involvement in, and support for, nuclear plant experience review programs. "Zack Pate's letter really brought the use of the lessons learned
from industry operating experience right up to the top levels of utility
management," in the words of one nuclear utility vice president. "The
letter emphasized to CEOs all over the country that, 'Hey, this is
something you folks need to be personally involved with.' Essentially,
the unwritten message there was, 'We're seeing too many repeat
events in the industry and we just can't go on this way. It's going to be
up to you folks to help fix it.'"

"Pate's letter to our CEO caused quite a bit of self-reflection at our
utility," a nuclear plant experience review official recalls:

> It made us go back and do a very extensive review of our pro-
> gram to make sure that we had a system that, besides imple-

menting the SOERs on a one-shot basis, kept them permanently implemented. As a matter of fact, we found that we had not done a very good job. We had initiated actions but hadn't completed them in some cases. And in a few cases we had changed a procedure to reflect that operating experience, and then it got scratched out when the procedures were revised.

So Pate's letter "increased upper management's attention quite a bit," he adds. "There's a lot more emphasis placed on the OE [operating experience] program now, more overall direction and oversight."

And that, explains an INPO official, is exactly what INPO was hoping to accomplish. "When the CEO starts asking, 'How come we got so many open SOER recommendations? And what the hell do we have to do to get them closed so I can answer this letter not looking like an idiot?' it gets done." The end result of all this: as of 1990, according to INPO, 96 percent of its SOER recommendations had been satisfactorily implemented by the nuclear utilities.[38] As for whether they stay implemented, that, of course, remains to be seen.

8
The Professionalism Project

In *The Truth about Chernobyl,* Grigori Medvedev, a nuclear power expert in the Soviet Ministry of Energy, points to a "criminally irresponsible act" as one of the basic causes of the world's worst nuclear accident. The Chernobyl operators, in violation of all safety procedures, deliberately shut off vital reactor safety systems in order to conduct a test.[1] Why? The answer, says Medvedev, can be traced to their "careless, slipshod attitudes," "overconfidence," and, most important, their basic "lack of respect for the nuclear reactor":

> They must have truly lost touch with the hazards all around
> them and forgotten that the most important parts of a nuclear
> power station are the reactor and its core. . . . They also could
> not have been particularly devoted to their work; if they had
> been, they would have pondered every move thoughtfully, show-
> ing the vigilance expected of true professionals. Without such
> devotion, it is better not to become involved with controlling a
> device as dangerous as a nuclear reactor.[2]

This example provides a good introduction to the theme of this chapter, the role of values—process values—in nuclear safety. When Medvedev says a nuclear plant operator should ponder every move thoughtfully, he is focusing on the operator's methods, his way of making judgments, and *the constellation of values, purposes, and sensibilities that should inform his course of conduct.* In short, he is focusing on process values, or, more precisely, their degradation at Chernobyl. "Every institution has process values," writes Selznick, "embodied in policies and procedures that reflect the institution's distinctive character and mission. . . . The spirit of a practice or institution is intrinsically elusive; it can seldom, if ever, be easily specified. But it is not ineffable or mystical. . . . What it means to 'do' science, to 'think like a lawyer,' or to absorb the special perspectives of any other discipline or enterprise must be learned in the course of practice."[3] Notice how this way of thinking also extends to Medvedev's analysis of what it means to "think like a nuclear professional"—pondering every move thoughtfully, vigilance, devotion to work, respect for the technology and its inherent dangers. And so on. These are some of nuclear power's subtle yet very real values, and they are also some of the values at stake in INPO's professionalism project.

"Although we would like to believe that an accident as awesome as Chernobyl can't happen at a U.S. designed plant, the same kind of problems that happened at Chernobyl . . . can happen . . . at a U.S. plant," INPO's vice president warned an audience of nuclear utility vice presidents. So the lesson of Chernobyl is clear: nuclear plant personnel must be "instilled with the proper attitude."[4] That, in a nutshell, is the professionalism project's essential purpose, and it is probably fair to say that, for the 1990s, instilling the proper attitude represents INPO's most significant and challenging task. In this chapter we seek an understanding of the professionalism project's aims and methods, and, in the course of doing so, there are at least three questions that must be answered: What exactly is the proper attitude that distinguishes a true nuclear professional? How is it instilled? And why the need for an attitude change in the first place? We start with the last of these questions.

The Professionalism Problem

In the seven or eight years following INPO's creation, according to INPO's president, virtually every serious accident could be traced to one or more of the following root causes: insufficient training, inadequate procedures, equipment failures, design problems, or inadequate supervision.[5] Now (1988), he continued, as a result of extensive efforts the industry has addressed these problems—"Not perfectly, but well."[6] The example of insufficient training illustrates the point. Remember (from chapter 2) how the post-TMI accident studies, after judging the system for training nuclear plant personnel inadequate and ineffective, called for a thorough overhaul. So technical training was at the heart of the industry's professionalism problem almost immediately after TMI, and ever since then INPO has devoted a great deal of energy to fixing it.[7] It is also worth recalling that, by the mid-1980s, INPO officials began to realize that technical training was only part of the industry's professionalism problem. "We are now seeing troublesome events that cannot be traced to inadequate training," said INPO's president. "Instead, our conclusion is that *the principal root cause is a shortfall in professionalism.*"[8] Think here of Peach Bottom's sleeping operators, and one can begin to see why, in INPO's view, the most troubling aspect of nuclear power's professionalism problem is no longer inadequate technical training; it now stems from more elusive aspects of institutional life involving, among other things, a sense of respect and responsibility for nuclear technology. At root, the problem is one of process values.

There is one especially important reason (among others) why INPO finds all this so troubling—the problem of "nonconservative decisionmaking." For simplicity, imagine a nuclear reactor running at full power when it starts behaving abnormally, and you, the operator, don't understand why. Nevertheless, in the face of uncertainty, rather than reducing power or shutting the reactor down, you continue at full power, confident that the safety systems will prevent any accident. If this seems reckless and dangerous, it is, according to INPO officials, who liken such behavior to a reckless driver speeding around sharp mountain curves, cocksure that the guard rails will save him from going over the cliff. This is a prime example of what INPO means by nonconservative decisionmaking.[9]

All this raises an obvious question—what accounts for such recklessness?—to which there is no simple answer, although a partial explanation can be found in the nuclear industry's lingering fossil fuel orientation and corporate management's preoccupation with producing electricity. Historically, "equivalent availability has been preached in the industry as *the* parameter of good operations," writes Commonwealth Edison's senior vice president in charge of nuclear operations. What this means in plain language is that "good" operations has been equated with keeping the reactor running—the longer and faster the better, so as to maximize the output of electricity—which is hardly surprising, of course, given the millions of dollars at stake in a nuclear plant's continued operation. This also puts into perspective the fact that many nuclear utilities, such as Commonwealth Edison (one of the nation's largest), staged production competitions among their nuclear reactors. So if you were a control room operator at one of these plants, the message was clear: "You are a 'winner' (and will be rewarded accordingly) if you have the longest running plant." Conversely, "You are a 'loser' if you have to shut the reactor down."[10]

Now consider the darker side to this bottom-line emphasis on electricity production. It tends to create an unnecessary sense of haste, say

INPO and industry officials, and, at some plants, has even led to a "hot rodding mentality." And that kind of orientation, observes an INPO official, is the "wrong environment" to foster at a nuclear plant: "If you look at the root cause of many of the recent events we've had in the nuclear industry, you'll find that many of them are caused by *an unnecessary sense of haste.* If management says this plant has got to stay on line for the next 100 days, the reactor operator gets that message and says, 'Well, I've got to keep it on line, and I'm going to do everything I can to keep it on line.'" (Emphasis supplied.) What makes that sense of haste a problem, he goes on, is that it induces plant personnel "to do some things that aren't very smart, like working around procedures that shouldn't be worked around, proceeding in the face of uncertainty [so they really don't understand the consequences of what they're doing], and not shutting the reactor down when it should be shut down to fix something."

Now it may seem that the solution to this problem is obvious: change corporate policy; downplay the emphasis on electricity production; and promote a more cautious or conservative approach to managing the reactor. In fact, Commonwealth Edison did just that in 1988. The operators' reaction? They resisted the change, according to the company's vice president in charge of nuclear operations. "Part of natural professional pride is to keep the reactor running," he explains, and the "operators thought some of the actions we were asking them to take were too conservative. . . . And when they're doing things they don't fully agree with, they don't do them very well."[11] Being conservative isn't "macho," as another industry official puts it. There are lots of "subtle pressures influencing operators," he explains, including certain kinds of values—"blue-collar," "macho" values—that convey messages like this: "'You aren't a good operator unless you can ride out the storm [such as a dangerous abnormality in reactor conditions], and you're chicken if you trip [shut down] the plant.'" "So you do find operators who feel a kind of internal responsibility to save the plant from a trip or from being shut down," he continues, "and they'll go to great lengths to keep the plant from coming off line."

Needless to say, those kinds of values, which remind us of the nuclear utilities' fossil fuel ("run it till it breaks") origins, are at odds with INPO's vision of the true nuclear professional and the process values he or she should embody. Which brings us to our next question: What precisely are the values and attitudes a nuclear professional should possess?

THE PROFESSIONAL IDEAL

In answering this question, we first need to look at INPO's definition of what it means to be a true nuclear professional: "The nuclear professional is thoroughly imbued with a great respect and sense of responsibility for the reactor core—for reactor safety—and all his decisions and actions take this unique and grave responsibility into account."[12] The keynote is responsibility—professional responsibility. "Just as a doctor must feel a special responsibility for his patients," INPO's president explains, "our nuclear professionals must feel a special and unique responsibility for the reactor—for not allowing damage to the fuel or the core."[13] So just as a doctor's professional training should inculcate her with a "great respect for the patient," the professionalism project should instill all nuclear plant workers with a strong sense of respect and responsibility for their "patient"—the nuclear reactor. An example: "We need to establish a climate at every plant such that . . . when an operator recognizes unexpected or anomalous behavior of the reactor, or its control systems, he *instinctively feels a great personal responsibility to take conservative action*, including reducing power or a reactor scram [shutdown] without hesitation." (Emphasis supplied.)[14] According to this line of reasoning, then, the antithesis of professional responsibility (nuclear as well as medical) is creating unreasonable risks of harm—in a word, recklessness.[15] That is why the nuclear industry must take process values seriously, according to INPO. One must foster the right "climate" at every plant—the matrix of values, purposes, and sensibilities that nurture and sustain conservative and thoughtful decisionmaking—in order to reduce recklessness. Otherwise, as INPO's president warned an audience of top-level nuclear utility executives, the industry will not "derive the full benefit of the enormous effort and resources expended over this decade to upgrade the fundamentals: training, procedures, equipment, etc."[16] Not only that, he continued, the "emphasis on professionalism and its attendant conservative decisionmaking is so vitally important" because its neglect courts disaster, a catastrophic accident that will shatter all the progress the industry has made since TMI. The message is clear: In matters of professionalism, as in all other aspects of nuclear safety, no nuclear plant is an island unto itself.

This way of looking at nuclear professionalism—both the problem and the ideal—leads to an important observation. What truly distinguishes the professionalism project from INPO's other regulatory activities is its overriding focus on culture, the nuclear plant's "climate" or "environment," and how it affects rank-and-file attitudes and sensibilities. If you look at some of the accidents involving a shortfall in professionalism, an INPO official explains, "they had the right procedures and the right hardware and still things went very wrong because something was missing . . . an intangible cultural kind of thing that has to permeate the whole organization." What was missing, in other words, were those subtle institutional values that should suffuse the nuclear plant's operating culture with a distinctive character or ethos. The professionalism initiative, says a nuclear utility vice president, "was really the first time INPO started going after cultural issues."

The final question: What steps has INPO taken to address the professionalism problem?

THE INDUSTRIAL MORALITY OF NUCLEAR PROFESSIONALISM

If one had to choose the most striking features of the post-TMI regulatory transformation, the list would certainly include the emergence of an industrial morality. We have seen its crucial role in unifying what once was a very fragmented industry around a common framework of industrial principles and practices, and now INPO is seeking to do much the same for the nuclear industry's professionalism problem. Similar yet different; for the professionalism project's focus on culture also makes it unique, as I just said, and from this fact follow some noteworthy differences in how this particular framework of regulatory norms was developed.

Meeting about a half-dozen times from early 1988 to early 1989, it was a thirteen-member industry committee (including ten nuclear utility vice presidents, two nuclear plant officials, *and no INPO officials*) that formulated the eighty-two principles underpinning the professionalism project: *Principles for Enhancing Professionalism of Nuclear Personnel.* Why did an industry committee, not INPO, develop these principles? "We wanted to avoid the appearance that this was an INPO document," a committee member explains. While the difference between an "INPO document" and an "industry document" may seem subtle and insignificant to an industry outsider, "it's a dramatic difference if you're from the inside of the industry," particularly in light of "INPO's nuclear navy background and their navy way of doing things." "When you're talking about writing a document as important as this one [the professionalism principles], the industry just wants a part in controlling its destiny."

To cite a small but revealing example, consider how the professionalism code's introduction stresses the principles' home-grown character: "The management principles that follow were developed by a committee of senior utility officials . . . with input from virtually all U.S. nuclear utilities."[17] "They are principles *that management in the nuclear industry considers important* for fostering professionalism."[18] As for INPO's role in all this, staff provided "assistance"—period. The subtext is clear: "This is not an INPO document—it is an industry document." A small point, perhaps, but apparently one with great significance for top-level industry officials pressed to adopt these character-defining principles "as their own."[19]

But if we conclude from these statements that INPO's role in all this was insignificant, we shall be very much mistaken. For it was INPO that prodded the nuclear industry to develop the principles in the first place; and working quietly behind the scenes, it was INPO that handpicked the professionalism committee members, brought them all together at its Atlanta headquarters, and actively assisted the committee in developing these principles. So without INPO's guiding hand in these developments there is no reason to think the industry would have created these principles. Yet they are nevertheless portrayed as a collective industry (non-INPO) document. And for one basic reason: the professionalism committee's "whole intent," says another of its members, "was to achieve a real sense of ownership and commitment to these principles."

RECONSTRUCTING MANAGERIAL AUTHORITY

Ask industry officials about this—why management ownership and commitment is so vital—and they will tell you that reforming a nuclear plant's environment or culture is no simple task. It is difficult and fraught with tensions because it requires INPO to "really get into management practices at a deeper level than ever before," in the words of a nuclear utility vice president. That makes it a risky business indeed. Alienating top-level industry executives is the last thing INPO needs, and yet, the professionalism project risks doing just that by directing INPO's critical energies at the management policies and practices at the root of the professionalism problem, many of which

involve jealously guarded managerial prerogatives. Unless INPO pro-
ceeds with caution, the reaction of many industry executives is quite
predictable: "Hey, you're trying to manage my business." More than
resentment and resistance, say industry officials, such reactions could
undermine the top-level utility support vital to the professionalism
project's success. All that is why the professionalism project "represents a unique initiative," in the words of INPO's president, and "more
so than anything else we have done" it requires a "full management
buy-in for the initiative to work."[20]

To understand what management is buying into, it is well to remember INPO's definition of a nuclear professional, as the professionalism code adopts INPO's formulation (word for word) as its starting
point: "The nuclear professional is thoroughly imbued with a great
respect and *sense of responsibility* for the reactor core—for reactor
safety—and all his decisions take this *unique and grave responsibility*
into account."[21]

Unless we imagine people are somehow born with this special
sense of responsibility, it seems reasonable to assume, as INPO does,
that it's an acquired trait produced by a variety of influences, particularly in the work environment. Hence, the professionalism project targets the nuclear plant's work environment as its major object of reform: "*The principles are aimed at creating an environment within a
nuclear power plant* that promotes a healthy respect for the unique
technology that nuclear electric power represents and, thus, to promote great care and conservative, thoughtful decision-making by the
nuclear plant staff."[22] According to INPO, then, if you are a nuclear
utility executive, and you want to build an organizational culture that
inculcates workers with a special sense of responsibility for nuclear
safety, what you need to do is follow the directions—the principles of
institutional design—spelled out in the professionalism code. In some
ways, the code's eighty-two principles thus resemble a blueprint; and
like a blueprint of a well-designed house, they also embody an implicit
image of the nuclear utility—the "well-managed" nuclear utility—
that represents a fundamental and far-reaching reconstruction of the
premises underlying the nuclear industry's traditional management
philosophy. There lies the professionalism project's broader theoretical
and historical significance, as we shall see, but first we need to know
something more about the industry's traditional methods of industrial governance.

Traditionally, says a top-level industry official, fossil fuel–based electric utilities have been "top-down type organizations" in which management exercises "domineering control over the workers." What is more, says another industry official, power plant workers have been treated like your "classic blue-collar worker"—not terribly bright or ambitious, disliking responsibility, and preferring to be led. As for nuclear plant workers, from what has already been said about the fossil fuel mentality—the nuclear reactor seen as just another way of boiling water—we would also expect to find this managerial perspective extended to them as well. As a professionalism committee member puts it, "What you find at a lot of nuclear plants (and it's a carryover from the fossil plants) is the attitude that the people running these plants are just blue-collar worker bees."[23]

What you also find, say industry officials, is a certain attitude among workers—a blue-collar mentality. "Basically, the workers view themselves as, well, you know, workers—come to work at the plant, do assigned tasks, carry out orders, and go home," as one nuclear utility executive puts it. More to the point, he explains by way of example: "If you [the plant worker] see something that's a problem, that needs attention, and it's not part of your job, why bother with it? It's not your problem." Another industry executive (and professionalism committee member) characterizes this orientation in much the same terms: "They come to work for their eight hours and get their paycheck. 'Management is somebody else. It's not me.' There's no ownership. No sense of having a stake in the plant's successful operation." These descriptions are to some extent caricatures, of course, but the essential point remains the same: The traditional system of industrial management *discourages acceptance of responsibility at the bottom of the organization.* That, says the professionalism committee member, is "the culture we want to turn around."[24]

Now there are at least two ways of construing this problem. One essentially blames the workers by defining it as a "personnel problem." (An industry executive might say: "If only we could find truly motivated and conscientious workers to run our nuclear plant. That would solve our problems.") The professionalism project rejects this approach, however. Treating workers more like victims than culprits, it considers the disengaged—"It's just a job"—blue-collar outlook as symptomatic of a flawed management system, and champions instead a very different perspective on industrial governance. Trust, respect, communication, professional development, teamwork, and responsibility—according to the professionalism project these are some of the core values a nuclear plant's work environment should embody when "senior management establishes an overall corporate philosophy that permeates the organization":

> * *People* and their *professional capabilities* are regarded as the nuclear organization's *most valuable resource.*
> * *Knowledge and skills are developed,* maintained, and enhanced through appropriate training and career development.
> * Management is . . . responsive.
> * Management practices and policies convey an attitude of *trust.* . . .
> * Management maintains an *atmosphere of open communication.* . . .
> * Management . . . promotes a *sense of pride and ownership* in the plant and its equipment.
> * Management provides an environment that is conducive to excellence and professionalism.[25]

So if anything distinguishes this new managerial perspective from the old one, it is an emphasis on the human contribution to an organization's performance: workers do their best, and their contribution to the nuclear plant is maximized, not when they are treated like foot soldiers or assembly-line workers, but when they are persuaded and motivated by a supportive management that treats them like professionals. "What we're really trying to do," says a professionalism committee member, "is build a solid, cohesive team where every individual is proud of and committed to the plant's overall objectives and performance." Or, stated more broadly, what they are really trying to do is transform the basic premises underlying the nuclear industry's management philosophy.

Now it must be said that the professionalism project's management philosophy is hardly new or exotic. For almost half a century management theorists associated with the "human relations" perspective have been discussing the need to reconstruct managerial authority, to humanize our machinelike bureaucracies so as to make them less authoritarian, more participatory and responsive—in short, more people-centered. So taking the long perspective, the professionalism project is an extension of well-established management trends, as its central premises closely approximate many of the human relations perspective's basic axioms, including, most important, the "principle of supportive relationships."

As sociologist Rensis Likert once wrote, the principle of supportive relationships is a "fundamental formula" used by "high-producing managers" to develop "highly motivated" organizations.[26] Think of the principle this way: Each of us wants "appreciation, recognition, influence, a feeling of accomplishment, and a feeling that people who are important to us believe in us and respect us. We want to feel that we have a place in the world." In short, workers want to be treated with dignity. Therefore, Likert goes on, organization leaders should create a work environment that ensures "a maximum probability that in all interactions and all relationships with the organization *each member will . . . view the experience as supportive and one which builds and maintains his sense of personal worth and importance.*" (Emphasis supplied.)

As for the benefits of this managerial approach, one is a strong sense of cooperation or teamwork. By harnessing every worker's "full potential," writes Likert, a supportive work environment produces "a maximum of coordinated enthusiastic effort." Equally important, a supportive work environment also encourages the acceptance of responsibility among workers. As a team member, writes management theorist Peter Drucker, "every man sees himself as a 'manager' and accepts for himself the full burden of what is basically *managerial* responsibility: responsibility for his own job and work group, for his contribution to the performance and results of the entire organization."[27]

Inculcating responsibility through teamwork and a supportive work environment—this serves well enough as a rough description of the professionalism project's overall aim. And all this, needless to say, stands in stark contrast to the utility industry's traditional managerial perspective: to oversimplify, a domineering work environment that treats nuclear plant workers like blue-collar worker bees.

At this point an inquisitive reader may wish to know exactly why the professionalism committee embraced this particular model of industrial management. The most obvious explanation is that these management ideas have become very popular in recent years—think of Peter and Waterman's best-selling *In Search of Excellence* as an example[28]—and like many other industrial institutions throughout American society, some of the more progressive utilities had already begun to adopt some of these ideas prior to the professionalism project. So it was an incipient trend in the nuclear power industry. And capitalizing on that trend, the professionalism committee raised up many of these unofficial norms, clarified and certified them, thus investing these principles with a new and much more authoritative status within the industry.

True enough. But it is also important to recognize that human relations principles do not entail one particular way of managing an organization, any more than democratic principles entail one and only one way of governing a country. It is clear, for instance, that participatory and humanized administration is central to the human relations perspective; but it is also apparent that these aspirations must be tempered by the practical need for authority, discipline, and subordination. But what *kind* of authority? discipline? subordination? Should it be the same for all organizations, regardless of task or technology? Obviously not; for what is wholesome discipline in one context (say, a nuclear submarine) may be suffocating domination in another (say, a university political science department). So what is the appropriate mix for a nuclear plant?

This brings us back to the nuclear navy's influence on INPO and the post-TMI regulatory transformation. Put simply, the nuclear navy model represents one particular way of implementing the human relations perspective, and it "definitely had a heavy influence on the formulation of our principles," says a professionalism committee member. "I mean, if you're talking about professionalism—getting people's attention focused on the need to do a superior job—the nuclear navy is the model that everybody ought to look at." And looking at the nuclear navy model, what the professionalism committee found was a military-minded version of the human relations perspective; a mixture of management ideas that strongly values not only a supportive work environment (teamwork, communication, individual initiative and responsibility, and so on), but also a high degree of soldierly discipline, such as strict adherence to procedures and dress codes. In short, the nuclear plant, like the nuclear submarine, cannot be a permissive place.[29]

To sum up, the root question under discussion is how to best organize human effort in the nuclear power industry, and it should now be clear that the industry has two quite different ways of thinking about these matters. Closely tied to the fossil fuel cultural orientation, the traditional approach leads to managerial policies, practices, and programs that regard workers like foot soldiers or assembly-line workers—in short, like "blue-collar worker bees." The professionalism project, on the other hand, inspired by a mixture of perspectives, human relations and nuclear navy, advances a very different image of the well-managed nuclear plant, that of a supportive yet disciplined work environment that encourages workers to think and act like responsible "nuclear professionals."

A TIME TO REFLECT

"Utility managers," states the professionalism code's Foreword, "are encouraged to make in-depth comparisons between these principles and their day-to-day policies and practices and to use such efforts as opportunities to communicate their organization's management philosophy to all nuclear personnel."[30] As a professionalism committee member explains: "Our main message to the industry was, 'Here's a framework of what we as a cross section of the industry think is important. What you need to do is take it back to your plants, read it, understand it, and translate what's in there into something that's meaningful to you and to your people.'" In other words, each nuclear plant organization should pause, turn inwards, and use these principles as authoritative instruments of self-reflection to criticize and change specific managerial policies, practices, and programs. And at INPO's prodding, many of the nation's nuclear plants have done just that, including, for example, South Carolina Electric's V. C. Sumner plant.

In responding to INPO's professionalism initiative, the plant's vice president, Ollie Bradham, first asked the employees to develop a professionalism code.[31] The workers refused. "I was irritated," recalls Bradham, "but I bit my tongue, I held on to my chair. I thought about it. And I said, 'You know, they are probably right.' *We had been issuing edicts to them, without getting their buy-in.* We had to change our approach."[32] Management had to change its approach because under the customary managerial regime—management by edict—workers were alienated and mistrustful. Consequently, a plant employee explains, workers were unwilling to "buy into" the idea of developing a professional code: "I would say buy-in and trust go hand-in-hand. You don't buy in unless you trust the system. And we didn't trust the system." So they dismissed their management's avowed commitment to the industry's professionalism principles as little more than lip service.

Management "needed to do something" to deal with this mistrust, Bradham recalls, so various committees were created to do an in-depth introspective analysis of the plant.[33] Says plant manager Jack Skolds, "We started looking at all aspects of how we do business."[34] One twelve-member committee, for example, drawn from a cross section of the plant, tapped the opinions of a broad range of employees in order to develop the plant's professional code.[35] Meanwhile, an eight-member committee interviewed 120 plant employees to critically evaluate their organization's culture in light of the industry's professionalism principles.[36] "We tried to get down to the root problems that concerned people the most," says one committee member.[37] Likewise, managers from the site as well as the corporate office were interviewed. General Manager Mike Williams: "We looked at all our policies, procedures, and programs. We talked to people from the CEO on down. We wanted to really know our strengths and weaknesses."[38]

As for INPO's role in all this, in August 1989 an INPO official visited the site to help get the self-assessment under way. This is a common practice, according to an INPO official close to the professionalism project, although the type of assistance INPO provides in this connection "varies a lot": "Sometimes people will ask us to come to them and talk about the conduct of a self-assessment and the lessons that other plants have learned from performing self-assessments. In some cases we help them on how to structure their interview process and be effective interviewers, because the whole self-assessment really is an interview process." In this connection, for example, INPO has compiled seventy-four pages of sample questions to help officials diagnose their plant's work environment.

What have been the fruits of all this soul-searching prompted by the professionalism initiative? One of the earliest and most visible results was the addition of 103 new employees to the nuclear plant's staff. Says Bradham: "We hadn't had an increase in the site staff since 1983. Employees began to see that corporate management was serious about supporting the nuclear division. We were allowed more money, more manpower to solve our problems."[39] The development of a professionalism code is another. Finally, and perhaps most significant from a long-term perspective, the self-assessment led to the creation of a program called "Nuclear Excellence." It includes eight "action plans" aimed at addressing a variety of management system deficiencies identified by the self-assessment, including, for instance, problems with "executive direction and control," "management effectiveness," and "human resource development."

Beyond that not much can be said, except that the plant's professionalism initiative is still very new and, judging from a recent (1991) company survey of employee attitudes, apparently has a long way to go in building a supportive work environment. The survey's results, a

Sumner plant official told me, were "not flattering." "Lost trust," he added, "is hard to recover."

It was just in this period, too, that another utility, Entergy Operations, conducted a similar self-assessment at its four nuclear plants. And one revealing product of that effort is a twenty-three-page booklet distributed to all nuclear operations personnel. Titled "Principles for Managing Nuclear Plant Personnel," it opens with this letter from William Cavanaugh III, the company's president and CEO:

> To Entergy Operations Personnel:
> . . . This document standardizes management responsibilities for providing a working environment that allows and encourages enhanced professional performance. Management is striving to put the principles outlined here in place. However, this is a process that cannot be accomplished overnight. The working environment that these Principles are intended to foster will be the result of consistent effort by everyone in the organization.
>
> *Implementing some of the principles will require a cultural change in our behavior. Many of the issues addressed here represent concepts that both we and our industry have only recently embraced. . . .*
>
> Management is ultimately responsible for providing an environment that is conducive to professionalism. Each individual has a responsibility to adhere to these principles, to assimilate the concepts they represent, and to be ever vigilant to take advantage of every opportunity for improvement.
>
> Management is committed to these principles, and they will be implemented in The Middle South Electric System's nuclear units in a timely manner.
>
> Please read this document carefully and make sure that your daily activities, your attitude and your professional judgement reflect and nurture these principles. History has shown us that even a momentary lapse in the pursuit of excellence and professionalism embodied in these principles can undo what may have taken years to accomplish.[40]

Suffice it to say that the dozens of principles listed in the booklet closely resemble the industry's professionalism principles. Three examples follow. On the principle of supportive relationships: "We recognize that our personnel and their professional capabilities are our most valuable resources. We also acknowledge that employees must have a professional environment to perform to their fullest capabilities and to achieve this standard of excellence. These . . . [principles] formalize management's responsibilities to provide an environment that is conducive to excellence and professionalism for those personnel involved in the management and safe operation of the system's nuclear plants."[41] On teamwork: "Management shall foster an environment which encourages a spirit of teamwork. This teamwork will be clearly visible from the chief executive officer down."[42] On conservative decisionmaking: "Management shall promote a culture which ensures that plant personnel will take prudent, conservative and safe action when unexpected and/or abnormal conditions arise."[43]

As of 1991, according to INPO, "nearly 40 percent of utilities have conducted professionalism self-assessments, and most others are putting the industry's *Principles for Enhancing Professionalism* to good use by other means."[44]

BUILDING COMMITMENT

"Because the principles are almost 'motherhoodish,'" says a nuclear utility vice president, "it's very easy for people to just give professionalism lip service." Making a similar point, another top-level executive tells how "everybody—I mean everybody—talks about professional codes and all that kind of stuff. They all want to be INPO number-one plants. So they all develop codes of professionalism with all the same buzz words. But do they really support the principles? That's the real question." The answer is far from clear, by all accounts, as the level of support for these principles varies considerably among utilities, ranging from strong and effective commitment in some cases to little more than lip service in others.

In practical terms this usually means that some utilities are much less willing than others to support the professionalism principles with needed money and manpower. And when that kind of support is not forthcoming, a utility's professionalism project may well do more harm than good to the plant's working environment. "Consistency is everything," a nuclear vice president explains: "It's sort of like saying, 'Hey, I'm going to run my own professional football team and my goal is to be the best and win the Super Bowl. But we're not going to give you first-class uniforms. We aren't going to have a weight room be-

cause it's too expensive.' There's this big discrepancy between the ultimate stated goal and all the supporting details. . . . Management has
to follow up with these professionalism codes," he continues: "Putting
a code on the walls causes a lot of problems for people if management
doesn't live up to it. You get everybody pumped up to do all these
wonderful things, and then they say, 'Oh sorry, we don't have the budget for that.' People quickly see that it's lip service. It's management
shooting off their mouth again and not following up. And that pisses
everybody off."

A partial explanation for management's hollow commitment can
be traced to a mixture of culture and budgetary politics. Culturally,
the fossil fuel orientation still colors the way some top-level utility
officials think about nuclear technology, and when it does, it tends to
obscure how the practical exigencies of running a nuclear plant differ
from conventional technologies. "There are utilities with nuclear
plants that haven't made the full transition from the board of directors
on down to what the nuclear ethic is," a nuclear utility vice president explains:

> A nuclear power plant is different from a fossil fuel one. It's not
> better; it's not worse; it's different. And what it takes to run a
> nuclear power plant is different. When the chairman of the
> company or the president of the company or the board of direc-
> tors don't really have that understanding of being different, it is
> very difficult for the station manager or the nuclear vice presi-
> dent to carry this [the professionalism project] off by them-
> selves. You need that very high-level support. And sometimes
> that's hard in coming because the sensitivity to the demands of
> a highly sophisticated technology like nuclear power just isn't
> there.

Reinforcing this cultural bent are political pressures that urge senior executives *not* to treat nuclear power technology differently. That
is because enhancing professionalism costs money (103 new employees at V. C. Sumner, for instance), and the competition for resources
within electric utilities has become very intense in recent years. This
makes for heated politics in the budgetary process, say industry officials, and nowhere is that competition more intense than between a
utility's nuclear and fossil fuel organizations. An example (as told by
a nuclear utility vice president with an exemplary professionalism
program) illustrates the point:

Our company has had a program in the last two years to cut manpower by approximately 10 percent. And in that two years we [at the nuclear plant] have gone up about 5 percent. That means every time I hire someone, somebody else loses someone. So we're taking money and manpower right out of the rest of the company. Obviously, that doesn't make me very popular with some people in the company because *they see all this talk about nuclear professionalism as extra perks for nuclear at the expense of the fossil fuel organization.* [Emphasis supplied.]

If this plant's professionalism program was not well supported by top utility management (and at many utilities they aren't, say industry officials), in all likelihood the outcome would have been very different. Siding with the fossil fuel organization, the utility's leadership would also judge the nuclear organization's request for special treatment—more money and more manpower in an era of shrinking budgets—not as a vital need arising from nuclear technology's special requirements, but as an unwarranted extra perk for nuclear.

As we saw in earlier chapters, one of INPO's essential tasks has been to change this way of thinking about nuclear technology. INPO evaluation reports, letters to the CEOs, annual CEO workshops—in one way and another these educational measures (among others) have sought to enhance the utility leadership's understanding of nuclear power's distinctive character and special needs. And all this has been quite successful—up to a point. For nuclear industry officials are also quick to add that such measures are no substitute for firsthand operating experience, that relatively few senior executives have such experience, and only when more board directors, CEOs, senior vice presidents, and other top industry officials come from the ranks of nuclear plant employees will there be a truly effective industry-wide commitment to transforming the nuclear plant's work environment and enhancing professionalism.

Which brings us to one of the professionalism project's less apparent yet fundamental long-term objectives. By reconstructing the industry's career track and elite recruitment patterns, it seeks to strengthen top-level utility commitment and support for nuclear professionalism. "There was a strong feeling on the [professionalism] committee," as one of its members explains, "that these plants would be safer if in fact you have senior levels of the company—all the way to the boardroom people—with true operating experience. Because what you find at some plants is that *they're not getting the resources they really need because the people making those decisions really don't understand what the operation of a nuclear plant really requires.*" (Emphasis supplied.) And so it is that, by changing the social composition of the industry's governing class, one of the professionalism project's long-term ambitions is to make nuclear power's leadership less "fossil-fuel-minded" and more "nuclear-minded."[45]

ACCOMPLISHMENTS

We must end this discussion by asking what the professionalism initiative has actually accomplished. If we measure by the yardstick of cultural change at the nation's nuclear plants, we cannot say much, at least for the time being. "If we implement them well, the professionalism principles should be able to change the environment," says an INPO official, although that remains to be seen: "I hope in five or ten years it's changing people's attitudes. But changing culture is really hard. All this is so new. And it's so difficult to measure. So I can't tell you how much difference it's made in reality, except that we have a long way to go."[46] Professionalism may have long way to go, but a moment's reflection suffices to remind us of how far the industry has already come in establishing an industry-wide infrastructure to support the professionalism project's long-term objective—building a new culture.

First of all, the professionalism project has mobilized the industry's attention. If you are a high-level business executive with a large corporation, chances are you're a very busy person confronting a wide array of job-related challenges, each making claims on your time. Your attention is a "scarce resource."[47] As for managing that resource, what you pay attention to and what you don't, organization theorists will tell you that all this is very much influenced by the attention-focusing institutional mechanisms of the organization you inhabit. Seen from this perspective, the professionalism project is a set of institutional arrangements that requires very busy nuclear industry executives (including the CEOs) to pay serious attention to the nuclear industry's professionalism problem. An example: INPO's November 1987 CEO conference, the time and place when, as a nuclear utility vice president puts it, professionalism became a "big issue" requiring the industry's "concentrated attention":

> It needed to get the kind of focus that comes only from Zack Pate [INPO's president] talking to the CEOs and saying, "Hey

guys, this is the number one issue in the coming years. Read my lips. Do I have your attention? This is number one." When Zack challenged the utilities at the meetings, *I knew that I had to do something about it.* I knew that we would have to come back and tell INPO what we've done on the professionalism initiative. And *I also knew that all my peers were going to be out there doing something, and that I had to do something that was going to stack up.* [Emphasis supplied.]

This was the first time ever that the industry's collective attention focused on these matters. I should also add that this meeting was the opening move in what has become an ongoing industry-wide campaign—workshops, training sessions, inspections, and so on—that in one way and another communicates a basic message to industry officials that goes something like this: "The professionalism problem threatens our industry's future. So pay attention and do something about it. That is our obligation—each and every one of us—as members of this industry."[48]

We are familiar enough with the second major step in laying the groundwork for the industry's cultural reconstruction. The professionalism project, by creating a common framework of principles—the professionalism code—has already moved the industry some way toward establishing a collective way of thinking about and responding to these issues. You may recall, for example, how the Sumner plant officials used these principles as instruments of self-reflection and self-criticism to reform their managerial policies and practices. Nor is there any reason to believe this is an isolated example, as all the utilities are under considerable pressure to pursue a similar course.

That pressure speaks to my third point. A moment ago I emphasized one nuclear utility vice president's initial response to the professionalism project. Knowing that all his "peers were going to do something about it," he also felt the need to "do something" in order to "stack up" in comparison to other utilities. What he felt, of course, was a kind of peer pressure owing to the fact that he knew, along with his peers, that the industry (through INPO) would be watching.

And INPO is watching. Although the principles occupy a somewhat ambiguous position in the formal inspection process, they "do impact how we look at management issues and how the plant is being managed," as an INPO inspector puts it.[49] That impact is well illustrated by the following excerpt from a 1989 INPO corporate evaluation. (Going back to an earlier point, it also illustrates how the professionalism project is reconstructing career tracks in order to raise the level of nuclear awareness.) INPO on the problem of inadequate corporate-level nuclear operating experience: "A lack of nuclear station experience exists at the corporate manager level and in key corporate staff positions. Only one member of the corporate staff at the director level has nuclear station experience . . . *This reduces the operational perspective in the corporate organization and restricts available career paths for station employees.*" (Emphasis supplied.) INPO on what corporate management should do to deal with the problem: "Establish career development for selected corporate and station personnel. . . . Revise corporate policies to include nuclear station experience as an important factor in employee development to advancement." The utility's response: "Career development . . . will be enhanced through the implementation of a Key Manager Development Program. . . . Revised job descriptions, which will indicate a preference for station experience for appropriate corporate positions, will be completed by September 1990."[50]

Here we see how INPO uses the inspection process to evaluate a utility's commitment to the professionalism principles, and, if necessary, pressures utility officials to convert those general principles into workable policies, programs, and practices. Broadly understood, moreover, this case can easily be translated into the theoretical concepts we have used to explain the movement toward community in the nuclear power industry. As a result of the professionalism project, there now exists a common industrial morality (the professionalism principles) backed by various forms of communal pressure (including INPO inspections) that is ultimately aimed at institutionalizing responsibility (particularly thoughtful and conservative decisionmaking). The professionalism project, in short, is a prime example of communitarian regulation.

I started this section by asking what the professionalism project has accomplished. Because it is in the early stages of a lengthy culture-building process, say five or ten years, the first and most obvious answer is "Not very much." But if we take a different view of the matter, one that focuses on methods and strategies rather than final results, it seems clear that the professionalism project is already well on its way toward instituting a supportive structure, industry-wide, that guides and goads industry officials along this difficult course of cultural reform. So perhaps the most important conclusion we can draw from all this is that the professionalism project, although it has a long way to go, does in fact represent a serious attempt to instill nuclear plant workers with the proper attitude—the constellation of values, purposes, and sensibilities that informs the thinking of a true nuclear professional. As to whether or not this attempt will succeed in its far-reaching aims, that, of course, remains to be seen. "Of all the initiatives," in the words of INPO's president, "this is the one where the greatest challenge remains." [51]

9
Conclusion

As I have repeatedly suggested in this book, one of the most remarkable features of the nuclear industry's post-TMI regulatory transformation is the emergence of community. "But this seems an odd notion of community," some will say, and reasonably. After all, when we think of community, we typically think of small face-to-face ones, such as the enveloping community seventeenth-century New Englanders knew. We think of a group of people living, like a big family, in the same locale and bound together by ties of warmth and intimacy. But at least 98,000 people work in the nuclear industry. What's more, they work for fifty-four different utilities that operate 111 nuclear plants located at seventy sites around the country.[1] A big warm family? Hardly. So in bringing this book to a close, this chapter invites you to consider a quite different notion of community, one that is central to understanding the nuclear industry's post-TMI regulatory transformation from a broader perspective.[2]

FORMS OF COMMUNITY

Although the idea of community is one of the "most fundamental and far-reaching of sociology's unit-ideas," it is also an idea that is exceedingly "difficult to define."[3] As a starting point, consider MacIver and Page's classic definition: "Whenever the members of any group, small or large, live together in such a way that they share, not this or that particular interest, but the basic conditions of common life, we call that group a community. The basic criterion of community is, then, that *all of one's social relationships may be found within it.*"[4] This formulation stresses the idea of social cohesion, and rightly so, for when we think of community we think of members of a group bound together by common ties. But also notice how much social cohesion this formulation presumes; if a group is to be a community, *all* of one's social relationships must be found within it. From this angle, unless one imagines a circle of nearly 100,000 nuclear workers living together, bound by feelings of warmth and intimacy, sharing a set of relationships comprehensive enough to encompass their entire lives, there is little reason to think of the nuclear power industry in communitarian terms.

Another way of thinking about this treats the concept as a continuum along which variation occurs. Thus: "A group is a community *to the extent* that it encompasses a broad range of activities and interests, and *to the extent* that participation implicates whole persons rather than segmental interests or activities."[5] Although this formulation (like MacIver and Page's) stresses the idea of social cohesion, it also emphasizes the significance of variation—that some communities are in fact more (or less) comprehensive than others—and therefore leaves open the question of *how much* social cohesion must bind group members.[6] Likewise, much the same logic also applies to the question of *what kind* of social cohesion binds members of a group into a community. A common history and culture? Geography? Kinship? Mutual interdependence? Common beliefs and values?[7] There is no single answer, as this line of questioning suggests, for the principal integrative mechanism may be a common history in some cases; in others it may be kinship, and in still others it may be common norms.[8] Thus understood, community is a variable concept.

At issue, then, is not whether the nuclear industry is a full-blown or comprehensive community, like an old-fashioned New England town, but whether, from this variable perspective, it is a form of community. And if so, *how much* social cohesion and *what kind* of social cohesion could hold such a seemingly heterogeneous group together?

For this task I will need the help of a number of ideas, and I begin by considering the role organizations can play in the development of community. In a classic work on the theory of organizations, Chester Barnard once discussed the "moral element" in organization and the "moral factor" in leadership. He was referring (more than fifty years ago) to what writers now call "organization culture." That moral factor, Barnard wrote, involves "the process of inculcating points of view, fundamental attitudes, [and] loyalties to the organization . . . that will result in subordinating individual interest . . . to the good of the cooperative whole."[9] For Barnard, then, because the moral element in organizations promotes group cohesion on the basis of shared values and beliefs, it is a *unifying force* that goes a long way toward explaining what unites organization members around a common organizational purpose.

A more fully developed statement of this perspective, Philip Selznick's theory of institutionalization, also maintains that values are of central importance for understanding what holds an organization together.[10] Organizations become institutions as they are "infused with value," to be more precise, and where institutionalization is well advanced, "distinctive outlooks, habits, and other commitments are *unified*, coloring all aspects of organizational life and lending it a *social integration*." (Emphasis supplied.)[11] Organizations can embody values, according to this view, and when they do, they acquire a distinctive character or culture. Or, put another way, culture is to an organization what personality is to an individual, as each reflects "a distinctive way of seeing and responding to the world," such as the nuclear navy's cultural orientation and its distinctive way of seeing and responding to the world of nuclear power.[12]

All this adds up to four basic points especially relevant to our discussion. First, because organizations become united on the basis of shared values, the process of value infusion and that of social integration go hand in hand. Second, because institutionalization is a *process*, the existence of an institution is a relative matter and one of degree; organizations are more or less infused with value, more or less institutionalized, more or less socially integrated. Third, because values are built into the organization's social structure, they have a social base. Finally, and most important, as the process of institutionalization advances, and as an organization becomes unified by shared beliefs and values, it may become a kind of community.[13]

Now the key point: A group of organizations within an industry can become a community in much the same way as members of an organization can become a community. In both contexts the process of value infusion and social integration can promote the development of community; in both contexts, the process is a matter of degree (like an organization, a group of organizations can be more or less infused with value and more or less socially integrated); in both contexts, finally, the development of community is *institution-centered*.

A focus on institutions turns attention away from the psychic cohesion so often associated with the idea of community. *Instead of seeing community in the emergence of like-minded, undifferentiated individuals, we see it in a network of distinct but interdependent institutions.* This does not eliminate the need for core values; indeed, if they are built into the premises and govern the operation of major institutions, core values are likely to be stronger and more effectively implemented than if they are manifested only in beliefs or feelings.[14]

Think of it this way. A vital part of what holds an "academic community" together is a common framework of values concerning (say) academic freedom and scholarly integrity. Yet it is more than a collection of individuals united by some common beliefs; it is also a network of institutions (universities, professional associations, and so forth) that help sustain the community's existence by safeguarding its unifying values. So what holds an academic community together is not shared understandings alone, but the embodiment of a particular set of values (a culture) in a particular set of institutions (a social structure).

With these general ideas in mind, we can better appreciate the distinctive form of community at stake in the post-TMI regulatory transformation. And perhaps the simplest way of showing that is to notice the union of culture and social structure produced by the two institutions central to nuclear power's community-building process—INPO and the nuclear utilities.

Take the new industrial morality INPO has created. With its performance objectives, good practices, professionalism principles, and so on, it should now be clear that INPO has gone a long way toward spelling out, for the entire industry, what conduct is esteemed and what goals are legitimate and desirable. Whether you are a nuclear plant chemistry technician or a nuclear utility CEO, INPO's normative system establishes an industry-wide framework for construing what it means to occupy your particular role and what it means to behave in a manner appropriate to that position. And when we add to this the numerous ways INPO inculcates those values, such as the industry-wide institutional mechanisms for allocating praise and distributing shame, there can be no mistaking the extent of INPO's effort to integrate the nuclear industry around this common framework of regulatory principles. In a vital sense, then, INPO is a *unifying institution.*

With the nuclear utilities, in turn, no consideration of the industry's community-building process can fail to include their role as *anchoring institutions.* The main reason this is so is that values require social support to be effective, particularly the precarious ones, such as learning from industry experience. Add to this the fact that values can be embodied in and supported by institutions—what INPO officials

call the "internalization of operating experience" in the case of learning from industry experience[15]—and you have one of the nuclear utilities' essential contributions to the community-building process: Like
anchors, they can enhance the stability and security of otherwise insecure values by giving them a solid base of support within the social
structure of the industry. As an example, think of the way INPO's
normative system calls for an effective operating experience review
program at each nuclear plant, including the various role obligations
that run to learning from industry experience; or the way INPO inspectors hold utilities accountable to those norms of appropriateness,
as when they translate particular instances of performance problems
into broader issues of management responsibility; or, perhaps most
important, the various ways INPO harnesses the CEOs' commitment
to such policies and purposes. It is all part of weaving the new industrial morality into a social fabric of utility-based institutional roles so
that the values at stake have a chance to become established and secure—in a word, institutionalized.[16]

THE VALUE OF COMMUNITY

This organization-centered perspective on community is not new. As
historian Thomas Bender reminds us: "Social theory in the nineteenth
and twentieth centuries has been concerned with the problem of re-
stating the value of community in an urban society increasingly dominated by large-scale organization. . . . Believing that the small, unique,
and particularistic units of life that make for the experience of community have been sentenced to death by historical necessity, the most
influential twentieth-century sociologists and social philosophers
have tried to recapture community by imputing it to large-scale organizations." I hasten to add that Bender rejects this viewpoint. It "trivial-
izes community," he charges, because the impersonal world of big organizations is hardly compatible with the feelings of intimacy and
brotherhood central to the experience of community.[17] And if this be
so, then ascribing community to a network of organizations in the
nuclear industry would only seem to aggravate the charge.

True enough, if we equate community (as Bender does) with the
Gemeinschaft model formulated by German social theorist Ferdinand
Tönnies—that is, a traditional folk community united by feelings of
intimacy and brotherhood. But our investigation of the nuclear industry's experience suggests a quite different image of community, not
cemented by warmth and intimacy, yet far from trivial either. To see

my point, turn your mind's eye to what it means to share a common life:

> A common life is not a *fused* life: in a fused life there would be no need for regulation or governance, no need to take account of individual differences, no need for adjustment, reciprocity, or cooperation. The tacit assumption here is that people and groups participate in any community, large or small, as individuated and self-regarding entities. They are independent as well as interdependent.
>
> *The distinctive function of community, then, is the reconciliation of partial with general perspectives. . . . [It is] to regulate, discipline, and, especially, to channel self-regarding conduct, thereby binding it, so far as possible, to comprehensive interests and ideals.* [Emphasis supplied.]
>
> What we prize in community is not unity of any sort, at any cost, but unity that preserves the integrity of persons, groups, and institutions. Thus understood, community is profoundly *federalist* in spirit and structure. It is a unity of unities. [Emphasis in original.][18]

And from the evidence we have, this kind of unity is quite similar to what nuclear industry officials seem to prize most in their new system of self-regulation. Recall comments of the chairman of INPO's board of directors:

> In establishing INPO, the nuclear utility industry took the unprecedented step of embracing the concept of self-improvement and self-regulation. In doing so, the industry assumed a major responsibility. . . . We adopted a philosophy by which all of the nuclear utilities would operate, and we committed ourselves individually and collectively to achieve a standard of excellence in the conduct of our nuclear power responsibilities.[19]

To put his observation in our terms, the main value of community lies in a distinctive kind of unity. It is a unity of distinctive yet interdependent organizations, one that is integrated around a shared framework of values (a common "philosophy"), one that is preserved by a well-developed capacity for regulatory ordering, and, most important, one that aims to cultivate responsibility ("excellence") among its members.[20] However we might want to describe this, it should now be apparent that this form of community is anything but trivial from the perspective of nuclear industry officials—and nuclear safety.

All right, you may say, but is the nuclear industry's experience with communitarian regulation a guide for anybody else? That's difficult to judge on the basis of a single case study. Now it could be argued that, given nuclear power's potential for incredibly catastrophic accidents, plus the relatively small number of organizations involved, we have a case for believing that the nuclear industry's experience with communitarian regulation is unique, if only because the fifty-four nuclear utilities are hostages of each other in an extraordinary way. If only it were so clear-cut. For there are growing signs that the chemical industry is making a concerted effort to unify itself around a common framework of regulatory principles, and, to this end, the Chemical Manufacturers Association is now (1992) examining the nuclear industry's experience with INPO for any lessons it may hold.[21] Perhaps the contrast between nuclear power and other industries is one of degree, not of kind, in terms of providing congenial conditions for the emergence of community. Perhaps a close look at other industries (such as chemical manufacturing) would reveal that the movement toward community has many paths, and that communitarian regulation has various forms. One can only speculate in the absence of comparative industry data. And yet, for all the uncertainties about generalizability, one thing seems clear enough in light of the nuclear industry's post-TMI regulatory transformation. Contrary to what many people suppose, the idea of community—and communitarian regulation—is well worth taking seriously, even in a complex technological society dominated by large-scale organizations.

Appendix, Notes, and Index

Appendix

The NRC and industry use various measures to gauge safety performance, including, most important, NRC performance indicators and INPO performance indicators. As the graphs below illustrate and a recent analysis by the National Research Council concludes: "The data show considerable improvements in the industry averages over the 1980's." National Research Council, *Nuclear Power: Technical and Institutional Options for the Future* (Washington, D.C.: National Academy Press, 1992), p. 56.

Two indicators—on scrams and safety system actuations—best make the point, as they are generally regarded as the leading proxies for measuring the overall safety of nuclear reactor operations. A "scram" refers to the rapid shutdown of a nuclear reactor in an emergency (like slamming on your car's brakes to avoid an accident), and from 1980 to 1990 the annual industry average dropped from 7.4 to 1.6 scrams per unit—an 80 percent drop. As for safety system actuations, picture (say) a nuclear plant's emergency core cooling system activated in response to an emergency. Because this ordinarily occurs when the limits of safe reactor operation have been reached, fewer actuations are a sign of greater care in plant operation, according to INPO and the NRC, and greater care contributes to a higher margin of safety. In 1985 (the first year this was measured by the NRC) the average number of actuations per unit was 2.74, while the average for 1990 was 1.05—a 60 percent drop.

On the data for these and other safety indicators, see NRC NUREG-1350, vol. 4, *Information Digest* (1992 ed.), pp. 44–45; also see INPO, "1990 Performance Indicators for the U.S. Nuclear Utility Industry." For a detailed discussion of what these and other indicators mean, and their safety-related significance, see NRC NUREG/CR-5437, "Organization and Safety in Nuclear Power Plants" (May 1990), pp. 135–54. For a different perspective, which highlights the limitations of these indicators as measures of nuclear safety, see Elizabeth Nichols and Aaron Wildavsky, *Safer Power: Understanding and Improving Organizational Design, Human Performance, and Governmental Regulation in Nuclear Power Plants* (unpublished manuscript, July 1992).

Unplanned Safety System Actuations

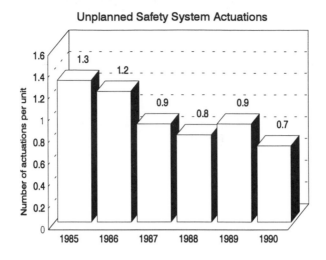

Automatic Scrams While Critical

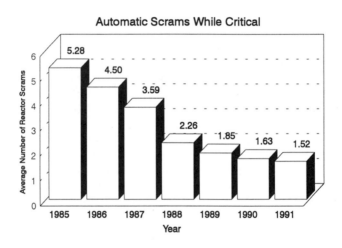

Safety System Actuations

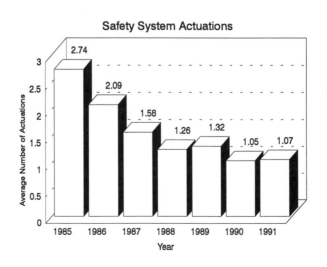

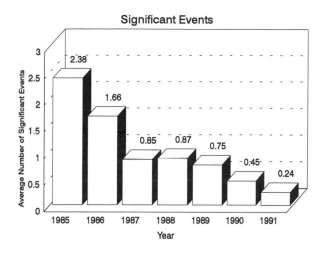

Significant Events

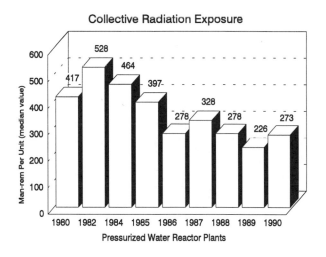

Collective Radiation Exposure

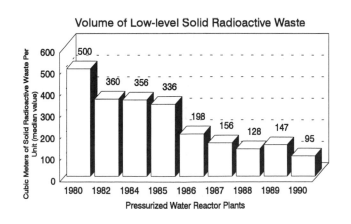

Volume of Low-level Solid Radioactive Waste

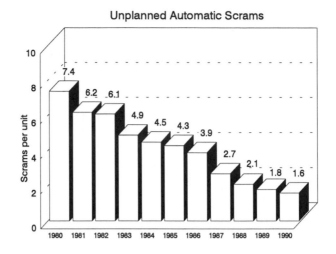

Unplanned Automatic Scrams

Scrams per unit

7.4 (1980), 6.2 (1981), 6.1 (1982), 4.9 (1983), 4.5 (1984), 4.3 (1985), 3.9 (1986), 2.7 (1987), 2.1 (1988), 1.8 (1989), 1.6 (1990)

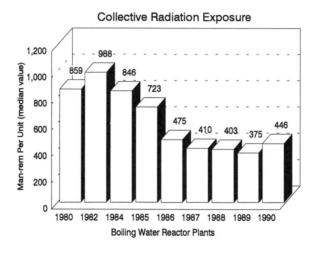

Collective Radiation Exposure

Man-rem Per Unit (median value)

859 (1980), 988 (1982), 846 (1984), 723 (1985), 475 (1986), 410 (1987), 403 (1988), 375 (1989), 446 (1990)

Boiling Water Reactor Plants

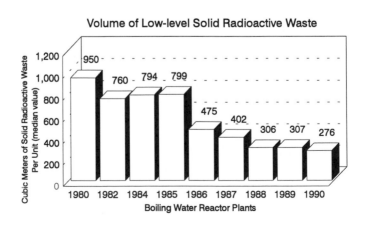

Volume of Low-level Solid Radioactive Waste

Cubic Meters of Solid Radioactive Waste Per Unit (median value)

950 (1980), 760 (1982), 794 (1984), 799 (1985), 475 (1986), 402 (1987), 306 (1988), 307 (1989), 276 (1990)

Boiling Water Reactor Plants

NOTES

Chapter 1

1. Random House Unabridged Dictionary, 2d ed., s.v. "Three Mile Island."

2. The industry group was the Edison Electric Institute's board of directors, and the committee it created was called the TMI Ad Hoc Nuclear Oversight Committee.

3. Walter J. McCarthy, "Industry Update—Progress and Challenge." Speech delivered at 1989 Annual INPO CEO Conference, pp. 7–8.

4. Letter from congressmen Kostemeyer and Markey to U.S. Government Accounting Office, quoted in James L. Franklin, "GAO Asked to Investigate Role of Nuclear Industry's Safety Agency," *Boston Globe*, 24 May 1990, p. 11.

5. U.S. Congress, House Committee on Interior and Insular Affairs, Subcommittee on General Oversight, 101st Cong., 2d sess., 14 March 1990. Testimony of Ralph Nader and Robert Pollard, p. 4.

6. Watkins added, "During the discussions with the Soviets, the United States delegation emphasized principles developed by INPO which define and govern safe reactor operational practices at nuclear power plants." James D. Watkins, "Approaches to Nuclear Safety," *Public Utilities Fortnightly* (24 May 1990), p. 22. As Watkins stated in another context, "I want to help the Soviets develop an INPO-like approach toward improving plant safety, because I believe they recognize the need to develop a culture of safe practices similar to that which INPO helped foster in our commercial industry after Three Mile Island." James D. Watkins, "Dinner Remarks." Speech delivered at INPO 1989 CEO Conference, Atlanta, Georgia, 1–3 November. See also *Nuclear News*, January 1991, p. 27; INPO *Review* (Jan./Feb. 1993), p. 6.

7. "WANO: Lord Marshall Replies," *Financial Times Limited* (London), 19 July 1990.

8. Keith Schneider, "New Mission at Energy Department: Bomb Makers Turn to Cleanup," *New York Times*, 17 August 1990, p. 1.

9. In 1987, for example, the DOE signed a contract with INPO that provided for, among other things, INPO technical assistance visits, INPO participation in DOE inspections, and DOE attendance at INPO work-

shops and training courses. In addition, INPO provided the DOE with its programs and methodologies for assessing the safety of commercial reactors. See Brian Jordan, "DOE Contract Provides INPO with Year-End Surplus of $6.5 Million," *Nucleonics Week*, 30 March 1989, p. 7; see also "DOE Responded to Criticism of Weapons Plant Safety with a Committee," *Nucleonics Week*, 5 November 1987, p. 5.

10. John Braithwaite and Brent Fisse, "Self-Regulation and the Costs of Corporate Crime," in *Private Policing*, ed. Clifford D. Shearing and Philip C. Stenning (Newbury Park, Calif.: Sage Publications, 1987), pp. 229–46.

11. *Nucleonics Week*, 26 April 1990, p. 7.

12. He added, "The question is: how much safer, and is that enough?" Quoted in Matthew Wald, "10 Years after Three Mile Island," *New York Times*, 23 May 1989, p. D1.

13. Todd R. La Porte and Craig Thomas, "Regulatory Compliance and the Ethos of Quality Enhancement: Surprises in Nuclear Power Plant Operations." Revision of a paper delivered at the annual meeting of the American Political Science Association, San Francisco, California, 31 August 1990 (rev. 9/10/91), p. 11, n. 16.

14. As an in-depth congressionally mandated study by the National Research Council recently stated:

> Over the past decade utilities have steadily strengthened their ability to be responsible for the safety of their plants. . . . *Self assessment and peer oversight through INPO are acknowledged to be strong and effective means of improving the performance of U.S. nuclear power plants.* . . . It is the Committee's opinion, based upon our experience, that the nuclear industry should continue to take the initiative to bring the standards of every American nuclear plant up to those of the best plants in the United States and the world. . . . Every U.S. nuclear utility should continue its full-fledged participation in INPO.

National Research Council, *Nuclear Power: Technical and Institutional Options for the Future* (Washington, D.C.: National Academy Press, 1992), 185. (Emphasis supplied.)

Even INPO's strongest critics express a grudging respect for its accomplishments. "If you look at INPO's own performance indicators, there's a downtrending of many of the problems that have plagued the industry in the past," says a member of Ralph Nader's Critical Mass Energy Project. "So it looks like INPO is doing a good job and that the plants are learning the lessons INPO has pointed out to them. Unfortunately," he adds, "INPO's doing what the NRC should be doing, and yet the public doesn't have any access to it."

Making a similar point, a nuclear power critic with the Washington-based Nuclear Information and Resource Service states:

> Our biggest beef with INPO is that everything is secret. But I'm certainly not complaining that INPO's out there, because I think INPO has clout within the industry and the concept of taking what

the utilities are doing well and spreading the information to other utilities is a good one. And given the few INPO inspection reports I've seen, if you compare them to the NRC's, the INPO ones tend to be more critical, broader in scope, and really more useful to both the public and the utility. So in some cases INPO seems to be tougher than the NRC. But has INPO brought about a vast improvement in safety? I just don't know, really, because it's all so secretive.

15. Because of global warming, for example, three environmental groups that have opposed nuclear energy—the National Audubon Society, the World Resources Institute, and the Union of Concerned Scientists— have recently recognized the technology's potential and accepted the need for more research. See Keith Schneider, "Is Nuclear Winter Giving Way to Nuclear Spring?" *New York Times*, 12 May 1991, p. E4.

16. See "NRC 20-year License Extension Plans Get Fair-to-Good Reviews," *Nucleonics Week*, 23 November 1989, p. 1.

17. On April 10, 1991, for example, the National Academy of Sciences urged the government to quickly develop and test a new generation of reactors. The DOE is spending $160 million to this end in 1991. See Schneider, "Is Nuclear Winter Giving Way to Nuclear Spring?" p. E4.

Chapter 2

1. Edwin Kintner, "After TMI-2: A Decade of Change." Speech delivered to American Nuclear Society meeting, 31 October 1988. (Emphasis supplied.)

2. This included the report of the President's Commission on the Accident at Three Mile Island:

> To prevent nuclear accidents as serious as Three Mile Island, fundamental changes will be necessary in the organization, procedures, and practices—and above all—in the attitudes of the Nuclear Regulatory Commission and . . . the nuclear industry.

> Popular discussion of nuclear power plants tends to concentrate on questions of equipment safety. . . . But as the evidence [uncovered by the commission] accumulated, it became clear [to us] that the fundamental problems were people-related problems and not equipment problems.

> When we say that the basic problems are people-related, we do not mean to limit this term to shortcomings of individual human beings. . . . We mean more generally that our investigation has revealed problems with the "system" that manufactures, operates, and regulates nuclear power plants. . . .

> Wherever we looked, we found problems with the human beings who operate the plant, with the management that runs the key organization, and with the agency that is charged with assuring the safety of nuclear power plants.

John G. Kemeny et al., *Report of the President's Commission on the Accident at Three Mile Island* (New York: Pergamon Press, 1979), p. 8. (Hereafter "Kemeny report.")

It also included the major NRC-sponsored study: "The one theme that runs through the conclusions we have reached is that the principal deficiencies in commercial reactor safety today are not hardware problems, *they are management problems.* These problems cannot be solved by the addition of a few pipes or valves. . . . *The most serious problems will be solved only by fundamental changes in the industry* and the NRC." Mitchell Rogovin and George T. Frampton, Jr., *Three Mile Island: A Report to the Commissioners and to the Public*, 2 vols. (Washington, D.C.: U.S. Nuclear Regulatory Commission, 1980), vol. 1, p. 89. (Emphasis supplied.) (Hereafter "Rogovin report.")

3. Institutions at a particular moment are a shifting residue of history, and lags in adjustment are important. . . . Ideas about appropriate behavior ordinarily change gradually through the development of experience and the elaboration of worldviews. Such processes tend to result in significant lags in the adjustment of institutions to their environments. The lags, in turn, make institutional history somewhat jerky and sensitive to major shocks that lead . . . to occasional periods of rapid change." James G. March and Johan P. Olsen, *Rediscovering Institutions* (New York: Free Press, MacMillan, Inc., 1989), pp. 168, 171.

4. Edwin Kintner, "After TMI-2: A Decade of Change." Speech delivered to American Nuclear Society meeting, 31 October 1988.

5. See Joseph G. Morone and Edward J. Woodhouse, *The Demise of Nuclear Energy* (New Haven: Yale University Press, 1989), pp. 47–52.

6. Rebecca Lowen, "Entering the Atomic Power Race: Science, Industry, and Government," *Political Science Quarterly* 102 (1987): 459–79.

7. Elizabeth Rolph, *Nuclear Power and Public Safety* (Lexington, Mass.: Lexington Books, D. C. Heath and Company, 1979), pp. 55–58.

8. U.S. Congress, House Committee on Energy and Commerce, Subcommittee on Energy Conservation and Power, Nuclear Reactor Safety, 99th Cong., 2d sess., 22 May 1986, testimony of Stephen J. Sweeney, Boston Edison CEO, pp. 269–75. (Emphasis supplied.)

9. Asked whether anyone had given any thought to how the utility industry would approach the operation of a nuclear power plant, a longtime industry executive, former Detroit Edison CEO Walter J. McCarthy, answered: "No one foresaw the complexity of modern-day nuclear power operations. . . . The feeling was that this new technology would just replace the boiler in a coil-fired plant. The immense difference between running a nuclear power plant and a conventional plant was never dreamed of." INPO *Review* (1 October 1989).

10. Philip Selznick, *The Moral Commonwealth: Social Theory and the Promise of Community* (Berkeley and Los Angeles: University of California Press, 1992), p. 321.

11. Ibid., pp. 321–22.

12. Kemeny report, pp. 22–23.

13. INPO, Maintenance Superintendent Workshop Proceedings and Discussions, 17–19 October 1982 (Atlanta: INPO, 1982), p. 135. Likewise,

INPO President Zack Pate stated: "Most of the industry's safety problems stem from the need for better training and just plain old management involvement." James Cook, "INPO's Race against Time," *Forbes*, 24 February 1986, p. 58.

14. INPO, "Foremost Safety and Reliability Issues," May 1983.

In TMI's case, for example, there were no direct reporting channels between the nuclear plant and top corporate management. With three organizational levels separating the on-site nuclear plant manager from the off-site president of the nuclear operating company, in effect the president was insulated from nuclear plant operations by three layers of bureaucracy, with all that that means for impeding effective communications between top management and plant officials. As a result of the accident, now the plant manager reports directly to the president of GPU Nuclear. Hyman G. Rickover, "An Assessment of the GPU Nuclear Corporation Organization and Senior Management and Its Competence to Operate TMI-1" (19 November 1983), p. 2. (Hereafter "GPU assessment.") The report was commissioned after the TMI accident by TMI's parent company, GPU Corporation, in order to evaluate GPU's organizational competence for managing and operating nuclear plants.

15. W. S. Lee, speech delivered at the 1981 INPO CEO Workshop, Atlanta, Georgia, 31 August–1 September 1981, p. 12.

16. He continues: "This lesson is not new. The Kemeny and Rogovin reports and many others shared it. . . . Full understanding of this lesson, however, is still incomplete." Philip R. Clark, "TMI Plus Five, Looking beyond the Lessons: A Utility Manager's Perspective," *Nuclear News*, April 1984, p. 63.

17. Quoted in David F. Salisbury, "Meeting Nuclear Energy's Challenge," *Christian Science Monitor*, 1 March 1984. Most of this paragraph is drawn from this article.

18. GPU assessment, p. 2.

19. Donald W. McCarthy, speech to INPO CEO Workshop, Atlanta, Georgia, 12 November 1986, p. 67.

20. He goes on:

You have to understand that in the fossil fuel plant, if something goes wrong with a boiler, you can shut it down, let it cool off, walk right in, inspect the pipes, and replace whatever doesn't look right. All that doesn't cost you much money. So you can afford to run things until they fail. That's no good for a nuclear plant. The potential consequences of a breakdown are too great. And if something breaks in a nuclear plant you can't just walk in and fix it like a coal fired plant. The damn thing is so radioactive people can't approach it. Everything has to be done with remote instrumentation. You're going to be down for months fixing the problem. And you're losing a million bucks a day. So in a nuclear plant things have to be done right. And they have to be done right the first time. And if anything might go wrong, you better find out what it is before you send it back into operation. You really have to treat a nuclear plant differently.

Reed is quoted in "Reactivity Management at Commonwealth Edison," *Nuclear Professional* (Winter 1990), p. 13.

Making a similar point, former NRC chairman John Ahearne observed: "Many of the problems that afflict the nuclear industry in the United States arose because the people making management decisions in the nuclear utilities were bright lawyers, accountants, and businessmen, but poor engineers." U.S. Congress, Senate Subcommittee on Nuclear Regulation, Committee on Environment and Public Works, testimony of John Ahearne, 99th Cong., 1st sess., 27 June 1985, pp. 50–52.

21. "We note a preoccupation with regulations. . . . However, we are convinced that regulations alone cannot assure the safety of nuclear power plants. Indeed, once regulations become as voluminous and complex as those regulations now in place, they can serve as a negative factor in nuclear safety. The regulations are so complex that immense efforts are required by the utility, by its suppliers, and by the NRC to assure that regulations are complied with. The satisfaction of regulatory requirements is equated with safety. The Commission believes that it is an absorbing concern with safety that will bring about safety—not just the meeting of narrowly prescribed and complex regulations." Kemeny report, p. 9.

22. U.S. Congress, Senate Subcommittee on Nuclear Regulation, Committee on Environment and Public Works, testimony of Thomas Pigford, 99th Cong., 1st sess., 27 June 1985, p. 89.

23. GPU assessment, p. 8. (Emphasis supplied.)

24. U.S. Nuclear Regulatory Commission, "Diagnostic Evaluation Team Report for the Dresden Nuclear Power Station," 25 November 1987, p. 21.

25. Kemeny report, p. 10.

26. Rogovin report, vol. 1, p. 89.

27. Kemeny report, p. 68.

28. "We found that in the past the NRC and the industry have done almost nothing to evaluate systematically the operation of existing reactors, pinpoint potential safety problems, and eliminate them." Rogovin report, vol. 1, p. 95.

29. "The structure of the nuclear industry has not been conducive to the effective sharing and integration of operating data," as one TMI accident study put it. Ibid., p. 96.

30. William S. Lee, "Management Involvement." Speech delivered at 1983 INPO CEO Workshop, Atlanta, Georgia, 22 September 1983, p. 6.

31. T. H. Pigford, "The Management of Nuclear Safety: A Review of TMI after Two Years," *Nuclear News* (3 March 1981), p. 42. To illustrate, consider these examples drawn from a lengthy list of training-related problems uncovered by the TMI investigations: (1) NRC standards provide for a shallow level of operator training. Even so, the TMI training program tended to concentrate on the narrow objective of getting the operators successfully through the NRC operator examination. Kemeny report, p. 49; GPU assessment, p. 12. (2) The place of training in the TMI organization was not high. For example, there was only a small commitment of physical resources and operator time to training. Furthermore, the seven-person training organization reported to the superintendent of TMI, competing for his attention with all of the problems of operating a site with 219 em-

ployees. GPU assessment, p. 12. (3) Operational considerations prevented as much as 50 percent of the scheduled attendance at training lectures; those not attending were assigned take-home packages for self-study. GPU assessment, p. 12. (4) "Operators were exposed to training material but they certainly were not trained." For instance, training was not directed at the skills and knowledge needed to satisfy job requirements. Nor did the training process measure the capabilities of the operators. Rather, the TMI training process took an approach to learning that bore little relation to actual plant procedures. U.S. Congress, Senate Subcommittee on Nuclear Regulation, Committee on Environment and Public Works, testimony of Mitchell Rogovin, 98th Cong., 2d sess., 27 June 1984, pp. 4–5.

Nor were these training problems limited to TMI. According to the nuclear industry's own assessment, issued in 1983, training-related problems "have broad applicability among nuclear utilities" and point up one of the "foremost safety and reliability issues confronting the industry." Some examples:

—Frequently, training is not completed and qualification is not verified prior to assignment of work that is not directly supervised.
—Excessive reliance is placed on unstructured "on-the-job" training.
—Licensed operator training concentrates on the licensing examination rather than the overall job.
—Lessons learned from operating experience are not being incorporated into training programs.

INPO, "Foremost Safety and Reliability Issues," 31 May 1983.

32. See chapter 8.

33. Zack Pate, "Professionalism and Conservative Decisionmaking." Speech delivered at 1989 INPO CEO Conference, 3 November 1989, p. 62.

34. Zack T. Pate, "Professionalism in Operations." Speech delivered at 1987 INPO CEO Conference, Atlanta, Georgia, 4–6 November 1987, p. 23.

Chapter 3

1. Remarks by Senator Abraham Ribicoff, *Congressional Record*, 93rd Cong., 2d sess., 13 August 1974, p. s14869. Quoted in the Union of Concerned Scientists, *Safety Second: The NRC and America's Nuclear Power Plants* (Bloomington: Indiana University Press, 1987), p. 5.

2. The NRC is a five-member commission. The commissioners, who are appointed by the president and confirmed by the Senate, serve staggered five-year terms. The commissioners' major responsibility is to oversee the administration of the agency, not unlike an active board of directors of a business corporation. With headquarters in the Washington, D.C., area, the agency also has five regional offices. In 1992, the agency employed 3,335 persons and had an annual budget of approximately $512 million.

3. Elizabeth Rolph, *Nuclear Power and Public Safety* (Lexington, Mass.: Lexington Books, 1979), p. 155.

4. Ibid.

5. Quoted in George T. Mazuzan and J. Samuel Walker, *Controlling the Atom* (Berkeley: University of California Press, 1985), p. 61.

6. Ibid.

7. Ibid., pp. 61–62.

8. Ibid., p. 87.

9. Note the "two generations" of the engineering safety approach. See Mazuzan and Walker, *Controlling the Atom*, pp. 61–62, for the first generation; for the second, see Joseph G. Morone and Edward J. Woodhouse, *The Demise of Nuclear Energy: Lessons for Democratic Control of Technology* (New Haven: Yale University Press, 1989).

10. Richard G. Hewlett and Francis Duncan, *Nuclear Navy* (Chicago: University of Chicago Press, 1974).

11. See Morone and Woodhouse, *The Demise of Nuclear Energy*, pp. 34–42.

12. Hewlett and Duncan, *Nuclear Navy*, pp. 240–42.

13. Mazuzan and Walker, *Controlling the Atom*, p. 91.

14. Ibid.

15. Ibid., p. 69.

16. Thomas Pigford, "The Management of Nuclear Safety: A Review of TMI after Two Years," *Nuclear News*, March 1981, pp. 47–48.

17. For a detailed discussion of the NRC's regulatory methods, particularly its emphasis on going by the book, see Elizabeth Nichols and Aaron Wildavsky, *Safer Power: Understanding and Improving Organizational Design, Human Performance, and Governmental Regulation in Nuclear Power Plants* (draft, July 1992).

18. Kemeny report, p. 64. (Emphasis supplied.)

19. NRC, NUREG-1355, "The Status of Recommendations of the President's Commission on the Accident at Three Mile Island," March 1989, p. 20.

20. NRC, *1987 Annual Report* (Washington, D.C.: U.S. Government Printing Office, 1987), p. 29. See also NRC, "Briefing on Diagnostic Evaluation Program," 23 November 1988.

21. NRC, SECY-90–189, "Reevaluation of the Systematic Assessment of Licensee Performance (SALP) Program," 25 May 1990, p. 4.

22. NRC, NUREG-1355, "Status of Recommendations," pp. 41–42.

23. NRC, "Systematic Assessment of Licensee Performance," chapter NRC-0516 in *NRC Manual* (Washington, D.C.: U.S. NRC, 1986).

24. NRC, NUREG-1395, "Industry Perceptions of the Impact of the U.S. Nuclear Regulatory Commission on Nuclear Power Plant Activities (Draft Report)," March 1990.

25. Ibid., p. 13.

26. Ibid., p. xix.

27. NRC, "Systematic Assessment of Licensee Performance," from 1990 NRC Inspection Manual.

28. Thomas W. Lippman, "Is Industry Usurping NRC Functions?" *Washington Post*, 26 March 1990.

29. Kemeny report, p. 64.

30. See NRC NUREG 737, "Clarification of TMI Action Plan Requirements" (November 1980), Item I.B.1.

31. NRC, "Guidelines for Utility Management Structure and Technical Resources," NUREG-0731 (19 September 1980).

32. NRC, NUREG-0988, August 1983. (Emphasis supplied.)

33. Public Law 97-425, Section 306.

34. NRC, "Policy Statement on Training and Qualifications of Nuclear Power Plant Personnel," SECY 85-1 (31 December 1984), p. 33.

35. *Federal Register,* 7 January 1992, p. 537.

36. Ibid.

37. *Federal Register,* 8 December 1989, p. 5061.

38. NRC, SECY-91-110, "Staff Evaluation and Recommendation on Maintenance Rulemaking" (26 April 1991). Also see "Maintenance Policy Statement: Advice But No Enforcement?" *Nucleonics Week,* 9 May 1991; "Commission to Get Staff Recommendation against Maintenance Rule," *Inside N.R.C.,* 22 April 1991. Although the commission did vote (3 to 2) for a maintenance rule that establishes performance (not programmatic) standards for nuclear plant maintenance programs, the NRC also seems well on its way to embracing INPO's maintenance program—how these programs should be managed and operated—as an industry standard. NRC, "Monitoring the Effectiveness of Maintenance at Nuclear Plants," *Federal Register,* 10 July 1991, p. 31306.

39. To coordinate their respective regulatory activities, the NRC and INPO have thus signed a formal "Memorandum of Agreement." It states (in part):

> This memorandum between the U.S. Nuclear Regulatory Commission (NRC) and the Institute of Nuclear Power Operations (INPO) reflects the desire for a continuing and cooperative relationship in the exchange of experience, information, and data related to the safety of nuclear power plants.
>
> The NRC has statutory responsibility for licensing and regulating nuclear facilities. . . . INPO is an organization sponsored by the nuclear utility industry whose mission is to promote the highest levels of safety and reliability in the operation of nuclear electric generating plants. As such, NRC and INPO undertake mutual and complementary activities, as defined in appendices to this Agreement. These appendices will help ensure that the goals of both organizations are achieved in the most efficient and effective manner without diminishing or interfering with the responsibilities and authorities of the NRC and the goals of INPO.

"Memorandum of Agreement between the Institute of Nuclear Power Operations and the U.S. Nuclear Regulatory Commission" (20 October 1988), p. 1.

For example, the Agreement includes a subsection titled "NRC Recognition of the INPO Evaluation Program," which states (in part): "NRC intends to recognize INPO evaluations and, in those areas deemed appropriate, to minimize NRC-sponsored evaluations or appraisals that duplicate INPO evaluations." "Appendix Number Two: Coordination Plan for NRC/INPO Appraisal and Evaluation Activities," p. 2.

40. As the TMI accident vividly illustrated, the nuclear industry was failing to collect and evaluate operational experience, so that each utility

could learn from the operating experience of other utilities. The industry, in short, had an information problem. (See chapters 2 and 7.) In response, the NRC approved in December 1980 the development of the "Integrated Operational Experience Reporting System." NRC, SECY 80-507 (November 1980). It included two principal features: the collection of detailed technical descriptions of significant events and the collection of nuclear plant hardware reliability data. In the end, however, the NRC deferred rulemaking and acknowledged INPO's information collection system. In 1982, the NRC recognized the INPO Significant Events Analysis and Information Network program (SEE-IN) by issuing Generic Letter No. 82–04. The NRC recognized INPO's Nuclear Plant Reliability Data System (NPRDS) in July 1983. See 48 *Federal Register,* p. 33850.

Chapter 4

1. Lelan F. Sillin, Jr., "Follow-up on INPO Programs." Speech delivered to INPO CEO Conference, Atlanta, Georgia, 22 September 1983, pp. 1, 5. (Emphasis supplied.)

2. *American Heritage Dictionary,* Second College Edition, s.v. "conscience."

3. Al Barker, quoted in "Plain Talk on the Institutional Plan," INPO *Review,* Fall 1983, p. 21.

4. William S. Lee, "Management Involvement." Speech delivered at the 1983 INPO CEO Workshop, Atlanta, Georgia, 22 September 1983, p. 6.

5. Rogovin report, vol. 1, p. 96.

6. William J. Lanouette, "Nuclear's Future after Three Mile Island," *National Journal,* 12 January 1980.

7. These regulatory activities eventually gave rise to the TMI Action Plan, which resulted in a total of 13,264 items to be implemented by nuclear plant licensees. NRC, Annual Report 1989, p. 33.

8. INPO, "1981 CEO Conference Proceedings," Atlanta, Georgia, 31 August–1 September, p. 105.

9. Lelan F. Sillin, Jr., "Follow-up on INPO Programs," speech delivered at 1983 INPO CEO Workshop, Atlanta, Georgia, 22 September 1983, p. 4.

10. Pat Haggerty, speech delivered to 1983 INPO CEO Conference, Atlanta, Georgia, 21–23 September, p. 22.

11. The TMI accident, according to an authoritative industry report, "served as a principal motivation for the INPO initiative": "[As a result of TMI, the] nuclear utility industry recognized that *all nuclear power facilities are affected by the performance at any one facility.* This understanding encouraged all U.S. nuclear utilities operating and building nuclear power facilities *to join together* and commit themselves to strive for standards of excellence as determined by INPO." Utility Nuclear Power Oversight Committee, "Leadership in Achieving Operational Excellence," August 1986, p. 2. (Emphasis supplied.) (Hereafter "Leadership in Achieving Operational Excellence.")

12. INPO, *Institutional Plan* (Atlanta: INPO, 1990), p. 5.

13. Zack Pate, "Closing Remarks" delivered to 1986 INPO CEO Conference, Atlanta, Georgia, 12–14 November 1986, p. 71. (Emphasis supplied.) INPO's "primary goal" and the "cornerstone of all it undertakes,"

according to the Institute's 1981 Annual Report, is to "reduce the probability of a serious nuclear plant accident. . . . Members and participants can be assured that INPO will concentrate on that primary goal as a cornerstone of all its undertakings."

14. INPO, "Plain Talk on the Institutional Plan: A Candid Account from Two Executive Committee Members," *Review,* October 1983, p. 22.

15. An INPO official describes this problem from another perspective. "The utility CEOs and president had heard about INPO, of course, because they were involved in its formulation. But what about the rest of their organization. 'Hey, what is INPO? Who are these people looking over our shoulder? We've got enough to do down here. We've got the NRC to worry about and the public utilities commissions. Hey, who are these INPO guys.' And even though we had the support of the CEOs (at least up front and on paper) we still had to earn our spurs. We did not come in with instant credibility and clout."

16. INPO *Review,* October 1989, p. 5.

17. "A lot of people," another industry official observes, "resented having to expend additional resources, that were above and beyond the regulatory process, because of INPO. . . . That was the utilities' biggest concern, having to go out and expend a lot of capital and O and M [operations and maintenance] dollars installing things they never had in before, because what they had there on the plant right now met the regulations."

18. Another industry official makes a similar point in these terms: "If you were being regulated or evaluated you would want to be evaluated by someone who you know has been there and has experienced your problems and the challenges that you face rather than someone who comes from a different culture, like the navy, and doesn't really understand your way of life."

19. INPO, Plant Managers Workshop Proceedings (1982).

20. Philip Selznick, *TVA and the Grass Roots: A Study of Politics and Organization* (1949; reprint ed., Berkeley and Los Angeles: University of California Press, 1984), p. 13.

21. Leonard Broom and Philip Selznick, *Sociology: A Text with Adapted Readings,* 5th ed. (New York: Harper and Row, 1973), p. 228.

22. INPO, Institutional Plan (1990), p. 3. As INPO's by-laws state, "The affairs and activities of the Institute shall be managed by or under the direction of the Board of Directors *which shall have all the powers and duties necessary or appropriate for the administration of such affairs and activities."* INPO, "Certificate of Incorporation and Bylaws," March 1987, p. 8.

23. INPO, "Looking Back on INPO's Early Years," *Review,* Fall 1989, p. 39. (Emphasis supplied.)

24. To help ensure its representativeness, elections are held each year. Further, board members are selected by a principle of sectoral representation, so to speak, thereby ensuring that each major "class" (INPO's term) of the nuclear industry is assured a seat on the board—nuclear plants owned by the federal government, nonfederal public agencies, electric cooperatives, and investor-owned corporations. See INPO, "Certificate of Incorporation and Bylaws," March 1987, pp. 1–3.

25. Lelan F. Sillin, Jr., "Follow-up on INPO Programs." Speech delivered at INPO CEO Conference, Atlanta, Georgia, 22 September 1983.

26. Quoted in INPO *Review,* Winter 1984, p. 23. (Emphasis supplied.)

27. Gregg M. Taylor, "INPO at Age Five: Setting Benchmarks of Excellence," *Nuclear News* (October 1984), p. 67.

28. Another review group member describes their role in similar terms: "We give the full-time INPO people guidance—how they are doing, whether they are looking at the right things or not. If there were areas they need to improve in. Basically, we evaluate how well INPO is doing their job. . . . For example, we went out with INPO on three different plant evaluations to see how they functioned. Were they consistently applying the standards that we'd set and endorsed? . . . We found a couple of areas for improvement. But nothing significant. They were looking at the critical items associated with the operation of nuclear stations."

29. W. G. Counsil, remarks delivered at INPO 1982 CEO Workshop, Proceedings, Atlanta, Georgia, 3–5 October 1982, pp. 185–86.

30. INPO, *1991 Annual Report,* p. 24.

31. INPO, *1990 Annual Report,* p. 6.

32. INPO, "The Peer-to-Peer Point of View," *Review,* April 1985, pp. 12–16. (Emphasis supplied.) As another peer evaluator puts it in another INPO story: "One of the benefits of serving as a peer was seeing how INPO does business. The process was more open than I thought it would be— issues were discussed in a candid and professional manner. I learned a lot about evaluations, and I was impressed with the depth of the discussions and amount of research. The evaluation process definitely makes more sense, and the role INPO is supposed to play in the industry makes more sense." INPO, "Information Exchange," *Review,* Summer 1991, p. 4.

33. INPO, "Information Interchange," *Review,* Summer 1991, p. 3.

34. INPO, "The Peer-to-Peer Point of View," *Review,* April 1985, p. 16.

35. More precisely, in 1991 there were 57 loaned employees at INPO's Atlanta headquarters, which brings the total number of loanees, past and present, to 428. INPO, *1991 Annual Report,* p. 25.

36. INPO, "A Loan That Pays Dividends," *Review* (Summer 1990), p. 23. (Emphasis supplied.)

37. INPO, *1991 Annual Report,* p. 25. According to INPO's vice president: "Forty-seven INPO employees have served on reverse loan. That's 20 percent of INPO's permanent nuclear technical work force. Most of these reverse loan assignments have occurred in the last few years, including one plant manager, one operations manager, seven training managers, three outage managers, five health physics or chemistry managers, and seven engineering or support managers." Terence J. Sullivan, "Building the Future—INPO's Role in the 1990s," INPO 1991 CEO Conference, p. 67.

38. INPO, "One Stop Shops," *Review* (Fall/Winter 1989), p. 27.

39. INPO's rate formula works as follows. In 1991, a nuclear utility paid INPO $120,292 for each "rating point." Each utility, in turn, was charged two rating points as a member, plus two points for each of their nuclear plants, plus one point for each operating reactor. If, for instance, the utility had one nuclear plant with two operating reactors, its total bill would be about $721,000.

40. James Q. Wilson, *Bureaucracy: What Government Agencies Do and Why They Do It* (New York: Basic Books, 1989), p. 95.

41. Ibid., p. 96.

42. Richard G. Hewlett and Francis Duncan, *Nuclear Navy* (Chicago: University of Chicago Press, 1974), p. 359.

43. Pate's duties included overseeing, coordinating, and guiding the navy's evaluation program for more than a hundred nuclear submarine and surface ship power plants. What is more, Pate was chosen to command the navy's first Trident-class nuclear submarine, though, because of construction delays, he retired before the first Trident submarine was commissioned.

44. Quoted in Norman Polmar and Thomas B. Allen's *Rickover* (New York: Simon and Schuster, 1982), pp. 315–16.

45. INPO, *Institutional Plan* (Atlanta: INPO, 1990), p. 5.

46. GPU assessment, p. 1. (Emphasis supplied.)

47. James D. Watkins, speech delivered to 1989 CEO Conference, Atlanta, Georgia, 1 November 1989, pp. 36–38.

48. INPO, *Institutional Plan*, p. 10. (Emphasis supplied.)

Chapter 5

1. A brief discussion of what I mean by industrial morality may be in order. In a classic work on the theory of organizations, Chester Barnard once wrote about a manufacturer that "was engaged in producing a certain type of vehicle of very high quality, using the best materials and a high grade of precision workmanship":

> It was decided to produce the same type of vehicle by mass production methods, using materials of lower quality and less precision in mechanical work. The manufacturer attempted to do this in the same plant, merely lowering standards and using some new machines, but with the same organization. The attempt was a failure. *The old organization simply could not produce effectively with lower standards,* so that finally a new plant in a distant city with a new organization was set up to produce the cheaper product. Note that this was not a case where new skills had to be learned. In general, less skill and less time were required. *The acceptance of lower standards was morally repugnant.*

Chester I. Barnard, "Elementary Conditions of Business Morals," *California Management Review* 1 (Fall 1958): 9. (Emphasis supplied.)

What this example illustrates, according to Barnard, is the "reality of the moral factor in much work commonly regarded as merely technical." He was referring to what many writers now call "organization culture," while others have variously characterized this form of normative ordering as an "internal morality" (see Lon Fuller, *The Morality of Law,* rev. ed. [New Haven: Yale University Press, 1969], pp. 33–94); a "practice" (see Alasdair MacIntyre, *After Virtue,* 2d ed. [Notre Dame: University of Notre Dame Press, 1984], pp. 187–96); and, most recently, as "norms of appropriateness" (see March and Olsen, *Rediscovering Institutions*).

Whatever the label, the general idea is an ancient one, dating back to the post-Homeric Greeks, who believed that "excellence is to be judged in terms of the standards established within and for some specific form of activity. . . . The concept of the best, of the perfected, provides each of these forms of activity with the good toward which those who participate in it move." Alasdair MacIntyre, *Whose Justice? Whose Rationality?* (Notre Dame: University of Notre Dame Press, 1988), 30–31. Take the "practice" of baseball as an example. "A practice involves standards of excellence and obedience to rules. . . . To enter into a practice is to accept the authority of those standards and the inadequacy of my own performance as judged by them. It is to subject my own attitudes, choices, preferences and tastes to the standards which . . . define the practice. . . . We cannot be initiated into a practice without accepting *the authority of the best standards realized so far*. . . . If, on starting to play baseball, I do not accept that others know better than I when to throw a fast ball and when not, I will never learn to appreciate good pitching, let alone to pitch." MacIntyre, *After Virtue*, p. 190. (Emphasis supplied.)

What makes baseball a practice, as these comments suggest, is that "individual excellence depends on *collectively maintained* codes of honor and discipline." Robert Bellah et al., *The Good Society* (New York: Alfred A. Knopf, 1991), p. 40. (Emphasis supplied.) Baseball is an institution, in other words, and at the core of any viable institution there is a "moral code" that gives shape to collective and individual experience by "providing the standards in terms of which each person recognizes the excellence of his or her achievements. . . . If the ideals embodied in an institution are not totally dead, they stand as a judgment against the corruption of their embodiment." Ibid., pp. 40–41.

Likewise, these ideals were far from dead among the workers in Barnard's example. The reality of the moral factor, alive and well, shaped their individual and collective expectations and moved them to resist lower standards of quality. What seems to be a merely technical matter thus turns out to actually involve standards of excellence that "provide criteria for what is worth striving for, and what is accounted as good reasons for actions." March and Olsen, *Rediscovering Institutions*, p. 161.

2. INPO, "The Development of Prospective Nuclear Plant Managers and Middle Managers" (Atlanta: INPO, 1988).

3. Ibid., p. i.

4. Ibid.

5. The list includes, for instance, the technical ability to assess the effectiveness of the plant's radiological protection program in minimizing worker and public exposure to radiation, the managerial ability to determine the appropriate management style for particular individuals and situations, and the moral commitment to the achievement of high standards. Ibid.

6. See p. 21.

7. See p. 30.

8. Rickover demonstrated "an intense concern for safety": "Since his first days at Oak Ridge . . . in 1946, Rickover had been aware of the dangers of radioactive materials and understood the exceptional emotional and political impact which a minor accident could have. From his experience

with the fleet he . . . realized that one major accident on a nuclear ship, especially if it caused damage or injury to the public, could jeopardize the use of nuclear power in the Navy." Hewlett and Duncan, *Nuclear Navy,* p. 342.

9. GPU assessment.

10. Ibid., pp. 1, 4. (Emphasis supplied.)

11. Ibid., p. 2.

12. Ibid., p. 4.

13. Ibid., p. 6. An internal morality, as Selznick writes, "is the set of standards that must be honored if the distinctive mission of an institution or a practice is to be achieved." "In a sense," he adds, "every developed craft has its own morality, which consists of the virtues that must be cultivated if standards of craftsmanship are to be met. The master virtue is commitment to excellence." Philip Selznick, *Moral Commonwealth,* pp. 714–15.

14. GPU assessment, pp. 1–2. (Emphasis supplied.)

15. Ibid., p. 2. (Emphasis supplied.)

16. Ibid.

So what would happen if a management is *not* imbued with one or more of these principles? How would that affect its ability to operate a nuclear plant safely and dependably? Consider two examples drawn from the NRC's "problem list," an annual inventory of the nation's half-dozen or so most dangerous plants.

Commonwealth Edison's Dresden plant was deeply troubled in 1987. And it was clear to all involved that one of the major reasons stemmed from the fact that Dresden's management was not expected or encouraged to do more than merely meet regulatory requirements. They were not imbued with the principle of rising standards, in Rickover's idiom, and were not striving to meet or exceed the best practices in the industry. "The fundamental or root causes of Dresden's poor performance history were attributed to . . . [an] attitude and approach that had not been devoted at achieving or maintaining a high standard of safety performance. Such a level of performance was not demanded, not funded, and not established as a way of life. Instead a . . . climate flourished where the minimum was good enough; if it is not required, don't do it; and fix it only when it's broken." NRC, "Diagnostic Evaluation Team Report for Dresden Nuclear Power Station" (6 November 1987), p. 21. This was one of several fundamental causes of Dresden's performance problems.

Now consider what can happen when management slights another part of nuclear power's industrial morality, the principle of technical self-sufficiency. It holds that a plant's decisionmaking managers should have expert analytical and engineering resources readily available within their own organization, and Florida Power and Light's Turkey Point management did not. That was the conclusion reached by a management consulting firm hired by the utility to diagnose Turkey Point's "history of persistent equipment and design problems." In the consultant's words: "One of the root causes leading to performance deficiencies at Turkey Point is *ineffective technical support.*" In fact, the deficiencies plaguing Turkey Point's operation were so severe—"missed schedules," "little proactive support," "less than satisfactory work quality, team work and communications," "lack of understanding of plant needs," "quick fixes . . . instead of effective long range solutions"—that the NRC almost ordered a halt to plant operations. ENERCON Services, Inc., "Independent Management Appraisal of Florida Power and Light's Turkey Point Units 3 and 4" (8 April 1989), pp. 37–39. (Emphasis supplied.)

These examples reinforce an important point. If there was a salient factor that put Dresden and Turkey Point on the nation's list of real problem plants, it had to do with the fact that their managements gave insufficient weight or consideration to what Rickover called the "principles of operation which are fundamental to all nuclear power activities." So what really led to incompetent and undependable operation at both plants, Rickover would conclude, was management's lack of motivation to act responsibly in light of those principles—in short, their lack of integrity.

17. Ross E. Cheit, *Setting Safety Standards: Regulation in the Public and Private Sectors* (Berkeley and Los Angeles: University of California Press, 1990), p. 5.

18. Ibid., p. 176.

19. INPO, "Leadership in Achieving Operational Excellence," August 1986, pp. 2–3.

20. Ibid., p. 11.

21. Ibid.

22. Ibid., p. 3.

23. Selznick, *Moral Commonwealth,* p. 60.

24. See Fuller, *Morality of Law,* chap. 1.

25. INPO, "Performance Objectives and Criteria for Operating and Near-Term Operating License Plants" (Atlanta: INPO, April 1987), p. i.

26. Grouped into two broad categories—one to evaluate a nuclear utility's corporate organization (26 objectives) and the other to assess a nuclear plant's performance (77 objectives)—there are 103 performance objectives. They are both mandatory and subjective; mandatory because all members of INPO are obligated to pursue them (and are evaluated accordingly by INPO inspectors); subjective because they are worded broadly and INPO inspectors must therefore exercise considerable judgment in their application. Suppose, for example, that you are an INPO inspector and that you must determine whether a utility's corporate practices do in fact serve to "ensure and enhance plant safety and reliability." Is the objective fully met? How safe is safe enough? Faced with questions such as these (and all the performance objectives raise similar sorts of questions), it is easy to see why, as INPO states, "considerable judgment is required" in applying the performance objectives. INPO, "Performance Objective and Criteria for Plant Evaluation" (Atlanta: INPO, January 1982), p. iii.

27. To cite but one example, take Rickover's principle of learning from experience—"An inability or unwillingness to learn from experience is intolerable in nuclear operations"—and compare with INPO's performance objective: "Industrywide and in-house operating experiences should be evaluated and appropriate actions undertaken to improve plant safety and reliability." INPO, "Performance Objectives and Criteria for

Operating and Near-Term Operating License Plants," April 1987, pp. 102–3.

28. "Deviation from any particular guideline would not in itself indicate a problem in plant operations. However, differences between the guidelines and the actual plant practice should be reviewed to determine if plant practice should be changed. A change to plant practices would be appropriate if a performance weakness were determined to exist." INPO, "Guidelines for the Conduct of Operations at Nuclear Stations," June 1985, p. 1.

29. "Before INPO," observes a nuclear utility vice president, "you didn't really have anywhere to turn to see who's doing better than anyone else in the industry." That soon changed, however, as a result of INPO's creation. INPO's president:

> The identification and sharing of best practices was one of INPO's assignments from the beginning. Early on, we thought it would be easy—not much more complicated than xeroxing documents and mailing them to our members. In fact, this has been one of our most difficult challenges. First, you have to have the experience and competence to recognize when a practice is really a good one. Second, it is important that people with a wide range of backgrounds agree that a practice is good before we offer it to our members. Different people from different utilities had quite different ideas about what constituted a Good Practice. . . . We rarely found Good Practices at a station that could be borrowed intact and disseminated to the industry. Instead, we found elements of Good Practices, and had to bring ideas from several plants back to Atlanta and put them together. Finally, to give them wide applicability and to ensure wide acceptance in the industry, we had to add in a considerable measure of experience and thought at INPO.

Zack Pate, remarks delivered at INPO 1982 CEO Workshop, Atlanta, Georgia, 3–5 October 1982, p. 49.

30. "The attached Good Practice provides a means to delineate responsibility within the operations department. It also provides basic standards for conducting routine operations department business. This Good Practice may be useful in the following ways:

> *original development of a procedure to guide the conduct of the operations department.

> *improve or enhance existing procedures that define the operations department's methods of conducting business." INPO, "Good Practice: Conduct of Operations," July 1984.

31. INPO also collects and disseminates industry good practices in two other ways. First of all, when INPO inspectors identify a good practice during an inspection, they must make a note of it in their evaluation report and enter that information into Nuclear Network, a computerized information system that links all nuclear utilities. Second, INPO receives nu-

merous telephone inquiries from industry officials as to which nuclear utilities have an exemplary program or procedure in a given area. Often, INPO has this information on file, and if not, INPO canvasses the industry for exemplary programs, asks for a copy, and sends it to the requesting utility.

32. "Good practices are provided to assist member utilities. They can be used as furnished, modified, or not used if an alternative approach is considered as good or better by the member utility." INPO, *Institutional Plan* (Atlanta: INPO, 1990), p. 7.

33. He continues: "Even if they don't have a problem that we call out as an issue [an official INPO finding that a problem exists], if we see an area and it looks like they can do a little better, we provide them with a copy of the good practice. 'This is an approach that has been effective at other stations. You may want to consider it.'"

34. Zack Pate, quoted in U.S. Nuclear Regulatory Commission, "Annual Briefing by INPO," 12 July 1988, pp. 16–17. (Emphasis supplied.)

35. As this example also shows, INPO's quest for the best maintenance standards included extensive industry participation, another salient feature of INPO rulemaking. Why? Because it "allows you to marshal more expertise," as a top INPO official puts it:

> When we write a standard, we do the best with the people we have at INPO. Then we send out the initial draft to a dozen or so leaders from the utilities who push it down in their organizations and get their guys to work on it. That way we've magnified our expertise a dozen times. For example, when we realized that we had to have corporate evaluations, I picked out nine leaders in the industry and I called them up and asked them to volunteer. *They were nine crackerjack people, some of the best in the industry,* and they formed an ad hoc group to give me input as to what we ought to put in the standards. We wrote the first draft at INPO, sent it to all of them, and got a lot of comments. After we went through several iterations, we finally developed a set of standards. Then we sent those standards out to all the utilities and told them to evaluate their corporate organization against the standards and tell us where you're weak. We went through iterations of that for three or four years before we finally honed down to a way of looking at a corporate organization's ability to monitor and support and take corrective action as required on discrepancies in its nuclear plants.

Thus, after several years, and after extensive industry participation, INPO promulgated its performance objectives and criteria for corporate evaluations.

Equally important, this extensive participation also allows INPO to marshal industry support for these standards. "One thing I'd like to make clear to you," says an INPO inspector, "is that those performance objectives and criteria were not developed by INPO. The driving force behind all the standards is the cumulative input from all the utilities. The utilities developed the standards by which they wished to be judged, and that's how the performance objectives and criteria came to be." While this over-states the industry's role, and understates INPO's, the essential point re-mains the same. Industry participation in the standards-making process leads to a sense of ownership among industry officials, a sense that the standards are home-grown, so to speak (especially compared to NRC regu-lations), and that enhances INPO's legitimacy as a community-based regu-lator in important ways. At the same time, however, it is also important to keep in mind how INPO establishes the orienting framework—the quest for the best—that sets industry participation on its distinctive course.

36. In thinking about the nuclear industry's normative unification from a broader perspective, we might notice how similar themes have been sounded by the new institutionalism in organizational analysis. This per-spective emphasizes that organizations are open systems strongly influ-enced by their environments, including, in some cases, industry-wide normative categories and practices. As Brint and Karabel write: "The stud-ies that comprise the new institutionalism in organizational studies are brought together chiefly . . . by a shared agreement that *much organiza-tional structure and change derives from efforts to create or conform to categories and practices [within the organization's institutional environ-ment] that give classificatory meaning to the social world."* Steven Brint and Jerome Karabel, "Institutional Origins and Transformations: The Case of American Community Colleges," in *The New Institutionalism in Orga-nizational Analysis,* ed. W. W. Powell and P. J. DiMaggio (Chicago: Univer-sity of Chicago Press, 1991), p. 336. (Emphasis supplied.)

Think of INPO's normative system in this light—as an industry-wide system of classification that gives meaning to, and shapes, the social world of nuclear power operations. Also note that insofar as an organization (such as a nuclear utility) patterns its formal structure after these norma-tive classifications in the institutional environment, it "demonstrates that it is acting on collectively valued purposes in a proper and adequate man-ner. . . . On the other hand, organizations that omit environmentally legiti-mated elements of structure or create unique structures lack acceptable legitimated accounts of their activities. Such organizations are more vul-nerable to claims that they are negligent, irrational, or unnecessary." John W. Meyer and Brian Rowan, "Institutionalized Organizations: Formal Structure as Myth and Ceremony," in *The New Institutionalism in Orga-nizational Analysis,* p. 50.

From this sociological perspective, moreover, we have in the nuclear industry's post-TMI normative transformation a prime example of how a "functional organizational field" or "societal sector" is constructed, in-cluding, most notably, how field-wide mechanisms—"mimetic" and "normative"—lead to "institutional isomorphism," in the terminology of sociologists DiMaggio and Powell. When organizations incorporate industry-wide institutional rules within their own structures, as DiMag-gio and Powell explain it, over time they become more homogeneous, in large part because the organizational field penetrates the organizations, thus "creating the lenses through which actors view the world and the very categories of structure, action, and thought." Paul J. DiMaggio and Walter W. Powell, "Introduction," *The New Institutionalism in Organizational Analysis*, p. 13.

On the concept of "institutional isomorphism," also see John W. Meyer and Brian Rowan, "Institutionalized Organizations: Formal Structure as Myth and Ceremony," in *The New Institutionalism in Organizational Analysis*, pp. 41–62. On "organizational field," see Paul J. DiMaggio and Walter W. Powell, "The Iron Cage Revisited: Institutional Isomorphism and Collective Rationality in Organization Fields," in *The New Institutionalism in Organizational Analysis*, pp. 64–65; and Paul J. DiMaggio, "Constructing an Organizational Field as a Professional Project: U.S. Art Museums, 1920–1940," in *The New Institutionalism in Organizational Analysis*, pp. 267–92. On "societal sector," see W. Richard Scott and John W. Meyer, "The Organization of Societal Sectors: Propositions and Early Evidence," in *The New Institutionalism in Organizational Analysis*, pp. 108–40. For a good review of this literature, see W. Richard Scott, *Organizations: Rational, Natural, and Open Systems*, 3d ed. rev. (Englewood Cliffs, N.J.: Prentice Hall, 1992).

37. Another way of saying this, following March and Olsen's terminology, is that INPO's normative system embodies a "logic of appropriateness": "To describe behavior as driven by rules is to see action as a matching of a situation to the demands of a position. Rules define relationships among roles in terms of what an incumbent of one role owes to incumbents of other roles. . . . *The terminology is one of duties and obligations*. . . . What is appropriate for a particular person in a particular situation is defined by political and social institutions and transmitted through socialization." March and Olsen, *Rediscovering Institutions*, p. 23. (Emphasis supplied.)

38. *Nucleonics Week* (15 February 1990).

39. Ibid. Several plants within the last year, Russell goes on to say, have begun to focus on the issue of INPO's role in rising O&M costs and costs associated with trying to win higher INPO ratings. "One of these years," Russell predicted, utility executives will band together and try to resist further demands from INPO and other organizations that increase costs. "It will come," Russell said. "It's being talked about."

As the article also reports: "One utility representative, during a discussion of O&M costs, said his management had decided that his utility could not afford the initiatives necessary to win a top rating from INPO and would settle for average or above average scores on its INPO evaluation."

> Mike Hill, manager of nuclear plant support at Carolina Power & Light . . . said the issue is how far the industry can go in pursuing excellence before it becomes noncompetitive and how to determine when a utility has achieved enough improvement in safety and performance. "I don't think anybody is in a position to stand up and say, 'We're excellence—we're good enough,'" Hill said. "I don't think we're able to define what is good enough or when excellence has been achieved. How much are we willing to pay for that increment of excellence? Nobody has defined that."

40. Still another industry official makes a similar point:

When INPO got started it was made up mostly of ex–nuclear navy people. The nuclear navy program has been run successfully for a number of years, but without some of the constraints and problems we face in the commercial nuclear industry. For instance, budget restrictions. The nuclear navy doesn't worry a lot about how much it costs to run a nuclear submarine. But we have to worry about what it costs to run a nuclear power plant. So the navy influence on INPO was let's do it this way, without regard to the costs, because this is the navy way.

Not that all industry officials are of one mind on this matter. Some utility officials, for example, taking issue with such complaints, argue that INPO's critics are too short-sighted on the cost question. As one industry official says:

Some utilities don't realize that the economics of nuclear power operation have to be viewed differently [from conventional power plants]. The most severe economic penalty in nuclear power is to get in trouble. Take some of the plants that are in trouble. These companies are paying a third of a million dollars a day every day the plant is out of service. If they spent the money on making the plant operate right in the first place, and stay in operation, they wouldn't have those problems. The economics are just different.

Another industry official makes a similar point:

In the navy the feeling is if something has to be done to maintain safety of the nuclear operation you do it. But you know, that's something the utilities have to accept; if something has to be done to maintain safety, you do it. As a matter of fact, you don't justify it only on a safety basis. You also can justify it on an economic basis. Because if you don't do it, you're likely to pay a price later on.

41. James D. Watkins, "Approaches to Nuclear Safety," *Public Utilities Fortnightly* (24 May 1990), p. 22. (Emphasis supplied.)

42. For a discussion of this matter in the context of learning from industry experience, see chapter 7.

Chapter 6

1. U.S. Congress, Senate Subcommittee on Nuclear Regulation, Committee on Environment and Public Works, 100th Cong., 1st sess., 8 October 1987, p. 313. In a 1983 speech to fellow nuclear utility CEOs, the chairman of INPO's board of directors explained the nature of INPO's enforcement mechanisms in similar terms. "How does it work when a utility is unresponsive and is not meeting its responsibilities to the whole industry. . . . That is the question the INPO called on me to address today. . . . In several forums, before the NRC . . . the financial community and the press, the question has arisen 'what will INPO do, or what will industry do, or what is the mechanism with which INPO has to deal for utilities that are unresponsive to the recommendations of INPO?' With consis-

tency, we have replied . . . knowledge of peer pressure." Lelan F. Sillin, Jr., speech delivered at the CEO Conference, Atlanta, Georgia, 22 September 1983.

INPO's *Institutional Plan* explains the central role of peer pressure in these terms: "In forming INPO, the nuclear utility industry took an unusual step. By committing to meet INPO's criteria and to implement improvements in response to INPO recommendations, the industry clearly established and accepted *a form of self-regulation by peer review*. . . . The nuclear industry . . . formed INPO and placed itself in the role of overseeing INPO activities, while at the same time endowing INPO with *ample authority to bring pressure for change on individual members.* That feature makes INPO unique." INPO, *Institutional Plan* (Atlanta: INPO, 1990), p. i. (Emphasis supplied.)

2. James Q. Wilson, *Bureaucracy* (New York: Basic Books, 1989), p. 46. (Emphasis supplied.)

3. U.S. Congress, House Subcommittee on Energy Research and Production, *Nuclear Safety Research and Development Act of 1980: Hearing on H.R. 7190,* statement of Admiral Eugene Wilkinson, 96th Cong., 2d sess., 19 June 1980, pp. 33–34. (Emphasis supplied.)

4. See INPO CEO Conference Topic, 21 September 1983.

5. *Leadership in Achieving Operational Excellence: The Challenge for All Nuclear Utilities* (Chicago: Utility Nuclear Power Oversight Committee, 1986). (Hereafter cited as "Sillin report.") The report's authors were Lelan Sillin, a retired nuclear utility CEO and former chairman of INPO's board of directors; Marcus Rowden, the first chairman of the NRC (who now works as an industry attorney in Washington, D.C.); and Admiral Eugene Wilkinson, INPO's first president (and the same person who five years earlier did not foresee any problems in terms of utility responsiveness to INPO directives).

6. "It was recognized by the industry leaders who commissioned this study that, despite the progress being made by the utility industry, not all utilities were contributing to this success nor were all meeting the commitment to excellence." It should come as no surprise, the report continued, "that the performance of some utilities is adversely shaping public as well as NRC perception of overall industry competence and performance. This fact reinforces the urgency for the U.S. nuclear utility industry to focus special attention on such utilities." Sillin report, pp. 12–13.

7. Ibid., p. 13.

8. Ibid., p. 14.

9. See, for example, Joseph Rees, *Reforming the Workplace* (Philadelphia: University of Pennsylvania Press, 1988), chap. 3.

10. The NRC's Special Inquiry Group on the TMI accident also recommended that INPO evaluations be linked to the industry's coinsurance plan: "If INPO is linked to a plan for coinsurance by a pool of utilities of the cost of replacement power that would have to be purchased by any one utility after a nuclear accident shut down its plant—so that a utility not receiving a passing grade from INPO's inspectors and auditors would be excluded from the coinsurance pool—this approach has some chance of success. We urge its rapid implementation." Rogovin report, vol. 1, p. 110.

Moreover, according to John Ahearne, an NRC commissioner at the time of INPO's creation, NRC commissioners were told by some industry officials that insurance and INPO would in fact be linked. U.S. Congress, Senate Subcommittee on Nuclear Regulation, Committee on Environment and Public Works, 99th Cong., 1st sess., 27 June 1985, pp. 61–62.

11. Since the early 1980s, the utilities do send a copy of their INPO evaluations to NEIL, and the better-performing utilities receive some form of credit on their premiums. Because the amounts involved are relatively insignificant, according to industry officials, their influence on nuclear safety has been negligible.

12. Hugh A. Barker, CEO, Public Service Company of Indiana, Inc., quoted in proceedings of INPO 1981 CEO Conference, Atlanta, Georgia, 31 August–1 September, pp. 93–94.

13. Sherwood Smith, quoted in proceedings of INPO 1981 CEO Conference, Atlanta, Georgia, 31 August–1 September, p. 75. (Emphasis supplied.)

14. U.S. Congress, Senate Subcommittee on Nuclear Regulation, Committee on Environment and Public Works, testimony of John F. Ahearne, 99th Cong., 1st sess., 27 June 1985, p. 62.

15. Lelan F. Sillin, INPO CEO Conference Proceedings (22 September 1983).

16. We should also remember that Admiral Rickover promoted a very different view of the CEO's role. "It is extremely important that senior management become technically informed and be personally familiar with conditions at the operating plant." GPU assessment, p. 2. In effect, the Sillin report championed the nuclear navy's approach, which is not surprising given the fact that Rickover's protégé, Admiral Eugene Wilkinson, coauthored the report.

17. "INPO should insist on the involvement of the chief executive officer . . . of each member utility in the review of [INPO] evaluation results and in the utility's responses to the concerns noted in the evaluation." Sillin report, p. 16.

18. "INPO should assure that the chief executive officer provide a copy to and review its plant evaluation report with the utility's governing board." Sillin report, p. 16. To this end, each INPO inspection report now contains this message to the CEO: "In keeping with the INPO response and commitment to the UNPOC report, Leadership in Achieving Operational Excellence—The Challenge for All Nuclear Utilities, *each CEO is strongly urged to furnish the attached information to his Board of Directors.*" (Emphasis supplied.)

19. Another nuclear utility executive makes a similar point:

The most valuable function of INPO performance indicators is that it allows you to compare your plant's performance with other similar plants and measure how well you're performing. Absent that, you had no way of really questioning your performance on various parameters. Was it too low? Too high? But now you can pick from dozens of other plants of very similar design and vintage and actually compare parameter by parameter your operation against others. The indicators are also useful for spotting problems. If, for example, you're shipping a great deal more radioactive water than similar plants, the indicators immediately focuses your attention on that. If you're not equal to the industry averages, it gives you a place to begin looking for difficulties.

20. He goes on, "At Public Service Electric and Gas, we do set performance targets for each indicator. When performance in an area does not meet our expectations, we attempt to identify the specific problems that must be overcome, and, if appropriate, we adjust our work practices to remedy these problems." It is also worth noting the pathological side of performance indicators. Again, nuclear utility CEO James Ferland:

> We have become very aware that overemphasis on individual indicators can lead to undesirable results. Each of us in this room can be sure that if we overemphasize a particular performance area, our innovative personnel will find some way to march toward this goal—possibly at the expense of other activities that may be more important in the long run. Overemphasis of a particular indicator can lead to "managing the indicator" rather than managing the plant. As an example, in an attempt to reduce radiation exposure, one utility significantly cut back operator rounds in areas where high doses would occur. This resulted in significant areas of the plant not being regularly inspected, allowing equipment reliability to degrade.

James Ferland, "Use of Performance Indicators: 1990 and Beyond" (1989 INPO CEO Workshop Proceedings, Atlanta, Georgia, 1–3 November, pp. 70–71).

21. INPO, "INPO Responses to the August 1986 Report Leadership in Achieving Operational Excellence" (31 August 1986).

In promoting excellence, said INPO's president, "the use of . . . performance indicators is wholly consistent with INPO's mission." INPO president Zack Pate, quoted in proceedings of INPO 1985 CEO Workshop, Atlanta, Georgia, 20–22 November, p. 30. Explaining how, the chairman of INPO's board of directors went on to observe that performance indicators "should *foster a spirit of competition* and assist in positive reinforcement for nuclear professionals—they should build pride." "The goals you set using performance data," he added, "should *stretch your organization to strive for INPO's standards* of excellence." INPO's chairman of the board, Lelan Sillin, quoted in proceedings of INPO 1984 CEO Workshop, Atlanta, Georgia, 28–30 November 1984, p. 47. (Emphasis supplied.)

If we turn from how this yardstick competition looks now to where it may be heading, it is fair to say that, like the Olympics, it is becoming an international tournament: "Since 1987, all of INPO's international participants with operating units have participated in the international performance indicator program. In 1990, that process expanded with adoption of an international set of indicators and definitions by the World Association of Nuclear Operators (WANO)." INPO, *1990 Annual Report* (Atlanta: INPO, 1990), p. 27.

22. March and Olson, *Rediscovering Institutions,* p. 60.

23. To be more specific, in 1985 and 1990 INPO had each nuclear plant set five-year (1990 and 1995) performance goals for most of the indicators. Those individual plant goals, in turn, were averaged to determine industry-wide five-year performance goals, thus setting the stage for what might be called a "yardstick competition" or "regulatory tournament" among the industry's nuclear plants. See Ian Ayres and John Braithwaite, *Responsive Regulation* (New York: Oxford University Press, 1992), pp. 141–42.

24. "INPO should establish an assessment category that identifies the industry standard of acceptable performance. In addition to this acceptable category, the levels above and below it should clearly describe the operational performance of the plant. Thus, INPO should establish and assign assessment categories, such as shown below:

Category
1. Excellent performance
2. Superior performance
3. Meets industry standard of acceptable performance
4. Need for improvement is indicated
5. Requires special attention and assistance." Sillin report, p. 15.

25. Note that some plants may have two or three nuclear reactors. INPO defines a category 1 rating thus: "Overall performance is excellent. Industry standards of excellence are met in most areas. No significant weaknesses noted." INPO defines a category 5 rating thus: "Overall performance does not meet the industry standard of acceptable performance. The margin of nuclear safety is measurably reduced. Strong and immediate management action to correct deficiencies is required. Special attention, assistance and follow-up are required." INPO, "Peach Bottom Performance Assessment," 28 October 1987.

26. William S. Lee, remarks delivered at 1983 INPO CEO Conference, Atlanta, Georgia, 22 September 1983.

27. *Financial Times* (London), "Making Nuclear Safety International" (21 June 1990).

28. John Braithwaite, *Crime, Shame, and Reintegration* (Cambridge: Cambridge University Press, 1989).

29. "This is a relatively small industry," observes a nuclear utility vice president. "There are fifty-four utilities that have nuclear plants, and most of us at the plant manager or senior executive level know everybody else. Which means that the grapevine in this business is quite effective. Word spreads quickly. So when we go to industry meetings, everybody pretty much knows who got rated high by INPO. And the converse also applies. If you get a poor rating from INPO, it spreads pretty fast in this industry and you get kind of a stigma to live with for a while."

30. To generalize, it operates through expressions of community disapproval (ranging from mild rebuke to degradation ceremonies), followed by gestures of reacceptance into the community of law-abiding citizens (ranging from a simple smile expressing love and forgiveness to quite formal ceremonies to decertify them as deviant). Braithwaite, *Crime, Shame, and Reintegration,* p. 55. "Our theory," writes Braithwaite, "predicts that cul-

tures in which the 'family model' is applied to crime control both within and beyond the family will be cultures with low crime rates." Braithwaite, *Crime, Shame, and Reintegration,* p. 57. In other words, wrongdoing in the community, as in the family, "is best controlled when members of the community are the primary controllers through active participation in shaming offenders, and, having shamed them, through concerted participation in ways of reintegrating the offender back into the community of law abiding citizens": "The theory of reintegrative shaming explains compliance with the law by the moralizing qualities of social control rather than by its repressive qualities. Shaming is conceived as a tool to allure and inveigle the citizen to attend to the moral claims of the criminal law, to coax and caress compliance, to reason and remonstrate with him over the harmfulness of his conduct." Braithwaite, *Crime, Shame, and Reintegration,* pp. 8–9.

31. "The fundamental societal conditions conducive to cultural processes of reintegrative shaming are communitarianism and interdependency. . . . For a society to be communitarian, its heavily enmeshed fabric of interdependencies therefore must have a special kind of symbolic significance to the populace. Interdependencies must be attachments which invoke personal obligation to others within a community of concern. They are not perceived as isolated exchange relationships of convenience but as matters of profound group obligations. Thus, a communitarian society combines a dense network of individual interdependencies with strong cultural commitments to mutuality of obligation." Ibid., pp. 84–85.

32. "Shame not only specifically deters the shamed offender, it also generally deters many others who wish to avoid shame and who participate in or become aware of the incident of shaming. . . . Nothing has greater symbolic force in community-wide conscience-building than repentance. . . . Because shaming is a participatory form of social control . . . shaming builds consciences through citizens being instruments as well as targets of social control." Ibid., p. 81.

33. Effective shaming presumes a context of community, as these comments suggest, particularly a shared understanding ("majoritarian morality") as to what conduct should be viewed as deviant. And those communitarian contexts, Braithwaite observes, can be found throughout society, to varying degrees, including business corporations: "The theory of reintegrative shaming leads to a similar analysis of the role of organizations in white collar crime control to that of families in delinquency control. The families and organizations that are effective at crime control will not be those that are most punitive, but those that sustain communitarian bonds, that secure compliance by expressing disapproval while maintaining ongoing relationships characterized overwhelmingly by social approval." Ibid., p. 139. According to this line of reasoning, then, "effectively self-regulating companies are those with means of drawing everyone's attention to the failings of those who fall short of corporate social responsibility standards (shaming) while continuing to offer them advice and encouragement to improve (reintegration)." Ibid., p. 135.

34. Ibid., p. 167.

35. Ibid., p. 150.

36. INPO, *Institutional Plan* (1990), pp. 10–11.

37. What about the last step in this special procedure? Has INPO actually suspended the membership of any utility? The answer is no. And the answer is worth stressing, as it points to another "critical feature of communitarian societies," according to Braithwaite: "They are both more capable of potent shaming . . . *and less willing to cast out their deviants.*" *Crime, Shame, and Reintegration*, p. 88. (Emphasis supplied.)

38. See Zack Pate letter to Robert D. Harrison (11 January 1988), p. 7.

39. Ibid., attachment A.

40. Letter from Zack Pate to James L. Everett, 3 January 1986.

41. As Pate wrote: "From my assessment, this pattern will not change, and personnel performance at Peach Bottom will not improve, until you personally acknowledge the need, and communicate the need, for real change to your organization. . . . Lee [James L. Everett, Philadelphia Electric's chief executive officer], it is vitally important that you let your organization know that, from your perspective, a substantial upgrade is necessary and that you and John [John Austin, Philadelphia Electric's president] become personally involved in formulating the action plan to achieve such an upgrade." Zack Pate letter to James L. Everett, 13 January 1986.

42. Progress-check visits are conducted by INPO when a plant is assessed in the lower performance categories.

43. Zack Pate letter to James L. Everett, 7 May 1986.

44. INPO, "Peach Bottom Post-Exit Point Paper," 12 November 1986.

45. Philadelphia Electric Company, "Philadelphia Electric Company Plan for Restart of Peach Bottom Atomic Power Station, Section II: PBAPS Action Revision 1" (8 April 1988), p. 42.

46. See Zack Pate letter to Robert D. Harrison, 11 January 1988, p. 4.

47. INPO, "Briefing for Special Committee of Philadelphia Electric Company Board of Directors," 28 August 1987, p. 3. (Emphasis supplied.)

48. Among the examples of faulty practices cited by Pate is the following: "A protectionist and overly paternal culture within the corporate organization that dwells on past accomplishments, rejects the need for change . . . and tends to place the blame for problems on someone else." Ibid., p. 7.

49. *Inside NRC*, 28 September 1987.

50. Quoted in Hannah Arendt, *Between Past and Future* (New York: Viking Press, 1961), p. 123.

51. E. Michael Blake, "INPO Censures Peach Bottom; PECo Chief Departs," *Nuclear News* (March 1988), p. 30.

52. *Critical Mass Energy Project v. Nuclear Regulatory Commission* (DC Cir. no. 90–5120). The case at issue was filed by Critical Mass in 1984 and had bounced between the district court and the appeals court ever since. It involved a dispute between Critical Mass and the NRC over access to SEE-IN reports prepared by INPO and voluntarily transmitted to the NRC under a memorandum of understanding by which the NRC agreed to keep the INPO reports confidential. The Supreme Court denied Critical Mass's appeal without comment.

53. As an INPO vice president argues: If INPO did not guarantee confidentiality, utilities might not be as candid with INPO as they now are.

Then INPO would not be able to provide as accurate information to the industry as it now does and nuclear plants might not be as safe as they could be. Elizabeth Tilley Hinkle, "Court Denies Appeal for NRC Release of Confidential Industry Reports," *Energy Report* 20:34 (August 31, 1992).

54. Says another critic: "I just don't buy their reasoning on why they won't make their reports public. What they're essentially saying is, 'This industry won't tell the truth if it has to talk to the public.' Basically, they're saying, 'Trust us.' Well, I'm sorry, but I just won't trust them. And I just don't believe that people in the plant won't come forward with their problems. It's not that working-level people won't come forward, but that management officials and nuclear power boosters *don't want them to come forward* in the public sphere."

55. Sillin report, p. 16.

56. National Research Council, *Nuclear Power: Technical and Institutional Options for the Future* (Washington, D.C.: National Academy Press, 1992), 185.

57. Asked about the chilling effect this might have on INPO-utility communications, he responds: "I don't think that's a problem. Because if one of those very bad utilities said we're not going to let INPO look at us, that itself could be made public and would be a strong indictment."

Beyond enhancing INPO's clout, less secrecy and more openness would also improve INPO's (and the industry's) public credibility, according to NRC Chairman Ivan Selin. Addressing a 1992 meeting of the American Nuclear Society, he said that everything he had seen and learned in his sixteen months at the NRC had confirmed to him how critically important it is to foster public credibility, and that this could not be achieved by anything other than candor and straight talking. He thought that the nuclear industry has sometimes acted as though public participation was a necessary evil rather than a positive force. "But like it or not, public credibility cannot be achieved without public participation, and without public credibility, nuclear power in the United States will never see renewal." "Reviewing 50 Years of Nuclear History," *Nuclear News* (January 1993).

Besides such considerations, Professor John Braithwaite offers another reason why it is important to have less secrecy and more public participation in INPO's regulatory activities:

> If it were my book, I would be concluding that though INPO has achieved a great deal during the past decade, the question is whether such achievement can be sustained historically in conditions that lack democratic accountability. *Secrecy allows good systems to gradually rust over time. Secrecy allows complacency to go unchallenged.* Bearing in mind work such as that of Marver Bernstein on the life-cycle of regulatory agencies that start out as energetic and effective before they decay into a comfortable complacency or capture, closed communitarianism can only secure fragile accomplishments. Open communitarianism is needed for robust improvement over the long haul. *Dialogue with critics is particularly crucial.*

Personal communication, 26 January 1993 (emphasis supplied); also see Ian Ayres and John Braithwaite, *Responsive Regulation: Transcending the Deregulation Debate* (New York: Oxford University Press, 1992), chap. 3.

There is much to be said for this argument. Yet it is far from clear how such dialogue with critics might operate in the nuclear power context. For the unexpressed premise of Braithwaite's argument—that the industry and its critics share common ground (and a basis for constructive dialogue) inasmuch as they both value the regulated activity in question—is hard to reconcile with the outlook of many (probably most) public interest groups involved in nuclear power matters. "We definitely want to phase out nuclear power. That's always been our overriding goal and it always will be." Comments like this one, by a key official with Ralph Nader's Critical Mass Energy Project, could be heard in various interviews with nuclear power critics. Because nuclear power production is an inherently pernicious activity, according to their view, *it should be eliminated altogether.* By way of contrast, INPO and industry officials consider nuclear power production a valuable social activity, one that must be regulated and disciplined *without doing undue damage to it.* However one might want to describe these differences between nuclear power's opponents and proponents, it does not seem to provide congenial conditions for meaningful dialogue and accommodation.

Chapter 7

1. NRC, NUREG-1410, "Loss of Vital AC Power and the Residual Heat Removal System during Mid-Loop Operations at Vogtle Unit 1 on March 20, 1990," June 1990.

2. The reader should keep in mind the limited focus of our discussion. Just as individuals can learn from their own experience as well as from the experience of others, so too organizational actors. In the nuclear industry this distinction is reflected in the development of two distinct types of programs. *In-house* operating experience review programs deal with a nuclear utility's ability to learn from its own (mainly problematic) experience with nuclear plant operations, while *industry* experience review programs are designed to learn from the operating experience of other nuclear plants. Although INPO has been equally concerned with strengthening both, we shall limit our discussion to learning from industry experience and focus on INPO's efforts on developing nuclear power's competence (both inter-organizational and intra-organizational) in this regard.

3. GPU assessment, p. 2. (Emphasis supplied.)

4. Joel Feinberg, "Responsibility Tout Court," *Philosophy Research Archives* 14 (1988–89): p. 82. He offers this example:

The very best will in the world will not qualify a person to occupy certain elevated offices; and obedience, trustworthiness, benevolence, and diligence, while they are surely important virtues of character, are far from sufficient to make a person a responsible executive or administrator. . . . The Mayor of New York, the President of the University of California, and the chief engineer of a major automobile company, must be more than "nice guys who are willing to work hard"; they must also be capable of exercising their own discretion at every turn. They must be self-reliant persons of independent judgment and firmness of will, calm under fire, and decisive in crises. Moreover, *they must have the specific talents and skills to achieve particular ends:* administrative efficiency, experience, and know how. It is precisely because of our lack of some of these capabilities that most of us are . . . *insufficiently responsible* for high and mighty offices. [Emphasis supplied.]

5. William J. Broad, "Cutting Corners Costly in Space Exploration," *Raleigh News and Observer* (New York Times News Service), 11 June 1991, p. 1.

6. GPU assessment, p. 7. He elaborates: "Since we are dealing with persons and machines which cannot be made perfect, it is important to recognize that mistakes will be made. We must do our best to design machines having tolerance for mistakes and to continue to improve them through experience. This process of evolutionary improvement, the basis for much of our most useful technology, depends on a capacity to acknowledge mistakes and to determine and correct their underlying causes, whatever the cost."

7. INPO Performance Objectives and Criteria.

8. Rogovin report, vol. 1, p. 96.

9. The program's basic goal is to ensure that "the cumulative learning process from operating experience works well and that the lessons learned are reported in a timely manner to improve both plant safety and availability." INPO, "Significant Event Evaluation and Information Network (SEE-IN): Program Description" (January 1982), pp. 1–2. The following paragraph draws from "Event Analysis: Bringing Industry Experience to the Table," INPO *Review* 11:1 (Summer 1991): 8–12.

10. While most of the department's reviewers are permanent INPO employees, several persons are on loan (usually for two years) from utilities and nuclear plant manufacturers (such as Westinghouse and General Electric). The reviewers have considerable nuclear industry experience, as they include individuals with Senior Reactor Operator licenses and individuals with plant operating experience on the plant involved or a similar unit, as well as designers and analysts who are familiar with the particular plant or plants that had the event. E. L. Zebroski, INPO Vice President for Analysis and Engineering, "Analysis of Operating Events and Priorities." Speech delivered on 18 October 1982 to the American Nuclear Society Topical Meeting on Government and Self-Regulation of Nuclear Power Plants, p. 3.

11. Each SOER is also color-coded to alert the utility as to its priority— red (immediate attention), yellow (prompt attention), and green (normal attention). Moreover, because the SOER involves the industry's most significant problems, and since its "recommendations" are mandatory, the issuance of an SOER requires ten or more concurrence signatures at INPO, including INPO's president and other senior INPO managers. On occasion, an event is considered so significant that it is designated a "major event." When this occurs, INPO conducts a detailed field investigation, analyzes

the causes, and distributes the findings in a technical report to the industry.

The SEE-IN program also includes other types of documents. These include the Significant Event Report (SER), the Significant by Others (SO) report, and a Recurring Significant Event Notification (RSEN) list. For more details, see "Event Analysis: Bringing Industry Experience to the Table," INPO *Review* 11:1 (Summer 1991): 11–12.

12. See Zack Pate, "INPO Progress Report." Speech delivered at 1984 INPO CEO Workshop, Atlanta, Georgia, 28–30 November 1984, p. 25.

13. INPO, Significant Operating Experience Report 84-2 (April 17, 1984).

14. Zack Pate, "Update on Selected Issues," INPO 1991 CEO Conference, p. 55.

15. John Swartout, "Industry Initiatives: Event Analysis." Speech delivered at the 1981 INPO CEO Workshop, Atlanta, Georgia, 1 September 1981.

16. In March 1983 (after two rounds of INPO inspections) INPO officials concluded that the utilities' inability to implement the lessons of industry operating experience was an extensive problem. Among the recurring problems identified were the following:

—The Operating Experience Review Program [within nuclear plants] is not periodically evaluated to assess its effectiveness.
—Improvements are needed in the [nuclear utilities'] methods used to track the development and completion of corrective actions resulting from operating experience review.
—Operating experience information is not distributed to appropriate personnel and departments in a timely manner.
—Evaluation of operating experience information, including Significant Event Reports and Significant Operating Experience Reports, and implementation of corrective actions are not completed in a timely manner.

INPO, *Recurring Findings, Recommendations, and Good Practices* (Atlanta: INPO, 1983), pp. 31–32.

17. Zack Pate, remarks delivered at INPO 1988 CEO Workshop, Atlanta, Georgia, 2–4 November 1988.

18. A nuclear plant operating experience review official offers this example: "When it comes to learning from the experience of other plants, it's been an educational curve for my management. Two or three years ago the emphasis [on learning from industry operating experience] wasn't there. Basically our manager didn't see much value in spending maybe fifteen minutes a day with the operating experience program. It's sort of like Bible reading. You should get up every morning and read the Bible, but it gets crowded out if you're not really that committed to it. That's what happened at our plant. Management viewed experience review as a low priority and it got crowded out."

19. On the idea of critical function, see Henry Mintzberg, *Power in and around Organizations* (Englewood Cliffs: Prentice Hall, 1983), pp. 166–70.

20. INPO Good Practice, "In-House Operating Experience Review" (June 1985), p. ii.

21. Once again we are in the presence of mimetic and normative pressures that encourage isomorphic organizational change. See, for instance, Paul J. DiMaggio and Walter W. Powell, "The Iron Cage Revisited: Institutional Isomorphism and Collective Rationality in Organizational Fields," in *The New Institutionalism in Organizational Analysis*, pp. 67–74.

22. INPO, "Performance Objectives and Criteria for Operating and Near-Term Operating License Plants" (INPO 85-001, April 1987), p. 101.

23. The ethic of responsibility that runs through INPO's normative system is also well illustrated by INPO's "good practice" on learning from industry experience. As we saw in chapter 6, when a nuclear utility develops an exemplary method of operation, one that INPO deems worthy of imitation, the method may be disseminated throughout the industry in the form of an INPO good practice. So what does a nuclear plant experience review program worthy of emulation look like, according to INPO? Suffice it to say that the document's core section is titled "Responsibilities," and that it details the various learning-related tasks key nuclear plant officials are responsible for performing. Above all, the Good Practice thus establishes a clear structure of organizational responsibility for learning from industry experience.

24. For this purpose, an INPO inspector explains, "INPO has a complete record of everything the plant has ever done with every SOER recommendation since day one."

25. INPO, Guidelines for the Use of Operating Experience (February 1989), p. 1.

26. Shifting from the particular to the general, this affords yet another example of how INPO's normative system embodies a "logic of appropriateness." See James G. March and Johan P. Olsen, *Rediscovering Institutions: The Organizational Basis of Politics* (New York: Free Press, 1989).

27. 'For example, 25 significant operating experience report recommendations were found to be not satisfactorily implemented, a number considerably higher than typically seen at other utilities."

28. "For example, approximately one quarter of approximately 1250 items on the integrated tracking system are past due. Many involve lessons learned from industry operating experience. In many instances, personnel are not held accountable for completing items on time."

29. In this instance the relevant obligation involves INPO's first "Performance Objective and Criteria for Corporate Evaluations," which requires (in part) that "managers are responsible and held accountable for performing" in the operating experience area. INPO, "Performance Objectives and Criteria for Corporate Evaluations" (1987), p. 3.

30. A nuclear utility vice president echoes this view, in a slightly different way: "INPO doesn't want us to do something because they said to do it. They want us to do what we think is right. Because of the NRC, you see, there's been a strong tendency in this industry to be compliant; whenever the NRC says do something you do it. Period. I think it's much healthier the way INPO does business. They say this is what we found wrong,

these are some examples of that finding, what do you want to do about it? It's up to us to decide what we're going to do about it."

31. GPU assessment, p. 2. (Emphasis supplied.)

32. "The purpose of the CEO meeting is to help the CEOs focus on areas that need management attention," a nuclear utility vice president explains. "Of course," he adds with a laugh, "I'm on the receiving end of this":

> You see, no CEO wants to have information that singles them out as being low man on the totem pole. So its effect on CEOs is to direct their attention to get their scorecard up. And wherever INPO puts their marks on the scorecard, that's where I want my team to direct its attention because I want to get that scorecard up. If INPO says we got a low mark in maintenance or operating experience or whatever, that immediately sends me a signal that we've got to focus more attention over there.

33. He continues:

> Our executives can tell you the average number of open SOER recommendations that are still not completed at plants throughout the industry. And wanting to be better than the other guys, they want our plant's number to be less than that. To be in the top quartile you can only have three SOER recommendations open. Of course, our VPs want to know how to get there, what we need to do. So that peer comparison does create pressure. And then upper management puts pressure on plant management to complete the items that need to be completed, and working these off is something my management is constantly talking to me about.

34. INPO, 1982 CEO Workshop.

35. Zack Pate, "INPO Progress Report," remarks delivered at INPO 1984 CEO Workshop, Atlanta, Georgia, 28–30 November 1984, p. 24.

36. To illustrate, a nuclear plant official offers the following example:

> Some years ago at our plant INPO audited certain SOER recommendations, found that we had taken action on them, and that they were appropriately closed out. So INPO said, "Okay, this plant is finished with this recommendation." Well, about three years ago we had an event which appeared to have been addressed by that recommendation. It shouldn't have happened. But upon closer inspection we found that the inhibitor for that event was gone. In other words, the procedure change that had been done to address that SOER recommendation was no longer in place anymore because, as it turned out, the operations department had revised the procedure and had taken out the barrier.

37. Pate, 1988 CEO Workshop.

38. "Event Analysis: Bringing Industry Experience to the Table," INPO *Review* 11:1 (Summer 1991): 12. Also see Zack Pate, "Professionalism and Conservative Decision-Making by Managers, Engineers, Operators, and

Technicians," remarks delivered at the INPO 1989 CEO Workshop, Atlanta, Georgia, 1–3 November 1989, p. 61.

Chapter 8

1. Grigori Medvedev, *The Truth about Chernobyl* (Basic Books, 1991), p. 50.

2. Ibid., pp. 48, 57.

3. Philip Selznick, *The Moral Commonwealth: Social Theory and the Promise of Community* (Berkeley and Los Angeles: University of California Press, 1992), p. 333.

4. Kenneth Straham, "Managing Reactivity Changes" (videotape of speech delivered at 1988 CEO Conference Alternate Session, Atlanta, Georgia, November 1988).

5. Zack Pate, "Professionalism and Conservative Decision-Making." Speech delivered at the 1989 INPO CEO Conference, Atlanta, Georgia, 3 November 1989, p. 61.

6. Zack T. Pate, "Professionalism and Conservative Decisionmaking by Managers, Engineers, Operators, and Technicians." Speech delivered at 1989 INPO CEO Conference, Atlanta, Georgia, 3 November 1989, p. 66.

7. In December 1979, President Carter asked INPO to develop an industry-wide training and accreditation program, and in September 1980 INPO formed a task force for this purpose. Although the new accreditation system was first established in mid-1982, it was not until 1985, when the National Academy for Nuclear Training was created, that the present-day system was in place.

The accreditation process is the system's centerpiece. Using INPO-developed training standards, the utility performs a self-evaluation to identify and correct weaknesses in its training program. Then the utility sends INPO a self-evaluation report describing how its training program meets INPO's accreditation standards, which INPO reviews before sending an accreditation team to the utility. The team, which is made up of training experts from INPO and other utilities, visits the plant, assesses its training programs, and offers recommendations to the utility. These recommendations, along with the utility's corrective actions, are then sent to an independent National Nuclear Accrediting Board. A formal presentation on the training program is made to the accrediting board, which makes the decision to award or defer accreditation. The process is repeated every four years in order to renew accreditation. See INPO, "National Academy for Nuclear Training" (March 1989).

By INPO's count, about 35,000 of the 90,000 people working in the industry other than security guards now get some kind of continuing training. Control room operators get the most, spending from 12 to 20 percent of their time in training. See Matthew Wald, "Can Nuclear Power Be Rehabilitated?" *New York Times*, 31 March 1991. In 1979, twelve control room simulators were in use in the United States. Since then, the utilities have built sixty-one more, at a cost of as much as $15 million apiece.

In May 1987 the NRC issued this evaluation of INPO's training program: "Significant progress is being made by industry in improving training. . . . While significant training improvements have been observed, training deficiencies and weaknesses have been identified. . . . [However, these] are to be expected given the magnitude of the effort involved. . . . On balance, . . . the industry's efforts to date to improve training have been successful." Victor Stello, NRC Executive Director of Operations, "The 2-Year Evaluation on Implementation of the Commission Policy Statement on Training and Qualification."

In June 1991, NRC Commissioner Curtiss affirmed this conclusion: "This is the one area [training] in which I think we [the NRC commissioners] all agree that large strides have been made, significant strides." He goes on: "It's been effective . . . because the industry and INPO in particular have taken the lead in carrying out that program." NRC, "Briefing on Proposed Rule on Training and Qualification of Nuclear Power Plant Personnel," 10 June 1991, pp. 41–42.

8. Pate, "Professionalism and Conservative Decision-Making," p. 62. (Emphasis supplied.)

9. Here are some real-life examples, as described by INPO's president:

—In July 1988 at a U.S. PWR [Pressurized Water Reactor], the first startup with a new low leakage core was conducted without proper adjustments to nuclear instrumentation or special briefings. As a result, the power instruments based on neutron leakage read way too low. Instead of properly analyzing the situation, the operators adjusted the delta temperature-based power level *in the nonconservative direction*. When reactor power was increased to 30 percent indicated, actual power level was about 44 percent. As a result, the plant was operated without adequate overpower protection.

—In December 1988 at a U.S. PWR, a safety group of control rods dropped into the core after initial criticality was achieved on startup. Instead of taking *the conservative and proper action to shut down the plant*, operators commenced recovery of these dropped rods even though this was not covered in plant procedures. . . .

—In December 1988 at a U.S. PWR, following failure of a steam reducing valve, plant personnel attempted to keep the plant on line for some four hours through manual operation of valves that control feed flow. This process was not provided for in procedures. The highly abnormal actions that were being taken eventually led to a loss of feedwater control, and a steam generator boiled dry. A severe and unnecessary transient was imposed on the plant. This was a clear-cut case of improper, *nonconservative decision-making*, over a sustained period of time, that involved plant managers at a fairly senior level.

—In March 1989 at a U.S. BWR [Boiling Water Reactor], air header system pressure was reduced to the point that 34 control rods drifted into the core. Even though this was clearly an abnormal and unanalyzed reactor core configuration, with abnormal flux patterns, *the shift crew did not take the proper and conservative action of immediately reducing power or shutting down*.

—In June 1989 at a U.S. PWR undergoing startup testing, an operations crew failed to scram the reactor when a test procedure limit involving low pressurizer level was exceeded. . . . The plant was operated outside prescribed test limits for some five minutes before the reactor was finally scrammed. Operations management was present in the control room, *but also failed to ensure that proper conservative action was taken.*

Zack Pate, "Professionalism and Conservative Decisionmaking," pp. 62–63. (Emphasis supplied.)

10. "Reactivity Management at Commonwealth Edison," *Nuclear Professional* (Winter 1990), p. 13.

11. Ibid.

12. Zack Pate, "Professionalism and Conservative Decisionmaking," p. 64.

13. Ibid. "A doctor can do many things wrong," Pate continues, "but if he brings unnecessary harm to a patient, he has failed professionally in an unmistakable way, with uniquely serious consequences. That is most especially true in the view of that patient and his family. Likewise, we in this industry can make lots of mistakes, but if we damage a reactor core, we have failed in our profession in an unmistakable way, with serious consequences. And in our case, that will be the view not of just a patient but of an entire nation, indeed *many* nations."

14. Other examples:

—When an engineer is involved in moving power range detectors, he *feels an overwhelming professional obligation* to personally see to it that the power range instrumentation is properly calibrated before the next startup.

—When an operations line manager knows that a new low leakage core is being installed, *he feels a deep professional obligation* to personally ensure that the necessary training and briefings and recalibrations are carried out.

(Ibid., p. 66.) (Emphasis supplied.)

15. As philosopher Joel Feinberg writes: "Perhaps the most common of the employments of the word 'irresponsible' is that in which it applies to the *reckless* person . . . the person whose conduct creates unreasonable risks of harm. . . . Causing harm recklessly is causing it in a way that is *almost* intentional; but whereas in intentional causing one *knows* or actively *desires* that the harmful consequences will result, in the case of recklessness, one knows only that there is a *risk* that harm will result and one is not moved by that knowledge to change one's course. Recklessness then involves an element of intentionality, a 'conscious indifference' or 'intentional disregard.'" Joel Feinberg, "Responsibility Tout Court," *Philosophy Research Archives* 14 (1988–89): 84.

16. Pate, "Professionalism and Conservative Decisionmaking," p. 66.

17. INPO, Foreword to "Principles for Enhancing Professionalism of Nuclear Personnel" (1 March 1989).

18. INPO, "Professionalism Principles" (30 March 1988 edition).

19. Zack Pate, "Professionalism and Conservative Decisionmaking," p. 65.

20. Ibid.

21. INPO, Foreword to "Principles for Enhancing Professionalism of Nuclear Personnel" (1 March 1989). (Emphasis supplied.)

22. Ibid.

23. As former NRC chairman John Ahearne observed in 1985 congressional hearings, the prevailing managerial perspective considers the task of operating a nuclear plant a "dull," "boring," and "tedious" job that is best suited to individuals without much "intellectual drive and ambition." This way of thinking, incidentally, helps explain why industry officials opposed any college degree requirements for control room operators. A high school diploma, this logic maintains, is more than enough for such a dull task. U.S. Congress, Senate Subcommittee on Nuclear Regulation, Committee on Environment and Public Works, 99th Cong., 1st sess., 27 June 1985, p. 51.

24. Another professionalism committee member makes a similar point:

> The guys that can save your bacon or lose it for you are the guys
> with their hands on the switches or the guys with the wrenches in
> their hands. But basically we've ignored that level of the organiza-
> tion when it comes to striving for excellence in the industry. Ask
> an operator about excellence or professionalism, and he'd say,
> "What the hell are you talking about. I'm just an operator." That's
> what this professionalism thing is all about—reaching out to the
> people that really have an impact on the day-to-day operations of
> the plant. They need to clearly understand what it means to be a
> good operator, a good mechanic, a good electrician.

25. INPO, "Principles for Enhancing Professionalism of Nuclear Personnel" (1 March 1989), pp. 1–3. (Emphasis supplied.)

26. Rensis Likert, *New Patterns of Management* (New York: McGraw-Hill, 1961), pp. 102–3.

27. Peter F. Drucker, *Management: Tasks, Responsibilities, Practices* (New York: Harper Colophon Books, 1985), p. 284.

28. One best-selling example of this genre, among many others, is Thomas J. Peters and Robert H. Waterman, Jr., *In Search of Excellence: Lessons from America's Best-Run Companies* (New York: Harper and Row, 1982).

29. As Peter Drucker has written, the nuclear submarine, though a good example of a supportive work environment, "cannot be a permissive place": "The captain has to be the final authority whose word nobody dares dispute. Yet the crew, regardless of rank, *acts and works as one unit.* . . . And while the captain decides what should be done, each man on his own station then has to decide how to do a specific job and do it as if the life of everybody depended on him as indeed it does." Peter Drucker, *Management Tasks, Responsibilities, and Practices* (New York: Harper and Row, 1974), p. 283.

On Admiral Hyman Rickover's human relations–oriented management style, see Richard G. Hewlett and Francis Duncan, *Nuclear Navy* (Chicago: University of Chicago Press, 1974), pp. 384–88.

30. INPO, Foreword to "Principles for Enhancing Professionalism of Nuclear Personnel."

31. Much of the following account is taken from "They Have Principles," *Nuclear Professional* (Summer 1990), pp. 21–27.

32. Ibid. (Emphasis supplied.)

33. Ibid., pp. 21–22.

34. Ibid.

35. It contains six principles: (1) "We promote open communications, teamwork and mutual respect." (2) "We accept responsibility for the quality of our work and strive for improvement." (3) "We demonstrate pride in our organization by our attitude and appearance." (4) "We understand that policies and procedures are essential and must be followed." (5) "We strive to provide positive recognition as well as constructive criticism." (6) "We maintain personal well-being so that we are physically, mentally, and emotionally prepared for excellent performance." Ibid., p. 25.

36. Assured anonymity, they were asked questions like the following: How would you define professionalism? How professionally do you think the plant is being operated? What improvements are needed? Are there management policies or procedures that need to be changed? How do you get feedback from management?

37. "Special Assignment: V. C. Sumner Employees Assess Their Performance against Industry Standards," *Nuclear Professional* (Summer 1990), p. 27.

38. "They Have Principles," *Nuclear Professional* (Summer 1990), p. 24.

39. Ibid., p. 22.

40. Entergy Operations, Inc., *Principles for Managing Nuclear Plant Personnel* (July 1990), p. III. (Emphasis supplied.)

41. Ibid., p. 1.

42. Ibid., p. 3.

43. Ibid., pp. 4–5.

44. INPO's executive vice president continues:

There is an active group of utilities that has really taken this [professionalism] initiative and run with it. Recently, representatives from 18 utilities gathered at INPO to share a wealth of information and new insights into how to conduct professionalism self-assessments. The lessons learned will also be available to other utilities. And many of the participants offered to help support self-assessments at other utilities. . . . INPO plans to continue to conduct professionalism assistance visits in 1992. But critical self-assessments are only a start. Building a sense of pride and professionalism is a long-term effort that will require continued emphasis throughout the '90s.

Terrence J. Sullivan, "Building the Future—INPO's Role in the 1990s." Speech delivered to INPO 1991 CEO Conference (6–8 November 1991), p. 64.

45. Here are three examples. On the value of corporate officers with nuclear operating experience: "The corporate management philosophy and structure ensure that . . . corporate officers . . . responsible for supporting plant operations possess the necessary knowledge and experience to understand nuclear plant activities, problems, and events." On the value of promoting nuclear plant workers to corporate management positions: "Individuals with experience in day-to-day plant operations are considered as an important source of management talent. The policies and practices that govern career development ensure that individuals are aware of the opportunity to develop into management positions and that selected individuals are encouraged and provided with opportunities to pursue this career path." On the value of grooming nuclear plant employees for corporate management positions: "Candidates for management positions or for promotions to higher-level management positions are provided with opportunities to work with and for individuals who can serve as role models to enhance the development of leadership and management capabilities." INPO, "Principles for Enhancing Professionalism of Nuclear Personnel."

46. He goes on: "You have to make sure that people have teamwork, and that takes a long time. And you have to make sure the people have sufficient resources, and that's something you have to do over five or ten years."

47. On control of attention as a means of influence, see James G. March and Johan P. Olsen, *Rediscovering Institutions: The Organizational Basis of Politics* (New York: Free Press, MacMillan, Inc., 1989), pp. 61–62.

48. In February 1988, INPO brought together 173 industry personnel at its Senior Reactor Operators Workshop in order to discuss means to improve professionalism at nuclear stations and to begin the development of operator professional codes. In March 1988, INPO sent a letter to each nuclear utility that contained the "Principles for Enhancing Professionalism of Nuclear Personnel," and that requested each utility's senior management to conduct an in-depth comparison of their utilities policies and practices to the professionalism principles, and report their findings to INPO. In September 1988 INPO's Plant Managers Workshop focused on the theme "Pursuit of Professionalism," and discussed further means to enhance the professionalism of plant personnel. In November 1988, the issue of professionalism was once again the central focus of the annual CEO conference. The list of activities could go on, but the essential point remains the same: INPO functions as an institutional mechanism for focusing the nuclear industry's collective attention on the professionalism problem.

49. He goes on: "We don't specifically audit or evaluate to these principles but we do try to get a feel for whether they're pursuing those principles. And if we do find a problem that shows a lack of commitment to some principle, we identify it." Soon after the professionalism project began, moreover, the following INPO criterion for corporate evaluations was created: "Corporate managers expect and insist on professionalism throughout the corporate and plant organizations. A set of principles is in place that promotes a climate of professionalism." INPO, "Performance Objectives and Criteria for Corporate Evaluations" (December 1987), p. 4.

50. INPO, "Corporate Evaluation of Public Service Company of New Hampshire" (December 1989), p. 4.

51. Zack Pate, "Update on Selected Issues." Speech delivered to 1991 CEO Meeting, p. 52.

Chapter 9

1. To be more precise, there are about 98,000 utility employees involved in nuclear plant operations and about 100,000 contract employees working at nuclear plants at any given time. See Brian Jordan, "Industry Focusing on Staffing as Key to Controlling Costs," *Nucleonics Week* (18 January 1990), p. 1.

2. For this chapter, I have drawn heavily on, and am much indebted to, Philip Selznick's *The Moral Commonwealth* (Berkeley and Los Angeles: University of California Press, 1992), chap. 13.

3. Robert Nisbet, *The Sociological Tradition* (New York: Basic Books, 1966), p. 47; Thomas Bender, *Community and Social Change in America* (New Brunswick: Rutgers University Press, 1978), p. 5.

4. Robert M. MacIver and Charles H. Page, *Society: An Introductory Analysis* (New York: Rinehart, 1949), p. 9.

5. Selznick, *The Moral Commonwealth*, p. 358.

6. Or, to put it another way, the existence of community is a matter of degree. For simplicity, imagine a spectrum. On one end we have full-blown communities that encompass *all* the social relationships of group members within a comprehensive framework of shared beliefs and values (MacIver and Page's definition, for instance). If you then proceed down to the spectrum's other end, moving slowly to consider how the communities change along the way (say, from a spiritual community, to an occupational community of police officers, to the European Economic Community), you will notice that they encompass an ever-narrowing range of activities and interests. Arriving at the other end, you will thus find communities that provide an extremely limited framework for common life. Call these partial or quasi-communities.

For a similar approach to the analysis of the concept of "legal system," see John Finnis, *Natural Law and Natural Rights* (Oxford: Clarendon Press, 1982), pp. 3–22; Herbert Lionel Adolphus Hart, *Concept of Law* (New York: Oxford University Press, 1972), pp. 15, 210; J. Raz, *Practical Reason and Norms* (London: Hutchison, 1975), p. 150.

7. For a discussion of how various writers have addressed this question, see George A. Hillery, Jr., "Definitions of Community: Areas of Agreement," *Rural Sociology* 20 (1955): 111–23.

8. This is not to suggest, of course, that a community is integrated by a single factor; most likely, a variety of unifying forces are at work *to varying degrees* in the development of a particular community. Also notice that the concept of community does not necessarily presume a common locality. Gusfield, for example, calls the nongeographical sense of community a "relational" community. Joseph Gusfield, *Community: A Critical Response* (New York: Harper and Row, 1975), p. xvi.

9. Chester Barnard, *The Functions of the Executive* (Cambridge: Harvard University Press), p. 279. Emphasis supplied.

10. For a general discussion of the "institutional school" of organization theory, see Charles Perrow, *Complex Organizations* (New York: Random House, 1986), chap. 5.

11. Philip Selznick, *Leadership in Administration* (Evanston: Row, Petersen, 1957), p. 40. (Emphasis in original deleted.)

12. James Q. Wilson, *Bureaucracy: What Government Agencies Do and Why They Do It* (New York: Basic Books, 1989), p. 93.

13. As Selznick writes, "special-purpose institutions may become communities or at least quasi-communities": "This form of community occurs most readily when purpose is not very rigidly or narrowly conceived, where leeway is allowed for controversy over ends and means, and when participation is an important part of the individual's life within the organization. Thus community is more likely to develop in military or police organizations, which encourage a shared lifestyle, than in, say, marginal business firms where employment is sporadic, personnel turnover is high, training is unimportant, and work is highly routine and specialized." (*Moral Commonwealth*, p. 359.)

14. Ibid., pp. 370–71.

15. See p. 146.

16. At the very heart of nuclear power's new industrial community one can thus find a union of culture (including shared values, beliefs, and practices) and social structure (including unifying and anchoring institutions). Which is why an institutional perspective is a useful way of thinking about industrial communities as well as complex organizations. Most important, it is a way of taking values and institutions seriously (1) because it centers attention on the role of unifying values and beliefs in the emergence of community, and (2) because it highlights the crucial work institutions can perform in creating an industrial community (the unifying role) and in supporting an industrial community (the anchoring role). In short, an industrial community is a network of industrial institutions embodying a distinctive set of unifying values.

17. Thomas Bender, *Community and Social Change in America* (New Brunswick: Rutgers University Press, 1978), pp. 143–44. For a similar critique, see Sheldon Wolin, *Politics and Vision: Continuity and Innovation in Western Political Thought* (Boston: Little, Brown, 1960), chap. 10.

18. Selznick, *Moral Commonwealth*, p. 369. Consider, for example, the case of Mrs. Hibbens, a member of the Puritan congregational community in colonial Boston, a group that worked laboriously to channel egotism and maintain communal identity:

> In 1640 Mrs. Hibbens . . . quarreled with Mr. Crabtree about his fee for carpentry work in her house. Mr. Hibbens proposed arbitration: he chose one carpenter and Crabtree selected another. The arbitrators set a revised fee, but Mrs. Hibbens remained obdurate. Indeed, she complained bitterly and publicly about "brother Davis," one of the arbitrators. The carpenters became incensed at Mrs. Hibbens' aspersions on their skills, which diminished their reputation in the community. Church elders approached Mrs. Hibbens, but she remained unmollified. After another arbitration attempt failed, the

dispute moved into the First Church of Boston. . . . Once in church, however, the essence of the dispute shifted—from a disagreement over wages to the stubborn recalcitrance of a church member who did not respect communal fellowship. . . . In a proceeding that required two meetings, a week apart, and elicited the participation of brethren, sisters, and elders of the congregation, Mrs. Hibbens' conduct was relentlessly scrutinized and criticized. . . . *The entire congregation participated in a process designed to reassert harmony and consensus . . . and thereby strengthen communal values.* The sanctions of admonition and excommunication were sufficient for this purpose. The church could neither arrest a wrongdoer nor seize his property, but the danger of expulsion . . . loomed ominously. That was Mrs. Hibbens' ultimate fate. . . . Expulsion, a dire last resort, *reasserted consensual authority and thereby preserved the community against those whose self-assertiveness would subvert it.*

Jerold S. Auerbach, *Justice without Law?* (Oxford University Press, 1983), pp. 23–25. (Emphasis supplied.)

19. Lelan F. Sillin, Jr., "Follow-up on INPO Programs." Speech delivered to INPO CEO Conference, Atlanta, Georgia, 22 September 1983, pp. 1, 5.

20. All this, of course, is a relative matter and one of degree.

21. See Emma Chynoweth and Karen Heller, "Wanted: A System to Audit Care," *Chemical Week* (17 June 1992), p. 28.

The Responsible Care program was adopted by the Chemical Manufacturers Association (CMA) in 1988, and, with 175 U.S. companies involved, covers 90 percent of this country's basic chemical production capacity. Why the industry-wide self-regulation program was developed in the first place is explained by the CMA thus:

In spite of past efforts there still are too many incidents involving chemical operations. Politicians and government regulators will respond to the public's concerns about chemicals and our industry if the chemical industry does not respond first. . . .

Public concerns about chemicals and the industry are *the result of collective experience with the entire industry.* If the chemical industry is to respond to public concerns effectively, it *must act as a total industry* and, therefore, must be both a commitment and a membership obligation of every company in the association. It is critical to achieve the cultural change needed for the industry to improve performance in a responsive manner.

Chemical Manufacturers Association, "Questions and Answers about Responsible Care" (April 1991). (Emphasis supplied.) Like the nuclear utilities, in short, the chemical companies are hostages of each other.

In consequence of this, the chemical manufacturers have also developed an industrial code to promote responsible conduct among its members—that is, the responsible care of chemicals. More particularly, the program is built around six codes of management practice: community awareness and emergency response, pollution prevention, process safety, distribution, employee health and safety, and product stewardship.

Take the process safety code as an example. Designed to prevent fires, explosions, and accidental chemical releases, the CMA requires (among other things) that all its member companies: (1) have an ongoing process safety program that includes a measurement of performance, audits, and implementation of corrective actions; (2) conduct thorough safety reviews on all new and modified facilities during design and before start-up; (3) conduct and document maintenance and inspection programs to ensure facility soundness; (4) develop and put in place sufficient layers of protection to prevent escalation from a single failure to a catastrophic event; (5) train all employees to reach and maintain proficiency in safe work practices and the skills and knowledge necessary to perform their job; and (6) share relevant safety knowledge and lessons learned from incidents with industry, government, and the community to help prevent others from experiencing similar incidents. Chemical Manufacturers Association, "Process Safety Code" (no date).

As for what motivates chemical companies to take these industrial principles and practices seriously, at least part of the answer has to do with peer pressure. As two chemical industry reporters tried to explain it: "Peer pressure is working at both company and countrywide level." Emma Chynoweth and David Hunter, "Delivering on Commitments," *Chemical Week* (17 June 1992), p. 8.

A growing sense of interdependence among chemical companies, a new industry-wide code of conduct, peer pressure, promoting corporate responsibility—it is beginning to look as though the chemical industry may be following in the nuclear industry's footsteps. If so, there is good reason to think that communitarian regulation is now emerging as the dominant pattern of self-regulation in two of our nation's most hazardous industries.

Index